ISRAEL IN EGYPT,

OR

THE BOOKS OF GENESIS AND EXODUS.

ILLUSTRATED

BY EXISTING MONUMENTS.

ISBN: 978-1-63923-956-6

All Rights reserved. No part of this book maybe reproduced without written permission from the publishers, except by a reviewer who may quote brief passages in a review to be printed in a newspaper or magazine.

Printed: March 2023

Published and Distributed By:
Lushena Books
607 Country Club Drive, Unit E
Bensenville, IL 60106
www.lushenabks.com

ISBN: 978-1-63923-956-6

PREFACE.

THE present work has a definite end in view. The discovery by Champollion of the mode of reading the inscriptions that cover the remains of Ancient Egypt, was first brought under the Author's notice more than thirty years ago. It at once struck him, that if this discovery be real, and if the Bible be a statement of facts, the one must of necessity illustrate the other. Under this conviction he has since devoted his life to the pursuit of it,—wisely or not, is no part of the question now in discussion.

There is yet another conviction which has aided him in making this somewhat costly sacrifice:—he writes thus, because such is the fact. He has always held it for certain, that the history narrated in the Bible must be true, strictly true, a record of things as they were, and of facts as they did occur, if its doctrines are from God, and therefore worthy to be received as religious teaching. If it be not true in this exact sense,—if the men, for example, named therein be nations, not individuals, if its positive dates be vague numbers, if its miracles be mere metaphors, then is the Bible a lie! " and every lie, O that men would believe it, is at best but a whited sepulchre." * However fair such a structure may be externally, it contains nothing but dead men's bones, and all uncleanness, and therefore nothing can issue from it but that which is noisome and pestilential. The reality of the Bible history is a condition indispensable to the genuineness of its moral teaching. This proposition, which appears to him very clear and self-evident, renders it absolutely necessary, that the truth of the history should be fully established. In the ensuing pages, the reader will find an attempt to establish its truth in this strict sense, by the collateral evidence of the monuments of Ancient Egypt.

The author is well aware, that this necessity is denied, and in quarters whence all opinions come forth with the authority and influence of oracles. He knows that, by one of the great schools of modern thinkers, all such enquiries are denounced as "idle attempts to collect evidence;" † and that from another class, his work will bring upon him the

---

* Archdeacon Hare's Life of Sterling, p. ccxxxi.
† Fronde's Remains.

charge of maintaining "ignorant, uncritical, baseless assumptions concerning literal inspiration." *

He deeply regrets this antagonism, but it is not in his power to modify at all the conviction he has expressed.

* Archdeacon Hare, u. s. cxxx.

CONTENTS.

		PAGE
	INTRODUCTION	xi
CHAP.		
I.	PRELIMINARY	
II.	JOSEPH IN EGYPT	21
III.	THE FAMINE	129
IV.	EGYPT DURING THE SOJOURN	176
V.	THE KING THAT KNEW NOT JOSEPH	238
VI.	MOSES IN MIDIAN	284
VII.	THE PLAGUES OF EGYPT	309
VIII.	THE EXODUS	383

INTRODUCTION.

THE mode of reading the hieroglyphics (that is, the writings inscribed on all the remains of ancient Egypt) has been recovered. How this recovery was effected, is an oft-told tale; but, nevertheless, it must be here repeated, for with the exception of one or two students, the subject is altogether neglected in England.

A piece of granite was found near Rosetta, on the western mouth of the Nile, in digging the foundation of a fort, by the French army, in 1798. On this stone was a long inscription in hieroglyphics, with a Greek translation, which explained that it was a decree appointing divine honors to Ptolemy Epiphanes, who began to reign over Egypt 204 B. C. This stone is now in the British Museum.

A small obelisc was brought to England by Mr. Banks, from the island of Philæ, which lies on the extreme southern borders of Egypt. This has a hieroglyphic inscription on the shaft, and at the base a Greek one, which tells us that it was dedicated to the gods of Philæ by Ptolemy Physcon, the second successor of Epiphanes, and by Cleopatra his wife. They began to reign 146 B. C.

The following group of characters (I *below*) is of frequent occurrence on both these monuments. This had been conjectured to be the transcription in hieroglyphics of the name of PTOLEMY, before the arrival of Mr. Bankes's obelisc in England. On this last monument (II.) was another group which (assuming the former conjecture to be correct) was in all probability the name CLEOPATRA. The complete proof of both resulted from the analysis of M. Champollion, who had long diligently studied the antiquities of Egypt. It was as follows :

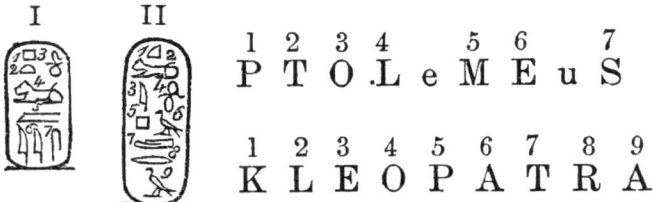

```
         1 2 3 4   5 6   7
         P T O L e M E u S

         1 2 3 4 5 6 7 8 9
         K L E O P A T R A
```

The first letter in Ptolemeus and the 5th in Cleopatra are both P. The first character in the ring supposed to be Ptolemy, and the fifth in that conjectured to be Cleopatra are both a square block, or rather package of linen. ▦ This character therefore was assumed to be *p*.

The third letter in Ptolemy and the fourth in Cleopatra, are both O. The corresponding characters in the two rings are also both the same,—a knotted cord 🪢, which was accordingly set down as *o*.

The fourth in Ptolemy and the second in Cleopatra, are both L. The corresponding characters are again the same in both rings. The lion was therefore put down for *l*.

The sixth and ninth letters in Cleopatra are both A. The sixth and ninth characters in the ring, assumed to be Cleopatra, are both a sparrowhawk, which we thenceforth write *a*.

The first letter in Cleopatra is not in Ptolemy, neither is the first character in the ring of Cleopatra to be found in that of Ptolemy. The triangular block was therefore added to the hieroglyphic alphabet; ◁ C, or the Greek K *kappa*.

The third character in Cleopatra's ring is one blade of a Nile reed ; the corresponding letter is a short ĕ. The last character but one in Ptolemy's ring is two such blades. This the discoverer rightly assumed from this analogy to be the long ē, which is the last letter but two in Ptolemy's name. From this approximation he was able to solve the difficulty which the comparison of the ring of Ptolemy with his name presents. There are nine letters in the name, but only seven characters in the ring. The intermediate vowels were often omitted in the ancient Egyptian writings, as in the Hebrew and other oriental languages. Long study of the Coptic, (which is the ancient Egyptian written with Greek characters) had rendered Champollion perfectly familiar with this fact. He therefore put down the fifth character in Ptolemy's name, a boat-stand ⌒ for *m*, and the seventh, a crotchet or yoke, ∫ for *s*. Both were soon verified from other names, and the hieroglyphic transcription of the name PTOLEMÆUS was read *Ptolmes*.

The penultimate letter in Cleopatra is R, which does not occur in Ptolemy. The last character but one in the ring is not found in the hieroglyphic transcription of Ptolemy. It is a human mouth, ⌒ which we put down from hence, *r*.

One step only was now required to complete the analysis of both rings: but here again was a difficulty. The second letter in Ptolemy and the seventh in Cleopatra are both T, but the corresponding characters are altogether different. In Ptolemy it is represented by a small stone shaped like the segment of a sphere, and used for polishing, ⌒; but in Cleopatra's ring a human hand ⬚ has the power of *t*. This comparison suggested that the same sound had many representatives in hieroglyphics— the system of *homophons*, as its discoverer well named it.

The key to the reading of these mysterious writings was now evidently recovered. There is no occasion to proceed further with its history. Its results will be far more likel to interest the reader.

NAMES OF THOSE WHO HAD BEEN SOVEREIGNS IN EGYPT.

These are always written in frames or cartouches.

ROMAN EMPERORS.

Augustus Cæsar, (from Esneh.) *autkrtr ksaars.*    Tiberius Cæsar, (from Philæ.) *tibris kesrs.*

THE PTOLEMAIC KINGDOM IN EGYPT.

Philip of Macedon. *plipos.*    Alexander the Great. (Karnak.) *alksantrs.*    Queen Arsinoe. *arsn.*

For Ptolemy and Cleopatra see p. xii.

PERSIAN KINGDOM IN EGYPT.

Cambyses. *kmbat.*    Darius. *triush.*    Xerxes. *shaershu.*

THE KINGDOM OF THE NATIVE PHARAOHS.

The 26th Dynasty, about 600 B. C.

The royal names at this period are all written in two rings. The second ring contains the name, and that only we translate.

Psammetichus. *psmtk.*    Pharaoh Necho. *nku.*

Pharaoh Hophra. *ht-haa-phra.*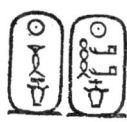

The 25th Dynasty about 700 B. C.

These kings came from Ethiopia. They are called Ethiops in the Bible.

Sabacho.  Tirhakah.
shvk. tiharka.

The 22nd Dynasty, about 800 B. C.

Shishak. This was the Pharaoh who invaded
Σεσωγχις. Judah in the days of Rehoboam,
LXX. the son of Solomon. The picture
Sesonchis. of his triumph afterwards, yet re-
shshnk. mains on the north external wall
of the palace of Karnak in eastern
Thebes.

The 20th Dynasty, about the time of the Exodus.

Sethos II.   Ramerri
stei.   his son,
The Pharaoh   who perished
who perished in   with the
the Red Sea.   first born.

Queen Thouoris. *thavrus.* The daughter of the king that knew not Joseph, the patroness of Moses.

The 19th Dynasty, about the time of Moses.

Ramses II. the final expeller of the Shepherds from the Delta: the king that knew not Joseph. *ra-mss.*

From this time the royal names, are often written in one rin onl .

The 15th Dynasty, Canaanite Shepherds
(so called.)

Aphophis the patron of Joseph. *aphaph.* 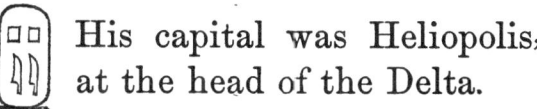 His capital was Heliopolis, at the head of the Delta.

The 3rd and 4th Dynasty, the builders of the Pyramids.

Suphis the builder of the great pyramid. *shufu.*   Soris the first king of the 4th Dynasty, *shure.* The builder of the middle pyramid of Abusir.

 Sephuris of the 3rd Dynasty, *sanfru.* The earliest of the kings of Egypt of whom any cotemporary monument has been found.

The 1st Dynasty.

Menes, the protomonarch of Egypt. *mnei.* (Hieroglyphic genealogies.)   His name as king of Egypt occurs in that of a prince of the court of Suphis, whose tomb is at Ghizeh. Josephus says that Menes reigned many years before the times of Abraham.

The subjoined alphabet is strictly artificial. It gives the characters employed in the foregoing table of kings, arranged under their proper sounds, and no other.

a e i o u

h b . u or h . h . b . h

c k . . . . .

d t . . . .

f [glyph]
l r [glyph]
m [glyph]
n [glyph]
p [glyph]
s [glyph]
sh [glyph]
ch (guttural) [glyph]

The ring or frame [glyph] which incloses these names is the ground plot of a cattle-pen made of "hurdles," [glyph]. The first king of Egypt, the founder of Memphis, was named *Menes.* [glyph] *mn-ei,* which means "hurdle-maker." He first enclosed his name thus as an indication of its meaning. All the kings of Egypt after him were, or professed to be, his descendants, and they also assumed it in token of this consanguinity. So strong was the feeling under the native Pharaohs that every king of Egypt must of necessity be of the race of Menes, that the priests pretended that Cambyses was the natural son of Amasis II, whom he conquered, and Alexander the Great, of Nectanebo, the last native king of Egypt.

We have found the meaning of these characters by taking the names to pieces. In order to show how the system was invented, we must put it together again.

All the letters or characters in this mode of writing, are pictures. It is generally supposed that the Egyptian system differs in this particular from other writings of the same antiquity. Such however is not the fact. They also were constructed throughout upon the same principle. All the letters in them were at first pictures of objects.

Three modes of writing only are known of an antiquity at all approaching that of the inscribed remains of Egypt. These are:

1. Hebrew. The language of the entire eastern coast of the Mediterranean. It was used with very little dialectic variation by all the Shemites and Hamites that first peopled the district. The oldest known monuments of it are coins of some of the later kings of Judah, 8 to 900 B. C.

2. Greek. The language of Javan, (*Ion*) the son of Japhet. (Gen. x. 9.) It was spoken by the first settlers on the north coast of the Mediterranean, both on the continent and in the islands. Inscriptions in it on stones and metal are very numerous, and some of them nearly as old as the earliest remains of Hebrew.

These two languages were at first written with the same alphabet.

3. Assyrian, or Ninevite. The wedge-shaped characters on the ruins in the valley of the Tigris and Euphrates, where once stood Nineveh and

Babylon. These likewise are degradations of the same alphabet, suggested by the hard glassy material in the neighbourhood, imperfect tools, and want of skill in engraving. The system seems to have been written in two or three different ways. It is the original whence were derived the Sanskrit, the Thibetan, and the rest of the square-lettered alphabets of Asia.

Of these three modes of writing, the Hebrew and Greek have both been perpetuated by means of their alphabets: so that the names and powers of the letters, the meanings of the words, and the structure of the languages in which the inscriptions were written, are well known. The Ninevite inscriptions, on the other hand, represent the sounds of lost languages. A few characters only have yet been deciphered, and a few proper names read in them. This circumstance, together with the fact that the system itself is a mere degradation, altogether excludes it from our present enquiry: even though some of the inscriptions in it may possibly be as old as the oldest known forms of the other two systems.

The following collation of the oldest forms of the Hebrew and Greek alphabets very clearly shews, that both were the same at first, that all the letters were pictures, and that the names of the letters were also those of the objects represented by the pictures.

NAME.		MOST ANCIENT FORMS		PICTURES.	MEANING OF NAMES.	PRONTIO
Hebrew.	Greek.	Hebrew.	Greek.			
Aleph א	Alpha A α				an ox	a
Beth ב	Beta B β				tent, dwelling	b
Gimel ג	Gamma Γ γ				camel	g
Daleth ד	Delta Δ δ				door	d
He ה	[rough breathing] ‘				window-lattice	h
Vau ו	[smooth breathing] ’				hook, peg	v, (sm breath
Zain ז	[see Tzade]				club, sword	z
Cheth ח	Eta H η				hurdle	ē
Teth ט	Theta Θ θ				lump of clay ready for potter	t, th
Yod י	Iota I ι				man's hand	i, y
Caph כ	Kappa K κ				wings	k
Lamed ל	Lamda Λ λ				ox-goad	l
Mem מ	Mu M μ				water, wave	m
Nun נ	Nu N ν				channel for irrigation	n
Samech ס	Sigma Σ σ				trellis or vine-prop	s
Ain ע	Omicron O o				eye	o
Ph פ Ph	Φ φ				mouth	p
Tzade צ	Zeta Z ζ				mountains	ts, z
Koph ק					drinking-cup	qu, k
Resh ר	Ro P ρ				man's head	r

The correspondence of the oldest forms with the original pictures is very traceable. But in the later forms they were lost, save in the names of the letters. The convenience of the writer, and a certain uniformity and neatness in the appearance of a written text, soon altered their shapes, so that they became arbitrary marks representing sounds only.

The principle upon which the form and the sound have been associated likewise appears from this table. The form is made to stand for the first sound in the name of the thing; like a, ape; b, bull; c, cat, in a modern horn-book.

The Mizraites who colonized the valley of the Nile, constructed their system of writing upon the same principle. Their first alphabet was this:

Form.		Thing.	Name in Coptic.	Power.	Form.		Thing.	Name in Coptic.	Power.
1		reed	*ake*	a, e, ō	8		vase for offering water	*nu* water	
2		quail	*oumt*	f, v u	9		cleft substance bound together	*pah* to cleave	p
3		leg	בוא Heb. βαινειν Gr.	b					
4		thread rope	*eiau*	h	10		crotchet or yoke	*sa* part	s
5		metal cup	*koph*	k	11		looped cord	*touot* to tie	t pronoun
6		mouth	*ro*	l, r	12		polisher	*taate* to polish	t medial & final
7		hurdle	*moone*	m interchange	13		plate paten	*shei*	sh ch

The principle upon which the forms and sounds are associated is the same here as in the other two alphabets. The form stands for the first articulation in the name of the thing. It also exactly corresponds with them in one or two characters. These are:—5 *koph* "the drinking cup" *k*. This is very evident. The Egyptian form of it was a metal dish with a loose ring; convenient both for hanging on a peg in the tent, and for packing on the journey. 8 *nu* "water," *n*. The Egyptians made the word for water *nu*, instead of מי *mu*, or מים *mem*, that it might coincide with the name of Noah the Patriarch whom they worshipped as the god of water. *nuch* נוח. The picture of water therefore stood for *n* in their alphabet, instead of *m* as in the other alphabets. They retained however in their language the primitive word for water. The original picture of it also "the wave," was very early adopted by them as another form of *n*. In some exceedingly ancient inscriptions it is interpreted by the earthen vase thus .* In the other alphabets this picture represents *m*. (*mem* or *mu*. See table.) But in the Mizraite dialect of the primitive language, the sounds m and n interchanged, or rather the one was inherent in the other. 9 *p* bears in some ancient transcriptions considerable resemblance to two rows of teeth.

* Tomb, No. 17, Saquara, &c. &c.

It may therefore have been *Phe* or *Pi*, adopted from the primitive alphabet. (See table.)

Thus plain is it that the framers of this Egyptian alphabet must have known the original whence the other alphabets were derived, and been familiar with the principle of its construction.

These thirteen letters are the foundation of the whole written system of Ancient Egypt. In the most ancient texts of it they are placed, either immediately before or after other characters denoting the same sounds, to interpret them. In later texts these characters are not so interpreted. Their powers had become perfectly well known, so that they no longer need interpretation.

The following are examples. ⌇ *ab* "flesh," is so written in texts of all ages except the oldest, where it stands thus, ⌇. The syllable *hl* or *hr* is likewise written ⌇ in all later texts; but in the most ancient tombs it is always written thus, ⌇. By thus comparing together the ancient with the more recent texts, we obtain the following alphabet:

INTRODUCTION. XXV

a, e, is interpreted by

f, u

h

k   ,,   ,,

n   ..   ..

p

s   ..   ..

sh

---

[1] Tomb of Nabrai, Benihassan Ins. c. 104.   [2] id. c. 152.
[3] id. c. 115.   [4] Name of Usercheres, Ghizeh, &c.
[5] Tomb at El Bersheh, Leps. II, 184.   [6] Tomb 91. Ghizeh.
[7] Tomb of Amenemes, Benihassan.   [8] Tablet, 567. Brit. Mus.
[9] Nahrai c. 157.   [10] Nahrai *pass.*
[11] Tomb 20. Saquara.   [12] idem.
[13] id. et *passim.*   [14] id. 17 Saq.
[15] Nahr. c. 174, &c.   [16] Amenemes.
[17] Nah. c. 18 &c. &c.   [18] Nah. c. 211, &c. &c.
[19] Ghiz. 26.   [20] id. c. 171 &c. &c.
[21] Nah. c. 206.   [22] Nab. *passim.*
[23] Amenemes.   [24] Nah. *passim.*
[25] Nah. c. 194.   [26] Ghiz. 49 &c.

b

All these additional characters are written, interpreted in the ancient, and uninterpreted in the later texts. The pronunciation of most of them had before been ascertained by modern students, from their occurrence in proper names and elsewhere.

This comparison of texts of different ages makes it very clear that the thirteen letters of our alphabet were the best known in the primitive times, and had therefore been the first invented.

The writing of Ancient Egypt then was alphabetic ; that is, its characters represented sounds, in exactly the same manner as the other two systems with which we have compared it. It differs from them however in a remarkable particular. Its inventors determined that its letters should always retain their first forms without degrading into mere arbitrary signs. They wanted them to be decorative as well as illustrative: so that their inscriptions might adorn the objects on which they were written as well as explain them.

The twelve sounds denoted by these thirteen letters were not enough to write the primitive language intelligibly in any of its dialects. They express the elementary articulations of the human voice only. But these may be uttered in many ways, and the sense of words often varies according to the mode of their pronunciation : so that a separate letter is required for each difference. Hence it was that the Hebrew alphabet came to have twenty-two letters, and the Greek twenty-four; and also, that so many of the letters in both alphabets are closely allied to each other in sound.

This necessity likewise contributed to the increase of the Egyptian alphabet. Many of the new letters were retained in the system to express modifications in the sounds of the primitive letters that at first interpreted them.

But the circumstance that every letter in this mode of writing remained a picture, supplied another and still stronger motive for the multiplication of the number of characters in it, and to an extent very far beyond that of either of the other systems. Such a writing requires, and of necessity, that the meanings of the words as well as the sounds should be suggested by the pictures of which it is composed; it could not be read without a help of this kind. This is so clear that it might have been known beforehand. It was found out by experience in Egypt. The most ancient texts are altogether alphabetic or nearly so: i.e. every character in them denotes a sound. They are likewise scarcely to be understood! This obscurity however was soon perceived, and two devices were framed to render them somewhat more perspicuous. These are just as simple and child-like as that by which the radical letters were formed.

A. Initials.

This device is merely an extension of the principle of the radical or first alphabet. The medial and final sounds of a word written with the letters already invented, were added to the picture of the thing it denoted, which was made the initial (or first) letter. In the earliest times this initial was accompanied by the radical letter, the sound of which it represented; but afterwards, through long use, the form and sound became sufficiently associated, and the interpreting or index letter was no longer needed. Thus the word *hotp* " a shew table of offering," was written 〖◌〗 in the oldest texts. The second character ◌ is a picture of the table itself, as set forth before the images of the gods. The cord 〖 that precedes it shows that it is to be pronounced *h*. But the pronunciation of this frequently used group soon became sufficiently known without the index letter: so that nearly everywhere it is written thus ◌. In the same manner *sha*, " a joint or cut consisting of the ribs of an ox," was at first written thus ◌ :* but very soon afterwards the power of the initial picture became familiar to men's minds, and in all later texts

* Tomb, No. 17 Ghizeh.

it is inscribed thus : 🦅. So also *nh*, the name of the black vulture, or turkey-buzzard, was at first written 〰️🦅,* but ever after 🦅, without the wave, because it was then well known that the picture was to be pronounced *n*.

These index letters generally go before the picture they interpret. They sometimes follow it. In one or two instances other signs are even interposed between them. So little were system and perspicuity understood in remote times.

This initial writing was very rigidly confined to a single class of thoughts or ideas. Words so written never meant the thing depicted, but some quality or abstraction not to be represented in a picture, of which it was suggestive. The group 🍞 *htp* did not mean " a shew table," but " union, combination," and from thence " peace, harmony," and many kindred ideas, because meats and drinks of different kinds were set forth together on these tables. The language exactly conforms to this group. The word in the Coptic texts denotes " a collective offering," and has also the sense of " union," " marriage," and many similar meanings. The group 🦴 never meant " the ribs of an ox," but " weighed in the balance," and thence " tried, approved," because the ribs of all animals are equal on both sides, in number and length. The con-

* Tomb at Benihassan, &c.

formity of the language to the group is equally striking in the present instance. The Coptic word signifies "to divide, to multiply by division," and a crowd of words derived from it signify "equal," "a balance," "to weigh," "to adjust &c." In the same way the name of the turkey-buzzard written initially meant "black," because that was its colour, and not the bird itself. Such is likewise the case with every other group so written throughout the language. There is no known exception.

B. DETERMINATIVES.

In its primitive mode of use this is the most infantile device possible. A picture of the thing intended followed the letters that spelt its name: thus ⟨⟩ *eh,* Coptic *ehe* "a cow," was followed by 🐂 No further exemplification is required of this mode, which may be called "the determinative of the thing."

Another application of this device displays more thought and ingenuity, though just as simple. Words denoting animals were followed by the prepared hide of an ox, ⟨⟩ . The names of all flying creatures were determined by the picture of a goose, ⟨⟩ . Violent actions of the arm are signified by an arm grasping a club ⟨⟩, gentler actions of the arm by a hand soothing, ⟨⟩ . Rapid motions were denoted by two legs running ⟨⟩ . Slower motions by a leg walking, 𓂻. Words implying speech were determined by the picture of a man with his hand to his mouth, 𓀁. These characters may be called "determinatives of kind," i. e. of the class of things or actions to which the word belongs. Their invention is by far the most profound and abstract thought that appears in the whole system.

In late texts both initials and determinatives are often used alone, as abbreviations of the groups to which they belong: but it cannot be too plainly stated that they always signify the word and never the idea. There was no ideography (strictly speaking) in the writing of Ancient Egypt.

Thus was the hieroglyphic system constructed upon thirteen letters. It was as strictly alphabetic as the Greek or Hebrew writings. The initials and determinatives were mere expedients, suggested by its necessities and defects.

ISRAEL IN EGYPT.

PRELIMINARY.

"MARVELLOUS THINGS DID HE IN THE SIGHT OF THEIR FATHERS, IN THE LAND OF EGYPT, IN THE FIELD OF ZOAN." Psalm lxxviii. 12.

THERE is a perfect consistency in God's dealings in all things. He has one measure towards one people; he administers to the same locality, according to the same laws, at all times. Towards the people of Israel, his dispensations of mercy and of wrath both come strictly within one category, "he hath not dealt so with any other nation." His mercies towards Israel of old were without parallel; equally unexampled are the present judgments of Israel; scattered among all nations, yet separate among them, with all the miseries of an extinct nationality: Yet, for eighteen centuries that extinction which terminates the sufferings of every other dispersed people in a very few generations, has not yet befallen him. Israel gasps in his last agonies; yet not to die, but to struggle and to moan—a living death. Truly "he hath not dealt so with any other nation."

In the same locality we may likewise often trace this consistency of administration at all times. In no country more remarkably than in the one whose history blends with that of Israel throughout so long a period;—Egypt, to which Abram went down immediately after his call from Ur of the Chaldees, and whence God long afterwards called his son. Throughout the wide interval that separates these two events, the histories of Israel and Egypt run parallel. Egypt, according to our quotation, was the land of wonders from the first. Egypt is also the land of wonders to this day; and the stranger who now visits the valley of the Nile will have to acknowledge, that in "his sight," as well as in that of the fathers of old, God "does marvellous things in the land of Egypt, in the field of Zoan."

Egypt is situated on the driest zone of the world, on both sides the equator. It is just to the northward of the tropical rains. They never extend beyond the Astaboras and the southern limits of Upper Nubia. On its other border, the more uncertain mutations of the weather which fertilize the temperate zone, die away on the coast of Egypt. It is only in the depth of winter, that the clouds which career over the stormy Mediterranean, reach her coasts, and sometimes discharge their rains at Alexandria or Rosetta. With this exception, rain is a phenomenon in Egypt, contributing in no appreciable degree to her fertility, and forming no element whatever in the calculations of the husbandman. Egypt is, moreover, very near the centre of by far the driest portion of the whole surface of the earth. The arid, unproductive sand-plains of the Sahara, commence at her western border, and stretch away from thence to the westward, for more than 4000 miles to the Atlantic. To the eastward are the sun-bleached, sterile mountains of the eastern desert, of the Sinaitic peninsula, and of Arabia Petræa; and beyond them, the salt, dusty, dry tracts of Persia and Beloochistan, for at least an equal distance; so that Egypt is a narrow strip of fertility, reclaimed in the midst of 8000 miles of desert by the waters of a vast tropical river. The rest of the earth's surface presents no parallel to this.

The phenomena strictly peculiar to Egypt arise out of these circumstances.

The annual overflow of the Nile is the result of the tropical rains on the mountains of Abyssinia and South Ethiopia. It first appears at Memphis, about the summer solstice. It reaches its height about the autumnal equinox. It has entirely subsided at the winter solstice. The diffusion of this fertile flood, over the arid surface of the desert, requires the mind and the labour of man to an extent unknown in any other country. The digging of canals, of overflow and recession, the close observation of the right moment when the waters are to be admitted through the flood-gates, and when, the flood-gates being closed, the sluices which allow them to return to the bed of the river must be opened, are niceties upon which the success of the husbandman entirely depends, and which keep both his mental and bodily faculties in constant exercise. A day's mistake in either, is fatal to his hopes. Then, by means of irrigation during the low Nile, the fertile loam of Egypt will produce yet another crop: and the governors of Egypt have never been slow or gentle in their exactions from the wretched slaves that till the soil; so that the creak of the water-wheel and of the *shadoof* or balance-bucket, never ceases. And "the land of Egypt is still the house of bondage" to the human race.

One other peculiarity of Egypt will also require some notice. The extreme dryness of the atmosphere tends to the preservation of all remains of ancient constructions and of every other monument of human labour, to an extent without example in any other country. From the granite of Syene, down to the coat of Nile mud, stuccoed, and inscribed with hieroglyphics in colours, nothing appears to have undergone any change from atmospheric causes since the day it was finished. Bread, fruit, flowers, bakemeats, corn, seeds, linen in quantities incredible, wooden figures of most delicate execution are found in the tombs of Egypt, as little changed by the 4000 years wherein they have lain there, as the gems in the metal rings that accompany them. From the first king that sat upon the throne of Egypt, down to Caracalla and Septimius Severus the Roman emperors, whatever memorial the hand of man has spared, the tooth of time has in no degree injured.

In addition to the preservation of the monuments of Egypt, their number also far surpasses those of any other ancient nation. Every city, town and village, of ancient Egypt, had its temple and its cemetery. There was not a pillar or a stone in the temple which was not covered with reliefs and inscriptions. There was not a tomb, or sarcophagus, or mummy-case in the cemetery which was not similarly decorated. All these inscriptions were, in a sense, historical. Those on the temples related the exploits in war, or the acts of devotion in peace, of the king who had constructed them. On the remains in the tombs are inscribed the names of the deceased persons whose property they had been, and whose mummies were deposited in them;—so that in a sense, there is scarcely a monument of ancient Egypt that does not throw light upon her history, and from the days she first became a kingdom until now, it would be hard to say that any one memorial had perished through the lapse of time.

'These inscriptions are written in very remarkable characters (called hieroglyphics, by the Greeks), the mode of reading which is now, as we have seen, to a great extent, recovered.

These monuments, however would be unavailable as history, were it not that the Greeks in the times that followed those of Alexander of Macedon, had very great curiosity in all that related to Egypt, and translated the histories on the walls of the temples. Little remains to us of these translations, save mere lists of royal names; but these are of great value, because they can be identified with the hieroglyphic originals, and by their help we can place the names of the kings we read on the temples in the order of their succession.

So that the climate of Egypt itself has combined with the curiosity of the Greeks regarding its early history, to preserve to us a far more copious and connected series of memorials of its ancient greatness, than of any other kingdom that ever existed on the earth.

That the history of Egypt bears some close and intimate relation to the inspired history of Israel, is a very obvious truth. So plainly is the Bible, the book which of all others belongs to, and requires the history of Egypt, that the connection between the two has been always acknowledged, both by Jews and Christians. Josephus the Jew has preserved to us portions of the lists and histories of the Greeks to which we have already alluded, in his works on the Old Testament; the remaining fragments of these lost works we owe altogether to the scriptural comments and illustrations of Eusebius, Syncellus and other early Christian writers. The same connection and necessity were perceived by the Christian scholars of the more modern era of the Reformation: and many learned and laborious efforts were embodied in ponderous folios, all directed to the illustration of Scripture from what was then known regarding Egypt. These all failed, for lack of knowledge of the subject, and of the means of acquiring it. That they were made, however, sufficiently proves the existence in their day, of the conviction we have explained. These details will suffice to show, that when we claim Egypt and her ancient history, as especially a Bible subject, and illustrative of, and illustrated by, the Bible far more than any other book, we are making no fanatical or bigotted appropriation, but are merely stating a fact which has at all times been acknowledged, and to the consciousness of which we owe the preservation of the Greek illustrative records by the early Jewish and Christian writers.

It is the object of the present work to show that the recovery of the mode of reading the inscriptions which cover the monuments of Egypt now in existence, has by no means disappointed these expectations; and that the principal purpose which the facts thereby elicited will subserve, is that of scriptural illustration.

The notices of Egypt in the Bible are to the full as remarkable, and as distinct from those which allude to any other ancient nation, as the natural and historical phenomena we have already explained. The name of Egypt in the Old Testament, was that of the third son of the patriarch Ham, so that the fact that Egypt was first colonized by him, rests on exactly the same evidence as that Assyria was colonized by Ashur, or Canaan by the patriarch's first-born. The names of Ashur and Canaan have been long forgotten; but the name of Egypt in the east, to this day, is that of Mizraim, the third son of Ham. The same fact, moreover, though not formally stated, flows as a clear inevitable inference from the tenor of the inspired narrative. In the tenth chapter of Genesis, the name of Mizraim occurs in the enumeration of the sons of Ham, verses 6, 13. In the eleventh chapter is the narrative of the dispersion of Babel. In the twelfth chapter, the event that immediately follows the call of Abram, is his emigration into the land of Mizraim; and that at this remote epoch, this epithet had the same meaning as at all subsequent times, is demonstrated by the context, where the king of Mizraim is called Pharaoh; which, we need scarcely explain, is a title common to all the kings of Egypt and peculiar to them. Verses 10, 15.

This is by no means the only inference regarding Egypt that flows from this portion of the inspired narrative. Egypt was a monarchy settled upon a basis very similar to that which obtained long afterwards at the time of the call of Abram. Pharaoh was surrounded by his princes when the patriarch sojourned in Egypt, and therefore ruled as a king over a considerable territory. This was not the case with any other ancient monarchy at this remote period. We find in the course of the same narrative, that Shinar, afterwards Babylon, Elam, afterwards Persia, (Gen. xiv. 1.) Damascus, afterwards Syria, (xv. 2.) were then small independent cities, each under its *Melek*,* or petty king.

All these specialties regarding Egypt in its connexion with the Old Testament, are equally to be noted in the subsequent periods of that history. The interpretation of the hieroglyphics has greatly increased both the number and importance of them. It has been a slow and tedious process, but many in-

---

* The word *melek* abbreviated *mek* is the name of the hereditary ruler of a town or village, to this day, in East Africa.

teresting, and, to the verification of the Bible, highly important results, have already been realized. It is to these results and not to the process, it is to the general reader and not to the student of hieroglyphics that we exclusively address ourselves.

We hope to show, first of all, that the anticipations so long entertained by believers in Revelation, of ample light upon its concise narrative from the records of Ancient Egypt, have been abundantly verified; and then that from this new, and by many altogether unsuspected quarter, we have large additional evidence that the Bible is true.

The two heads under which the illustrations we have to submit in the present introductory chapter arrange themselves, are THE FIRST COLONIZATION OF EGYPT, and THE STATE OF EGYPT AT THE TIME OF THE VISIT OF ABRAM.

§ 1. THE FIRST COLONIZATION OF EGYPT.

The Scripture narrative has already presented to us Mizraim the son of Ham, with his posterity, as a clan or sept in the tribe of his father on the plains of Shinar, before the dispersion; and after that event, as having given his name to the valley of the Nile, in which his descendants had settled. It clearly follows that, on its occurrence, the clan of Mizraim emigrated to Egypt. Now the only direct route from Shinar to Egypt is across the isthmus of

Suez; and it is perfectly obvious in itself, as well as a fact with which all history makes us familiar, that large bodies of men emigrating under circumstances of misfortune, invariably plant themselves on the first convenient and safe locality at which they arrive, and afterwards extend gradually from thence in other directions. Under this view, the geographical position of the remains of Ancient Egypt, relatively to their antiquity, becomes a question of the deepest and most vital importance to the inquiry before us. The present author was the first to point out the facts that bear upon this question many years ago; and subsequent researches in Egypt have now established them beyond all possibility of contradiction. The remains of the most ancient kings all lie immediately opposite to the isthmus and to the ancient city of Heliopolis, at the crown of the Delta, just at the spot where the weary immigrant, after crossing the sands of the desert, and being entangled in the swamps of the Delta, would first find rest for the sole of his foot. Not only is this fact remarkably in accordance with the Scripture narratives: it is equally in harmony with the Greek tradition regarding the origin of the Egyptian monarchy, according to which the first king of Egypt was the first to cross the river and found the city of Memphis. The ruins of Memphis are part of the locality we have indicated. That this is the spot where Egypt was first settled, is further demonstrated by the circumstance, that immediately to the southward of it are found the names of the kings that, in the Greek lists, come next in antiquity; and this graduated order obtains for the whole valley, as to the great mass of the monuments; so that the Greek lists of kings and the geographical position of the kings' names in Egypt are in exact agreement, and the gradual progress of the first immigrants, and their occupation of each location in the valley in succession yet remain memorialized on the rocks that hem it in.

Another very unexpected identification has still more securely clenched the proof that Egypt was first colonized by the immediate descendants of Noah. The primitive idolatry of Egypt was a hero-worship, and its most ancient gods were merely the patriarchs of the Bible deified. The god of Heliopolis, for example, was Athom, or Adam. The tutelary of Memphis was Ptah; that is, Phut the brother of Mizraim. No, or Noh, was the god of the annual overflow, and a deification of the patriarch Noah. Mizraim was also made the local god of a city of the eastern Delta, under his primitive name of Osiris, that is יוֹצֵר, *Iozar*, "the potter." The patriarch Ham, in like manner, took the form of Ammon. The demonstration of all this belongs to the history of Egypt: I have there fully worked it out, and have now merely to refer to it.*

The monuments found in the Delta (the district immediately to the northward of Memphis and Heliopolis) all belong to a much later period of the history of Egypt. An interval of many centuries separates the two. This circumstance also we shall find to harmonize with beautiful exactitude with that which is inferred in the inspired history.

§ 2. THE STATE OF EGYPT AT THE TIME OF THE VISIT OF ABRAM.

The events that immediately followed the call of Abram from Ur of the Chaldees are thus related in the concise narrative of them embodied in the Bible.

" And Abram passed through the land unto the place of Sichem, unto the plain of Moreh. And the Canaanite was then in the land. And the Lord appeared unto Abram, and said, Unto thy seed will I give this land; and there builded he an altar unto the Lord who appeared unto him. And he removed from thence unto a mountain on the east of Bethel, and pitched his tent, having Bethel on the west and Hai on the east: and there he builded an altar unto the Lord, and called upon the name of the Lord.

* The Monumental History of Egypt. (Binns and Goodwin.)

And Abram journeyed, going on still toward the south." Gen. xii. 6—9.

This is the history of the period that elapsed between the call of Abram from Ur of the Chaldees, and his going down into Egypt. It presents to us Abram as the chief or head of a nomade tribe, pitching his tent in the places most favourable for the pasturage of his many cattle, and for this reason often changing his place. We infer from these considerations, that but a brief period is comprehended in this portion of the narrative. It proceeds thus:—
" And there was a famine in the land : and Abram went down to Egypt to sojourn there, for the famine was grievous in the land. And it came to pass when he was come near to enter into Egypt, that he said unto Sarai his wife, Behold now, I know that thou art a fair woman to look upon : therefore it shall come to pass when the Egyptians shall see thee, that they shall say, This is his wife ; and they will kill me, but they will save thee alive. Say, I pray thee, that thou art my sister, that it may be well with me for thy sake, and that my soul may live because of thee. And it came to pass, that when Abram came into Egypt, the Egyptians beheld the woman that she was very fair. The princes also of Pharaoh saw her, and commended her before Pharaoh : and the woman was taken into Pharaoh's house. And he entreated Abram well for her sake : and he

had sheep, and oxen, and he-asses, and men-servants, and maid-servants, and she-asses, and camels. And the Lord plagued Pharaoh and his house, with great plagues, because of Sarai, Abram's wife. And Pharaoh called Abram, and said, What is this thou hast done to me? Why didst thou not tell me she was thy wife? Why saidst thou, She is my sister? so I might have taken her to me to wife: now therefore behold thy wife, take her and go thy way. And Pharaoh commanded his men concerning him: and they sent him away, and his wife, and all that he had. And Abram went up out of Egypt, he, and his wife, and all that he had, and Lot with him, into the south [of Canaan]. And Abram was very rich in cattle, in silver, and in gold." Gen. xii. xiii.

This passage, like those we have already quoted, receives large and important illustration from the recovery of the mode of reading the inscriptions that cover the remains of Ancient Egypt. The remarkable circumstances arising out of it, we take to be, the settlement of a monarchy in Egypt at so early a period, and the migration thither. The question of the existence of a kingdom so early has already been mentioned. We only state here that the monuments, when compared with the lists of kings, distinctly elicit the fact, that at the time of Abram's visit, the Egyptian monarchy had existed for some centuries.

In regard of Abram's migration into Egypt, a difficulty seems to arise from another passage in the same inspired book, which declares that " every shepherd is an abomination to the Egyptians." (xlvi. 34.) Yet not only does Abram go down into Egypt, following the exclusive occupation of a shepherd or cattle-feeder, without scruple, when the famine befals the land of Canaan, but he sojourns there ; and with his family is received at the court of Pharaoh. The political condition of Egypt, and especially of the Delta, the northernmost portion of the valley into which Abram must have emigrated, which the reading of the hieroglyphics has disclosed, obviates this difficulty.

The narratives which the Greeks had copied from the temples of Egypt relate, that at a remote period of her history, shepherds of Canaan invaded the country, drove the reigning native Pharaoh from Memphis, and retained possession of that capital, and of the rest of Egypt for a long period. They proceed with long accounts of the destruction of temples, the massacre of the Egyptians, their sale as slaves, and other indignities, and barbarities committed by the Shepherds upon the aborigines. The monuments however, tell altogether a different story. According to them, there were at this period two dynasties of kings reigning in Egypt at the same time, each pretending to be kings of all Egypt. Both were the lineal descendants of MENES, the first king, who also first crossed the Nile and built the city of Memphis, on the western bank, overcoming the children of Phut who were settled in that locality. He then married the daughter of the Phutite king whom he had conquered, and ruled over his kingdom which he added to Egypt. He still further benefited his country by diverting the course of the Nile, causing it to flow more to the eastward than heretofore. By this work he greatly increased the fertility, not of the land around his new city of Memphis only, but also of Heliopolis, and one or two other localities on the eastern border of the Delta, where cities were at this time also in process of being founded by the Migraites. Menes was the son of the founder and petty king of one of these rising cities, Tanis, the Zoan of our quotation. Such was the reputation which Menes acquired by these good works among his tribe and kindred, both for himself and his family, that he was unanimously elected king of Upper Egypt, or Egypt on the left bank of the Nile, and his father or brother king of Lower Egypt, or Egypt on the right bank. This division of the kingdom and these two co-regent families of kings, both of the race of Menes, continued actually up to the period of the Exodus, and formally up to the extinction of the monarchy. Both lines pretended to the whole kingdom, and never waived this pretension,

c

even when there was peace between them. It was in these strange political circumstances that the fable of the shepherd invasion originated. The dominions of the Lower Egyptian Pharaohs had, at the time of it, been for more than two centuries circumscribed within the limits of a province or two, on the extreme eastern border of the Delta, by the successes of the rival pretension. They were compelled by this their position, to seek the alliance of the Canaanites, who, as shepherds or merchants, ranged the desert of Suez. Abram's visit to Egypt took place at this period. The Pharaoh with whom he had intercourse was a Lower Egyptian king, one of the 10th dynasty of the lists. Sebennytus in the eastern Delta was his chief city.* This explanation, for which we are altogether indebted to the monuments, converts our seeming difficulty into a high probability.

The alliances with Canaan of these Sebennyte Pharaohs, enabled them about a century afterwards, with the help of their auxiliaries, to become once more the aggressors upon the dominions of the Upper Egyptian Pharaohs. They retook Memphis,

---

* It is called Heracleopolis in the lists of Manetho, who was a native of it, because Hercules was its local god, and because Manetho did not care to expose what he felt to be a disgrace to his native city—viz. that it had been the capital of a race of shepherd-kings. Sebennytus is the סונה *Seveneh* of the Bible, Ezek. xxix. 10, where it is translated by mistake, Syene.

and expelled the rival pretension from the whole of Egypt. The history of this war was written by the partizans of the defeated faction. They therefore named the Lower Egyptians, foreigners; and the Sebennyte Pharaohs, shepherd-kings, in reproach and derision. The monarchs thus designated were nevertheless natives of Egypt, and the lineal descendants of Menes. The monuments declare this fact clearly and unequivocally. It cannot be too early or too plainly stated.

The circumstance that "every shepherd was an abomination to the Egyptians," was a far older rivalry than this. It began with Cain and Abel. It was that between the husbandman and the herdsman. Egypt was especially the land of the former, and therefore the latter was unclean in it; and remained so, even to the end of the monarchy.

These, and many more such facts, have appeared from the reading of the writings on the ruins of Egypt. They are highly interesting and important; needful to be known, not by the Biblical critic only, but also by every reader of the Bible. Yet do they remain to this day absolutely inaccessible to either class of students. The knowledge of them is strictly confined to the few who have devoted themselves to a most laborious and uninviting subject, and they are themselves altogether the issue of their long-continued and unnoticed labours. It is the practical results of those labours in the illustration and verification of the portions of Holy Writ which discourse of Israel in Egypt, that we purpose to lay before the general reader; omitting the processes and analyses whereby they have been worked out, as not essential to the matter in hand. We do not fear to state that, as we proceed with the history of Israel in Egypt, we shall find the illustration thrown upon the inspired narrative by the monuments of the latter, progressively increasing in value and importance, so as triumphantly to establish the validity of the anticipations of great light upon the Bible from Ancient Egypt, and also to afford a proof of the Divine purpose in the wondrous preservation of her monuments.

CHAPTER II.

JOSEPH IN EGYPT.

An interval of 215 years elapses after the sojourn of Abram in Egypt, and then the valley of the Nile becomes once more the scene of the inspired narrative :—

" And Jacob dwelt in the land wherein his father was a stranger, in the land of Canaan. These are the generations of Jacob. Joseph being seventeen years old, was feeding his flock with his brethren ; and the lad was with the sons of Bilhah and with the sons of Zilpah his father's wives. And Joseph brought unto his father their evil report. Now Israel loved Joseph more than all his children, because he was the son of his old age ; and he made him a coat of many colours. And when his brethren saw that their father loved him more than all his brethren, they hated him, and could not speak peaceably unto him. And Joseph dreamed a dream, and he told it his brethren, and they hated him yet the more. . . .

"And his brethren envied him, but his father observed the saying.

"And his brethren went to feed their father's flock in Shechem. And Israel said unto Joseph, Do not thy brethren depasture in Shechem? come, and I will send thee unto them. And he said unto him, Here am I. And he said to him, Go, I pray thee, see whether it be well with thy brethren, and well with the flocks; and bring me word again. So he sent him out of the vale of Hebron, and he came to Shechem. And a certain man found him, and behold he was wandering in the fields; and the man asked him, saying, What seekest thou? And he said, I seek my brethren; tell me, I pray thee, where they depasture? And the man said, They are departed hence, for I heard them say, Let us go to Dothan. And Joseph went after his brethren and found them in Dothan. And when they saw him afar off, even before he came near unto them, they conspired against him to slay him. And they said one to another, Behold this dreamer cometh. Come now, therefore, and let us slay him, and cast him into some pit, and we will say some evil beast hath devoured him; and we shall see what will become of his dreams. And Reuben heard it, and he delivered him out of their hands, and said, Let us not kill him. And Reuben said unto them, Shed no blood, but cast him into the pit that is in the wilderness, and lay no hand upon him; that he might rid him out of their hands to deliver him to his father again.

"And it came to pass when Joseph was come unto his brethren, that they stript Joseph out of his coat, his coat of colours that was on him. And they took him and cast him into a pit: and the pit was empty: there was no water in it. And they sate down to eat bread: and they lifted up their eyes, and behold a company of Ishmaelites came from Gilead with their camels bearing spicery and balm and myrrh, going to carry it down to Egypt. And Judah said unto his brethren, What profit to slay our brother and conceal his blood? Come, let us sell him to the Ishmaelites, and let not our hand be upon him, for he is our brother, and our flesh. And his brethren were content. Then there passed by Midianites, merchantmen, and they drew and lifted up Joseph from the pit, and sold Joseph to the Ishmaelites for twenty pieces of silver; and they brought Joseph into Egypt. . . .

"And the Midianites sold him into Egypt unto Potiphar, a prince (*saris*) of Pharaoh, and *sar hattabachim*. Gen. xxxvii. 1—5, 11—28, 36.

So familiar are the words of this narrative become through frequent use, that we often overlook the truthful touches with which it abounds, and which show out into bold relief and reality, the lives and the thoughts, and the habits of those primitive rangers of the Sinaitic desert. This however, is not the object with which we quote it on the present occasion. Joseph is gone down into Egypt, and we hasten to follow him thither.

The merchants or traders to whom Joseph was sold were Ishmaelites by descent, and Midianites by nation. Midian was the portion of the Sinaitic desert which lay immediately adjacent to the eastern frontier of Egypt. At the time now under consideration (that of the so-called shepherd-kingdom) Midian was apparently common ground to Egypt and Canaan. In the days of Moses, when the shepherds had been expelled, the limits of Egypt were better defined, and we shall find that then Midian was out of her jurisdiction. No monument has been found in this part of the desert whence it could be inferred that Egypt ever pretended to it: though somewhat to the southward, the minerals of the Wady Meghara had in the days of Joseph been the object of contention between the Pharaohs and Canaan for some centuries. The records of their strife remain written on the rocks at this day. But Midian was a country presenting no attractions whatever to the Egyptian colonists. Its sterile plains and dreary precipitous valleys afforded no home to those who had dwelt in cities on the banks of the fruitful Nile. The scanty innutritive herbage called forth by the thin rills of brackish water that here and there showed themselves, scarcely sufficed to keep alive the lean herds with which the hardy sons of Ishmael depastured it in their periodical wanderings over this dreary waste. By profession they were merchants. They carried to Canaan the corn, the wine, the oil, the linen of Egypt. They returned to Egypt with the spicery, the balm, the myrrh, the precious woods, the minerals of Canaan. Spicery only is mentioned in the inspired narrative before us. The clan to which Joseph was sold traded in this article alone. The demand for it in Egypt was enormous. The careful examination of the mummies of different epochs establishes the fact that at these remote periods it was used in the embalmment both of men and sacred animals, to an extent which was not practicable in after times, through the failure of the supply.

The twenty pieces or rings of silver, which these merchants paid the hardened profligates, as the price of their brother, was, at this age of the world, by no means the small amount that it sounds in modern ears. Silver always takes the precedence of gold, when both are enumerated in the earlier portions of the inspired narrative. The same is the case in the hieroglyphic texts; silver is always mentioned before gold, as the more precious metal, both on account of its comparative rarity, and because of its more extensive use in the adornment and utensils of the temples on account of its colour. Whiteness and purity were inseparably connected in the Egyptian mythology.

That these desert merchants brought into Egypt Canaanite slaves amongst other commodities, is a fact which is abundantly confirmed and amply illustrated by cotemporary remains of the times of Joseph and of those that immediately preceded him. As early as the epoch of the Pyramids, three centuries before Joseph, Canaanite men and women perform as posturers, tumblers, and jugglers, before the princes of Egypt as they sate and banquetted.* About 150 years afterwards, hundreds of Canaanite slaves are depicted wrestling and fighting as gladiators before Chetei, a prince of the court of Osortasen I., of the 12th dynasty. The tomb of this prince is at Benihassan. In the same locality is a still more remarkable proof of the traffic in slaves with Canaan, and of a period approaching still nearer to that of Joseph. It is the picture of the ceremonies that took place on the delivery of thirty-seven makers (or pounders) of stibium (or powdered antimony for the eye), which were purchased by Noh-hotp II., one of the excavators of the tomb, of a chief or petty king of the Jebusites. The chief, his clan, and his

* e. g. the tomb of Imai, one of the princes of Suphis.

presents are represented in the picture, but not the slaves. The picture is well known in England; for since the publication of it twenty years ago, by Rosellini,* it has been frequently copied into English

to its import. The hieroglyphics that accompany it explain very clearly what it means. It is " the delivery of the stibium-makers which the great chief of the Jebusites hath brought, even thirty-seven captives of his club." The transaction took place in the sixth year of Osortasen II., the second successor of the former monarch (as we shall presently see), scarcely a century before the times of Joseph. It is impossible therefore for any fact to rest on a firmer basis of monumental evidence, than that the Canaanite traders to Egypt were in the constant habit of bringing thither for sale slaves from among their own countrymen, whether enslaved as prisoners of war or by other circumstances. To a rightly constituted mind, evidence like this to the truth of a narrative is the most valuable of all.

The meaning of the name Potiphar is, " he who belongs (is devoted to) the sun," the local god of On or Heliopolis, at the head of the Delta. This is a point of great importance for the locality in which Potiphar was a resident.

The title rightly translated " prince" is of constant

* M. R. Part 26, seq.

occurrence in the tombs of the magnates of Egypt of the period before us: and, wonderful to tell, the inspired penman has copied it almost letter for letter from the hieroglyphic original—*srsh*. This title was highly honourable, and always heads the enumeration of the honours of those to whom it is ascribed.

The office borne by Potiphar is also one peculiar to Egypt, and described by two Egyptian words, which at a very late period have been assimilated to two later Hebrew words. We believe Potiphar to have been *sar toje*, i. e. " prefect (inspector) of the plantations." This is a common office with the princes in the tombs of Ghizeh.

The Pharaoh to whose court Potiphar was attached, and who afterwards became the patron of Joseph, was the king Phiops or Aphophis. All the ancient authorities who have mentioned the subject agree in this with such perfect unanimity, that to reject their testimony is simply to throw overboard all antiquity. Aphophis was one of the Memphite Pharaohs.

The history of Egypt in the interval that has elapsed since it was last the scene of the inspired narrative, will now require our attention.

Josephus, the Jewish historian, relates that when Abram first came into Egypt the Egyptians were engaged in a civil war, arising out of differences in religion; but by the good offices of the patriarch, the two belligerent parties were reconciled, and he left Egypt at peace. The only parts of this story of the slightest historical value are the statements that there was a religious civil war in Egypt when Abram came thither, and that it had ceased when he departed thence. Had such not been the fact, Apion and the keepers of the temple-records, with whom Josephus was in controversy, would have been too happy to have pointed out the error. The rest of the story they would treat as a mere *kompology*, as it was called, that is, a boast for the purpose of magnifying his own nation, and for which his own books furnished him with the authority. This was the universal mode of writing history in those days. Now it is the fact that shortly before the times of Abraham a great religious feud arose in Egypt. The cotemporary monuments are the unerring witnesses to this fact. An imperfect hint at such an event may be detected in the account of Egypt in Herodotus the Greek historian; but without their interpretation no human sagacity could have eliminated the truth from his legend. He however visited Egypt in utter ignorance of the language, and was therefore altogether at the mercy of the mendacious priesthood, and of his far from honest interpreter. According to the legend in question, the names and memories of Cheops and Cephrenes, the builders of the two great pyramids at Ghizeh, a part of the cemetery of Memphis, were held in great detestation, whereas Mencheres, the monarch who constructed the third and smaller pyramid in their immediate vicinity, was honoured as one of the most eminent of the benefactors of Egypt. The closing of temples was one of the atrocities ascribed to the two delinquent Pharaohs. Their re-construction was one of the blessings conferred upon Egypt by Mencheres.

Such is the legend; and the present condition of the three pyramids certainly sanctions the assumption, that it is not altogether without some foundation in fact. The external casing of granite that once covered the pyramids of Cheops and Cephrenes, had been removed in the days of Herodotus, B.C. 450: their appearance at this day is exactly that which he describes. But their bases are encumbered with chips and splinters of this material, worked off by the sculptor's chisel, to an extent and depth of which no one who has not actually visited them can form any conception. These pyramids, after their desecration, have evidently served for ages as the quarry whence the adjacent cities drew their supply of this (in Lower Egypt) precious and costly material. But of the neighbouring pyramid of Mencheres, more than one half of the granite casing now remains, and of the rest, many huge blocks, untouched, lie strewn about its base, bearing all the marks of comparatively recent removal. Visibly it was not until the final extinction of the Egyptian idolatry, and for the construction of churches and mosques, that the dilapidation of the pyramid of Mencheres was begun. Yet, if we examine the tombs of the princes, the nobles, and warriors of these three monarchs that surround their pyramids, in numbers incredible, we shall find that for the reclaiming of waste lands, and for the conquest of foreign enemies, Cheops and Cephrenes were far greater benefactors to Egypt than Mencheres. The comparison of the monuments of the three bring out nevertheless a difference which solves the difficulty. It is in the religious tenets of the two epochs, and may be thus explained. In the days of Cheops and Cephrenes, every king of Egypt became a god on his decease, and was worshipped in his pyramid, and associated in divine honours with the dead patriarchs of their original pantheon. But in the days of Mencheres (about a century afterwards, according to the monuments,)* this king-worship ceases altogether, and the dead patriarchs are the only gods. Osiris also, who is Mizraim, the tutelary of Abydos, and who is never once mentioned on the tombs of the former epoch, first assumes on the monuments of Mencheres the office of king of the dead, which he ever afterwards retained in the

* The Greek lists are not to be relied upon.

Egyptian mythology. The motive for this elevation is a perfectly obvious and natural one, according to the modes of thought that prevailed in the ancient world. The deceased patriarch who founded the Egyptian monarchy was *jure divino*, the king of all dead Egyptians. Mencheres merely gave him his rights.

A civil war in Egypt was the consequence of the changes in religion effected by Mencheres. The monuments and the lists combine in their indication of trouble and confusion in the times that follow his. Now, if Abram, (according to the uncontradicted tradition of Josephus), came into Egypt while this civil war was raging, and if it ceased before his departure, the time of this cessation corresponds, of course, with that of Abram's visit. We know the time in the history of Egypt, when this peace was concluded. It was at the commencement of the 12th dynasty of kings, as it is called in the lists. We know it by this: the lists then come once more into perfect harmony with the monuments; whereas, for the five preceding dynasties, nothing can be made of the lists when compared with the monuments. They tell of hundreds of kings, mostly nameless; whereas the monuments interpose five kings only between the last monarch of the sixth dynasty, and the first of the 12th, and of those five, four are found nowhere but in genealogies. The conclusion regarding the lists which this comparison suggests, is fully established by the recurrence of the same confusion in every other period of anarchy throughout the history of the monarchy. Advantage was afterwards taken by the priesthood, of such times, to insert in their lists dynasties of nameless kings reigning through fabulous centuries, for the purpose of exaggerating thereby the antiquity of Egypt.

The inspired narrative very satisfactorily confirms this our assumed date for the visit of Abram to Egypt. The commencement of the 12th dynasty precedes the times of Phiops or Aphophis by about two centuries :—which is also the proximate interval between the epochs of Abram and Joseph.

A time of great prosperity, lasting for upwards of a century, is the combined indication of the monuments and the lists, as the consequence of this pacification. The adherents of Mencheres were clearly in the ascendant, and were the unquestioned rulers of all Egypt. They extended the bounds of Egypt far to the southward. The greater part of Nubia was added by them to the monarchy, and it is in this quarter only that their monuments shew their territorial acquisitions to have been made. Their northern frontier must in the nature of things have been comparatively neglected :—for at this earlier period it is not possible that their forces would be sufficient adequately to maintain both frontiers.

We have said that the religious tenets prevalent were those of Mencheres. This sufficiently appears by their writing their names in two rings; a practice which commences with the immediate successors of Mencheres.

That the adherents of the old religion would be exceedingly depressed, and probably persecuted during this period, we may readily suppose; but at the same time it is not at all likely that the schism should have been healed. We therefore find, without any surprise, that the shepherd-kings have left us the evidence that they still received the old religion, by writing their names in one ring only. Nothing is more likely, than that their co-religionists in Egypt proper, would flee from the persecution of the opposite party, to the strongholds which the shepherds had built in the swamps of the Delta, and that thereby the shepherds would receive a considerable accession of force. The attention of the native Pharaohs was so centred upon the Southern frontier of the kingdom, that they would scarcely perceive the danger that threatened it from the North. These considerations render natural and probable the event that actually followed. During the reign of the seventh monarch of the 12th dynasty, who is called in the lists Ammenemes, in a fragment of their temple histories preserved by Josephus,* Amun Timœus,

---

* Against Apion. Vol. I. c. 14.

and on the monuments Timœus Amenemes, the Shepherds or Lower Egyptians, under a king named Saites, made a sudden incursion into Middle Egypt, defeated Amun Timœus, and obtained possession of Memphis, which they made their ecclesiastical capital during six successive reigns, and for a period of somewhat more than a century.

The conquests of the Shepherds or Lower Egyptians extended far to the southwards. There is monumental evidence that they were at Essiout, which is near Abydos, on the southern frontier of Middle Egypt. Amun Timœus seems to have fled before them. The later monuments of his long reign, and those of his few obscure successors, are all found very far in Ethiopia. These, however, are matters which belong to the history of Egypt. We return to the Delta and the Lower Egyptian kingdom : Aphophis, or Phiops, was the third or fourth successor of Saites. His political capital was Heliopolis. The proof of this, which is perfectly irrefragable, we shall consider hereafter.

Joseph, then, is at On, or Heliopolis, at the crown of the Delta, a magnificent city, famous in after ages for the number, magnitude and beauty of its temples, all dedicated to Re Athom,—i. e, to the sun as the father of the gods, impersonate in Adam, the father of mankind. The obelisks with which ancient Rome was adorned, and which still remain in modern Rome, were all brought from the ruined temples of Heliopolis. This is the united testimony of their inscriptions, and of the classic authors. One obelisk remains upright to this day, amid its sand-covered ruins. It is of a more ancient date than any in Rome, of the times of Osortasen I. of the 12th dynasty. When Joseph arrived at Heliopolis, it had stood where it now stands, for more than a century.

The Hebrew boy has been sold to Potiphar, one of the princes of Pharaoh Aphophis, and the inspector of the royal plantations.

" And Joseph was brought down into Egypt; and Potiphar, a prince of Pharaoh, and inspector of the plantations, an Egyptian, bought him of the hands of the Ishmaelites, which had brought him down thither. And the Lord was with Joseph, and he was a prosperous man, and he was in the house of his master the Egyptian.

" And his master saw that the Lord was with him, and that the Lord made all that he did to prosper in his hand. And Joseph found grace in his sight, and he served him; and he set him over all his house, and all that he had he put into his hand. And it came to pass, from the time that he had set him over all his house and over all that he had, that the Lord blessed the Egyptian's house for Joseph's sake; and the blessing of the Lord was upon all that he had in the house and in the field.

And he left all that he had in Joseph's hand, and knew not ought he had, save the bread which he did eat." Gen. xxxix. 1—6.

An expression is used in this portion of the inspired narrative, of a very remarkable character. We are told that Potiphar was an Egyptian. This would appear, at first sight, to be a very needless piece of information regarding a prince of Egypt residing in his native city; yet is the expression thrice repeated. In this very concise narrative, wherein no words are wasted and nothing is written in vain, we cannot doubt that the peculiar circumstances of Egypt at the time of Joseph's deportation thither, have suggested this expression. In ordinary cases it would have been a mere pleonasm to write that a prince of Egypt residing at Thebes, or any other city of Egypt, was himself an Egyptian: that would follow as a matter of course. But, at Heliopolis, in the days of Aphophis, when there were Canaanites both in the court and camp of Pharaoh, the case was very different; and it was of the last importance to the descendants of Joseph, in after times, to know that their progenitor had been a bond-slave in the house, not of one of the accursed and devoted race of Canaan, but of a prince of Egypt, a lineal descendant from Mizraim, and the first settlers,—having his estate at Heliopolis, and named hereditarily after the local god of his native city. In these circumstances have originated the triple repetition of the fact that Potiphar was an Egyptian.

The office held by Joseph in the house of Potiphar, is frequently represented in the paintings on the tombs of this epoch. Their testimony also amply confirms that of the inspired narrative. All the servants in the houses of the princes of Egypt were bond-slaves.

"And Joseph was a goodly person and well-favoured. And it came to pass after these things, that his master's wife cast her eyes upon Joseph; and she said, Lie with me. But he refused, and said unto his master's wife, Behold, my master wotteth not what is with me in the house, and he hath committed all that he hath into my hand; there is none greater in his house than I; neither hath he kept back any thing from me but thee, because thou art his wife. How then can I do this great wickedness, and sin against God?

"And it came to pass about this time, that Joseph went into the house to do his business; and there was none of the men of the house there within. And she caught him by his garment, saying, Lie with me; and he left his garment in her hand, and fled, and gat him out.

"And it came to pass, when she saw that he had left his garment in her hand and was fled forth, that she called unto the men of her house, and she spake unto them, saying, See, he hath brought in an Hebrew unto us to mock us; he came in to lie with me and I cried with a loud voice. And it came to pass when he heard that I lifted up my voice and cried, that he left his garment with me and fled, and gat him out. And she laid up his garment until his lord came home.

" And she spake unto him according to these words, saying, The Hebrew slave which thou hast brought unto me, came in unto me to mock me; and it came to pass as I lifted up my voice and cried, that he left his garment with me and fled out." Gen. xxxix. 9—18.

For any illustration of the barefaced profligacy of this scene we shall search the tombs of Egypt in vain. They are exclusively devoted to the praises of their inmates, and in no country that ever existed were sins of this character more rigorously prohibited, or visited with severer punishment; but we shall find there that which renders our narrative in the highest degree probable, in the ample details of the lives of luxury and ease and self-indulgence which were led by the haughty dames of Ancient Egypt. Scores of the princesses and noble ladies of these times have left on the walls of their tombs the imperishable records of the state and magnificence in the midst of which they lived. The luxury of their couches, the long trains of attendants that made their sumptuous toilettes, the stibium-boxes, the metal mirrors, the numberless little appliances connected therewith, buried with their owners as their most valued property, and remaining to this day the visible tangible witnesses of their luxury; their rings and jewels, their robes in endless variety, of all these likewise we can produce the yet existing testimonies; while we learn from the reliefs in the tombs where they were found, the sumptuous banquets of most elaborate cookery that were spread before them, and the soft music that played, and the lascivious dances that were performed by male and female slaves in attendance, while they partook of them. Ocular demonstration of "the pride, the fulness of bread, and the abundance of idleness," of the ladies of Egypt would thus be laid before the reader, and all of the precise time now before us. These pictures, we repeat it, would form the most instructive and perfect comment upon the passage now under consideration that could be imagined.

"And it came to pass when his master heard the words of his wife, that his wrath was kindled. And Joseph's master took him and put him into the prison, a place where the king's prisoners were bound: and he was there in the prison." Gen. xxxix. 19, 20.

The "king's prisoners" in Egypt were prisoners of war. They were incarcerated in cells built of brick, around the precincts of the temples and palaces during the night; in the day-time they were employed in making bricks and other drudgery connected with the building, which apparently was never considered to be finished, For the fact that delinquent slaves belonging to the households of Pharaoh and his princes were associated with the prisoners of war, we are altogether indebted to this narrative. The arrangement was a highly probable one.

" But the Lord was with Joseph, and showed him mercy, and gave him favour in the sight of the keeper of the prison. And the keeper of the prison committed to Joseph's hand all the prisoners that were in the prison, and whatsoever they did there, he was the director of it. The keeper of the prison looked not to any thing that was under his hand, because the Lord was with him, and that which he did, the Lord made it to prosper." Gen. xxxix. 21—23.

Joseph was the officer or task-master over the prisoners. His duties coincided exactly with those of the task-masters over his descendants long afterwards. A fixed amount of labour was required of the jailor, and his superiors never enquired into the means whereby it was exacted. The skill and tact of Joseph in obtaining this, recommended him to his keeper. These prisons were apparently regarded as an indispensable appendage to every great construction in Egypt. The reliefs upon the walls of the temples give fearful indications of the cruelties exercised upon their unhappy inmates. Yet the Divine blessing can send prosperity even into such a den of misery! This is a consolatory reflection to those who believe the Bible.

"And it came to pass after these things, that the cellarman, [keeper of the drinks] of the king of Egypt, and his cook, had offended their lord the king of Egypt. And Pharaoh was wroth against two of his princes [*saris,*] against the *sar* of his vineyards, and against the *sar* of his cooks."

These princes were equal, probably superior in rank to Potiphar. Their offices were of the highest possible consideration. In all pictures of banquets, the eldest son hands the viands and the cup to the father of the family, the eldest daughter to the mother. This is especially the case with Pharaoh, so that in all probability these were *princes of the blood* . It is very important that this should be understood, as otherwise the force of the succeeding narrative is greatly weakened.

The very ample illustration of which both these offices are susceptible, from the paintings on tombs contemporary with the epoch before us, again suggests the regret we have already expressed, at the want of interest in the question, that withholds all public encouragement from its pursuit, and renders such illustration impossible.

It will be perceived that the principle of the law of Egypt we have before explained, is also in force in the present instance. The superior alone is held responsible for the whole of the acts of his subordinates. Both the departments here in question were of an extent and importance in Ancient Egypt, of which our modern notions will receive but a faint impression. Even in the establishments of the princes and nobles, hundreds of men were employed in gathering the grapes and pressing and storing the wine, and also in the preparation of the viands, for a single banquet of frequent periodical recurrence. There were more than a hundred dishes served in the tri-monthly festivals in honour of the dead, held in the tomb of Nahrai at Benihassan. The bill of fare yet remains. This is also the case with many other tombs. The offence with which those two princes were charged must have been of a very grave character, connected in all probability with some attempt to administer poison. They would not otherwise have been committed to the slave prison.

" And they (the captive princes) dreamed a dream both of them, each man his dream in one night, each man according to the interpretation of his dream, the vintner and the house-steward of the king of Egypt, which were bound in the prison. And Joseph came in unto them in the morning and looked at them, and behold they were sad. And he asked Pharaoh's princes that were with him in the prison, saying, Wherefore look ye so sadly to-day? And they said unto him, We have dreamed a dream, and there is no interpreter of it. And Joseph said unto them, Do not interpretations belong to God? Tell me them, I pray you. And he that was over the vineyards told his dream to Joseph, and said unto him, In my dream behold a vine was before me. And in the vine were three branches; and it was as though it budded, and her blossoms shot forth; and the clusters thereof brought forth ripe grapes. And Pharaoh's cup was in my hand, and I took the grapes and pressed them into Pharaoh's cup; and I gave the cup into Pharaoh's hand. And Joseph said unto him, This is the interpretation of it: the three branches are three days. Yet within three days shall Pharaoh lift up thine head and restore thee unto thy place; and thou shalt deliver Pharaoh's cup into his hand, after the former manner when thou wast his vintner." Exod. xl. 5—13.

This passage clearly indicates the office held by the functionary in the court of Pharaoh. He had the oversight both of the king's vineyards and the king's cellars, as well as the function of cup-bearer to Pharaoh. The office was highly esteemed in Ancient Egypt. Many of the princes of the courts of Suphis and Sephres have inscribed it in the long catalogue of their titles. The peculiarities of the climate and soil of Egypt are especially suited to the culture of the vine, and of these days of old scarcely a tomb remains in which the entire process of the vintner's art, from the planting and watering of the vine-stocks up to the pouring of the expressed juice from vessel to vessel, and storing it in earthen jars, is not most carefully and elaborately depicted. That the oversight of the royal vineyards was also associated with the function of cup-bearer to the king is highly probable, though for the formal statement of the fact we are indebted altogether to the passage before us. It was once imagined that the vine did not grow in Egypt in ancient times, because Herodotus and the Greek authors do not mention it. We believe one of the infidel objections of the last century to the passage before us was founded upon this circumstance. The tombs, however, have a voice to answer it.

"But think on me when it shall be well with thee, and show kindness, I pray thee, unto me; and make mention of me unto Phoraoh, and bring me out of this house. For indeed, I was stolen away out of the land of the Hebrews, and here also have

I done nothing, that they should put me into the dungeon."

"And it came to pass the third day, even Pharaoh's birthday, that he made a banquet for all his court (*entourage*),—and he restored the prince of the vineyards to his office again, and he gave the cup into Pharaoh's hand.". . . .

"Yet did not the prince of the vineyards remember Joseph, but forgat him." Gen. xl. 14, 15, 20, 21, 23.

For the elucidation of this passage, there is no occasion to dig among the burning sands of Egypt. It is human nature, and every man's experience will amply illustrate it. Happy they who are taught by a trial somewhat less severe, than that undergone by the poor Hebrew boy in the dungeon, that "it is better to trust in the Lord, than to put any confidence in princes." Psalm cxlvi. 3.

"And when the prince, the high steward (of the cooks, *litt*), saw that the interpretation was good, he said unto Joseph, I also was in my dream, and behold I had three baskets of white (probably pure) *meats* upon my head. And in the uppermost basket was all manner of bake-meats for Pharaoh; and the birds did eat them out of the basket upon my head." Gen. xl. 16, 17.

The illustration of this passage to be found in the cotemporary tombs of Egypt, is to the full as important and interesting as those we have already considered. The entire process from the slaughtering and flaying of the oxen, the capture and plucking of the birds, and the netting of the fish, up to the serving of the bakemeats upon the guest-tables, are all minutely and elaborately commemorated in these wondrous records of times and customs that have so long past away. The most trifling particular in the passage finds its illustration there.

When the sons and daughters of the princes of Egypt served their parents at table, they carried upon their heads three baskets, one piled upon the other, and in the uppermost are the bakemeats.

That in crossing the hypæthral courts of the palaces of Egypt, the viands would be exposed to the birds, is a trait of every-day life in hot countries, receiving such familiar illustration in our own possessions in India, that we only notice it for the purpose of reminding the reader, that in ancient Egypt the vulture, the eagle, the ibis, and other carnivorous birds were held sacred, and to destroy one of them was to incur the penalty of murder. Flights of these voracious creatures haunted the cities of Egypt, and occasioned no little inconvenience to the inhabitants.

"And Joseph answered and said, This is the interpretation thereof. The three baskets are three days. Yet within three days shall Pharaoh lift up thy head from off thee, and shall hang thee on a tree; and the birds shall eat thy flesh from off thee. And it came to pass the third day, which was Pharaoh's birthday, that he made a banquet for all his court: and he hanged the high steward, as Joseph had interpreted." Gen. xl. 18, 19, 20, 22.

The birthday of the reigning king of Egypt was a high festival at all periods of its history. One of the objects of the Rosetta inscription is, to decree the observances to take place on the birthday of Ptolemy Epiphanes.* Many similar decrees of earlier periods are also extant.† That it would also be a day for the exercise of justice in a jail delivery, is highly probable, and in accordance with ancient custom:—though here again our text illustrates ancient Egypt, instead of receiving illustration from it.

The tombs of Egypt contain no records of crimes. It is to the text therefore that we are once more indebted. Capital punishment was by decapitation in ancient as in modern Egypt at this day. After the execution, the bodies of the criminals of Egypt were hung on trees, to be devoured by the gods of Egypt. Our text alone affords us this information likewise.

" And it came to pass at the end of two full years, that Pharaoh dreamed a dream, and behold he stood

---

* Hieroglyphics, line 10. Greek line 46.
† At Medinat Abou, Luxor, &c.

by the river. And, behold, there came up out of the river seven well-favoured kine and fat-fleshed; and they fed in a meadow. And, behold, seven other kine came up after them out of the river, ill-favoured, and lean-fleshed, and stood by the other kine upon the brink of the river. And the ill-favoured and lean-fleshed kine did eat up the seven well-favoured and fat kine. So Pharaoh awoke.

And he slept and dreamed the second time: and, behold, seven ears of corn came up upon one stalk, rank and good. And, behold, seven thin ears and blasted with the east wind sprung up after them. And the seven thin ears devoured the seven rank and full ears. And Pharaoh awoke, and, behold, it was a dream." Gen. xli. 1—7.

We have already explained, that the Pharaoh of whom this history is related, was the shepherd king Aphophis. This Greek transcription of his name is an opprobrious epithet, as is also the case with all the other names of the shepherd-kings in the Greek lists. His real name was Phiops, or Apappus. He was, as we have seen, a native Pharaoh. His monuments are all found at El Birsheh, Souade, and other localities in the south of Middle Egypt, on the eastern bank of the Nile. His capital, as we have already stated, was Heliopolis. Notwithstanding the ill odour in which all the shepherds stood in the fables of the Egyptian priesthood, Aphophis is admitted by them to have been a great benefactor to Egypt.

How completely the dreams of Pharaoh are Egyptian, how every peculiarity connected with the productiveness of Egypt is introduced in them, how the river and its overflow are clearly pointed out as the only causes both of the plenty and the famine, are points with which all readers of the Bible have long been familiar. Again, the point is susceptible of ample and most satisfactory illustration, from the tombs of princes cotemporary with the epoch. The great cattle of Egypt and their diseases are frequent subjects of the reliefs that cover their walls. From them we learn how large a part of the wealth of the princes of Egypt consisted, in these remote times, of their herds.

" And it came to pass in the morning that his spirit was troubled; and he sent and called for all the magicians of Egypt and all the wise men thereof; and Pharaoh told them his dream, but there was none that could interpret them unto Pharaoh." Gen. xli. 8.

Not much is known as yet of the etymology of the words translated "magicians" and "wise men." We can however explain generally that wisdom in ancient times was connected with the ideas of secrecy and of hidden things. The "magicians" were literally "the whisperers," and "the wise
m   " " he   ho h ."

The Egyptian priesthood was noted at all epochs for its pretensions to oneirocriticism. Papyri of the Greek and Roman periods, containing the dreams of the professional dreamers of the Serapœum at Memphis and of other temples, are not uncommon in the collections of Europe.

The divine agency was directly interposed in the present instance, or the oracles of Egypt would not have been dumb on such an occasion.

" Then spake the overseer of the vineyards unto Pharaoh, saying, I do remember my faults this day: Pharaoh was wroth with his servants, and put me in ward, even me and the overseer of the cooks. And we dreamed a dream in one night,—I and he; we dreamed each man according to the interpretation of his dream. And there was with us a youth, a Hebrew, slave to the overseer of the plantations, and he interpreted to us our dreams..... And it came to pass, as he interpreted, so it was; me he restored unto mine office, and him he hanged." Gen. xli. 9—13.

This passage is quite conclusive as to the high rank of the overseer of the vineyards. No mere menial would in this manner have been admitted into the councils of Pharaoh and allowed to advise upon the emergency. This is a point of much importance to the full intelligence of the entire narrative.

" And Pharaoh sent and called Joseph, and they brought him hastily out of the dungeon : and he shaved and changed his raiment, and came in unto Pharaoh.

" And Pharaoh said unto Joseph, I have dreamed a dream, and there is none that can interpret it : And I have heard say of thee, that thou canst understand a dream to interpret it. And Joseph answered Pharaoh, saying, It is not in me : God shall send Pharaoh an answer of peace. And Pharaoh said unto Joseph, &c. .... And Joseph said unto Pharaoh, The dream of Pharaoh is one : God hath shewed Pharaoh what he is about to do. The seven good kine are seven years; and the seven good ears are seven years : the dream is one. And the seven thin ill-favoured kine that came up after them are seven years; and the seven empty ears blasted with the east wind shall be seven years of famine. This is the thing which I have spoken unto Pharaoh : What God is about to do he sheweth unto Pharaoh. Behold, there come seven years of great plenty throughout all the land of Egypt : and there shall arise after them seven years of famine; and all the plenty shall be forgotten in the land of Egypt ; and the famine shall consume the land; and the plenty shall not be known in the land of Egypt by reason of the famine following; for it shall be very grievous." Gen. xli. 14—31.

The Nile, the waters, and the loam thereof, are the only agents whereby a single blade of grass springs up, or a single corn-blossom expands throughout the land of Egypt. This most patent and unanswerable fact is as fully acknowledged in all the different versions, both of the prediction and the fulfilment of this remarkable narrative, as its importance demands. Such being undeniably the case, we have no difficulty in saying what would be the causes of the events predicted. Both the plenty and the famine would originate in some great and marked disturbance of the course and measure of the annual overflow. No such events have since taken place; and the circumstances are altogether of so extraordinary a character, that we may fairly look for some traces of such a disturbance remaining to this day in a land where nothing alters. This point we shall consider hereafter.

" And the thing was good in the eyes of Pharaoh and in the eyes of all his court. And Pharaoh said unto his courtiers, Can we find such an one as this, a man in whom is the spirit of God? And Pharaoh said unto Joseph, Forasmuch as God hath shewed thee all this, there is none so discreet and wise as thou art." Gen. xli. 37, 38.

This full acknowledgment of the Divine Being who had imparted such wisdom to the Hebrew slave, comports but ill with our notions of an

Egyptian idolater; but, nevertheless, we find in the inspired narrative of these very remote periods, many similar proofs that, however mixed up with fable, a conviction of the existence and power of the true God had by no means entirely departed from among men, as at later periods of the history of idolatry. See Gen. xii. 17, 18, &c.

"And Pharaoh said unto Joseph, Forasmuch as God hath showed thee all this, there is none so discreet and wise as thou art. Thou shall be *over my house;* and according unto thy word shall all my people be ruled; only in the throne will I be greater than thou." Gen. xli. 39, 40.

The office of Joseph is a not uncommon one among the princes of Egypt. 𓂀𓏤𓉐 It corresponds to the mayor or prefect of the palace of the old French court.

"And Pharaoh said unto Joseph, See, I have set thee over all the land of Egypt. And Pharaoh took off his ring from his hand, and put it upon Joseph, and arrayed him in vestures of fine linen, and put a gold chain about his neck. And he made him to ride in the second chariot that he had; and they cried before him *ab rech,* and he made him *ruler over all the land* of Egypt. And Pharaoh said unto Joseph, I, Pharaoh, declare, that without thee shall no man lift his hand or foot in all the land of Egypt." Gen. xli. 41—44.

The princes of Egypt gloried in a long array of titles. Two more titles are here conferred upon Joseph. That of *ab rech* 𓉼𓏺 i. e., a pontifical prince, or "pure prince." This is a common title in the ancient tombs. The other title is also often read there, 𓈖𓈖 "the overseer, steward of the land." The ceremonies that attended his inauguration admit of pictorial illustration from the temples of Egypt, of those somewhat later periods when royal monuments first appear. Of these remote times, all, save the pyramids, that remains, is of individual princes.

"And Pharaoh called Joseph's name *tsaphnath paaneah*, and he gave unto him to wife *Asenath* the daughter of *Potipherah* the priest of *On*. And Joseph went forth (from Pharaoh) a prefect over the land of Egypt." Gen. xli. 45.

All these words are confessedly Egyptian. They have never been otherwise interpreted. This circumstance justifies our search, in the cotemporary remains of ancient Egypt, for the other names and titles which have already occurred to us. The attempts that have been made to interpret *tsaphnath paaneah*, began with the Greek translators of the Septuagint version of the Bible, which was made in Egypt about 240 B. C., when all tradition had past away, and before the faculty of critical examination had been imparted to men. They are mere paranomastic guesses, only proving the persuasion of those who made them that the words are Egyptian. The names of offices with which we have already dealt, were at a somewhat earlier period (in the times of Ezra) assimilated to other words from other languages, their original Egyptian meanings being also entirely lost. Thus the office ⟨𓏏𓊪⟩ *saris* was then made identical with a Persian word of somewhat similar sound, but meaning "eunuch:" a gloss which throws into intolerable confusion both the inspired narrative, and, with some writers, the history of Egypt also. The word *sar* underwent the same fate. Its root is common, both to the Hebrew and the Egyptian languages, but with widely different modifications. The Hebrew שַׂר *sar* means a "prince:" the Egyptian word *sar* means a "mayor," or "prefect" only. The former meaning was applied to the Egyptian word at this time also, with much confusion to the narrative. The cotemporary monuments of ancient Egypt have restored both to us.

Tsaphnath Paaneah will now require our attention. It is evidently two words. Similar examples of names of princes consisting of two words might be cited from the cotemporary monuments. The first of these words has not yet been found in the name of any prince of the epoch of Joseph. But if we assume that it must have embodied some allusion to the qualities in Joseph, on account of which it was conferred on him, it presents but little difficulty. It was probably ⸺ *tseph-nath,* "he who receiveth *Neith,*" i. e., the inventrix of the art of weaving, and the goddess of wisdom. With the other name we have still less difficulty. It actually occurs in a tomb at Sacchara, as the name of one of the princes of Userchères, about 150 years before Joseph's time, *pah noech.* Its import also corresponds exactly with the occasion on which it was given. It means, " he who flees from (avoids) pollution," especially " adultery." So that the first name conferred by Pharaoh upon Joseph, commemorated the divine wisdom to which he owed his exaltation ; and the second, his innocence of the crime for which he had so long suffered imprisonment. It is not easy to conceive of a more perfectly satisfactory identification than this, when we consider that in these times all names, especially new ones, were directly significant allusions to the circumstances to commemorate which they were conferred. So Abraham, Gen. xvii. 5 ; Israel, Gen. xxxii. 28 &c.

The names of Joseph's wife and father-in-law were long ago identified by Champollion. Asenath is *asnth* " she who sees Neith," and Potipherah is *petephre* " one devoted to the sun." Both the names are compounded with those of the tutelary idols of On, or Heliopolis. The formal mention of the circumstance that Potipherah was priest of On, reduces to certainty the strong indication embodied in the names of these tutelaries. The scene of the narrative before us was the city of Re-Athom, called On, by the Canaanites. To make this demonstration appear to the general reader, it is needful to explain that whenever the proper name of an Egyptian was a compound of that of an idol, it was the tutelary of the city of which the individual was an inhabitant. There is absolutely no exception to this rule, in the remote times now before us. One other circumstance corroborates the same fact, which scarcely needs such confirmation. His nuptial ceremonies were a part of the honors conferred upon Joseph by Pharaoh on the first interview. This is the clear import of the narrative, and it is moreover strictly in accordance with the customs of the east, both then and at the present day. Such being the case, it must have been in the native city of Asenath that the interview took place : any other supposition for a citizen of these remote times is extravagant. Thus strong is the proof that the scene we are contemplating took place in On, or Heliopolis.

" And Joseph was thirty years old when he stood before Pharaoh king of Egypt. And Joseph went out from the presence of Pharaoh, and went throughout all the land of Egypt. And in the seven plenteous years, the earth brought forth by handfuls. And he gathered up all the food of the seven years which were in the land of Egypt, and laid up the food in the cities: the food of the field which was round about every city, laid he up in the same. And Joseph gathered corn as the sand of the sea, very much, until he left numbering, for it was without number. And unto Joseph were born two sons before the years of famine came, which Asenath, the daughter of Potipherah, priest of On, bare unto him. . . .

" And the seven years of plenteousness that was in the land of Egypt were ended. And the seven years of dearth began to come, according as Joseph had said: and the dearth was in all lands; but in all the land of Egypt there was bread. And when all the land of Egypt was famished, the people cried to Pharaoh for bread; and Pharaoh said unto all the Egyptians, Go unto Joseph: what he saith unto you, do. And the famine was over all the face of the earth: and Joseph opened all the storehouses, and sold unto the Egyptians; and the famine waxed sore in the land of Egypt. And all countries came into Egypt to Joseph for to buy corn; because that the famine was sore in all lands." Gen. xli. 46—50, 53—57.

It would appear upon the face of the narrative, that Joseph had been thirteen years in Egypt at the time of his exaltation. (see xxxvii. 2). By this long course of trial and adversity his whole character would be ripened for the high office to which God had destined him, and for the great work he had to do. He would also have perfectly acquired the language and the customs of the house of his bondage.

The plenty and the famine appeared exactly as he had been inspired to foretel them. We have already remarked upon the extraordinary disturbance which the natural phenomena of Egypt must have sustained at this time. The nature of them we have now to consider. It may be safely stated that in Egypt and the adjacent countries one natural cause, and one only, could possibly have given rise to either of the visitations in question; and that cause was rain. The abundance of it made the plenty; the want of it made the famine. This is perfectly, unanswerably certain.

There is a point in the history before us which has not been noticed. The plenty was confined to Egypt. The famine was in all lands. We have now to describe another of these strange things whereby Egypt in the present day still vindicates her claim to the title of "the land of wonders." When Dr. Lepsius visited the upper portions of the valley of the Nile in 1843, he found engraven upon a cliff rising perpendicularly from the water's edge, at Samneh, which is far in Upper Nubia, an inscription dated in the 23rd year of Amun-Timæus, purporting to register the height of the overflow that year. Other registers are also written on the same rock in the reigns of his two immediate successors. With trifling variations they all give about the same height for the overflow, which averages 30 feet above the highest point ever reached by the water in the present day. Sir Gardner Wilkinson went over the same ground three years afterwards, and pursued the investigation still further. He found above the point in question vast plateaux of Nile mud on both banks, but many miles away from the present course of the river, and as barren as the sand that drifted over them, except when they are cultivated by hand irrigation. He traced the same visible proofs of the far greater elevation of the waters in former times downwards to the bar of red sandstone rock that crosses the Nile at Djebel Silsili, in Upper Egypt, where they ceased altogether.*

Many important conclusions may be arrived at from these premises. The tradition of the Egyptian priesthood preserved by many of the Greek authors, that the Nile had its source in the ocean, and flowed into the ocean again,† doubtless originated in the circumstance that when the first settlers

---

* Trans. Roy. Soc. Let. Vol. iv. p. 93, seq.
† Herodotus, lib. 2. c. 21, 23, 28, &c. &c.

in Egypt explored the valley, the waters of the Nile expanded themselves into a vast lake over what are at this day the plains of Darfur.

The bursting of this lake took place at a period concerning which we are able, on monumental evidence, distinctly to say that it was after the reign of Sukophthis II.—the second successor of Amun Timæus; and as the register of this year is the last of many entries, the probabilities are highly in favor of its occurrence but a little time afterwards. But Amun-Timæus was the Pharaoh whom Salatis expelled from Memphis, and afterwards they both reigned cotemporaneously: Amun-Timæus and his successors in Upper Egypt and Ethiopia, and Salatis and his successors in the Delta and Middle Egypt. But again, Aphophis also was the second or third successor of Salatis. The times of Sukophthis II. and of Aphophis must, therefore, have closely approximated.

Let us now consider the mode in which the disruption of this barrier must have occurred.

It certainly was not occasioned by the cleavage of the rock by an earthquake, or by any other great accident which would have set the entire body of water at liberty at once. Had this been the case, the rush of such a tide would have swept every thing before it, and the valley would have been depopulated: an event which we know did not take place.

There is but one other mode possible, and that is, the unusual prevalence of rains in the tropical mountains wherein are the sources of the river. The effect of them would be to elevate the waters of this lake, so that they would come into contact with and undermine some mud-bank, not ordinarily within reach of the inundation. This would allow the escape, not only of the superfluous waters of the flood, but also of some portion of those of the lake. Such an increase as this of the yearly overflow would be highly disastrous at the present day, when all the artificial means for irrigation (both the dykes and the mounds) have been for so many years adjusted to one scarcely varying measure; but at the remote period, now under consideration, we apprehend the case would be very different. The valley was, of necessity, but imperfectly cultivated any where, and it would only be in those narrow portions of it where the culture had already reached the mountains, that any mischief would be done. In the Delta (of which alone the inspired narrative seems to speak), where the cultivated surface is bounded on both sides by mere plains of sand, the only effect of this assumed disruption would have been, the diffusion of the teeming flood over a surface vastly more extended than in ordinary years. Of this circumstance the prescience of Joseph would direct him to take the utmost possible advantage.

Labourers would be sent everywhere to construct, for these new lands, sluices of recession and other necessary works for their productiveness, and the corn that was afterwards gathered by handfuls would now be sown by handfuls. This is God's invariable rule in all things.

The ordinary issues of the lake in Ethiopia would soon relieve the broken bank from the pressure of the overflow, and the Nile would subside to its wonted volume: but a large portion of the waters of the low or blue Nile would still flow through the vast *crevasse* formed by the disruption, and the surface of the lake would be lowered several feet. The effect of this is well known in engineering. The softer portions of the bank which retained the lake, and which were quite equal to sustain the inert pressure of the whole, would be worn away by the attrition of the currents that would now flow over them; and even in the low Nile the lake would go on decreasing. After eight months of incessant sun and dry sand-winds, cracking and parching the portions of this bank that had hitherto been under water, the Nile would rise again. We have now no occasion to assume another excess of rain in the mountains of Ethiopia. The ordinary flood would all but certainly be more than the bank thus injured could sustain, and another disruption would still further lower the surface of the lake in Ethiopia, and originate the second year of plenty in the Delta.

By the repetition of this process, it is, we contend, no unreasonable supposition, that it would take seven successive annual floods to wash away entirely the embankments that sustained the lake of Ethiopia, and to bring down the Nile to its present level, and that in this increase of the ordinary measure of the overflow, consisted the cause of the seven plenteous years in the Delta.

We have now to consider the seven years of famine that followed them. The same phenomena will, we apprehend, go far to account for them also. On the first year, after the final subsidence of the lake, the annual overflow (supposing it to have been an ordinary one) on first reaching what was formerly the head of the lake, would enter an endless tissue of devious and intricate channels among rocks and mud-banks; and through this labyrinth it would have to work and wind its way for hundreds of miles. At the same point, only in the year preceding, the annual flood joined a vast body of water, and the wave of its first impulse would convey the commencement of the inundation to the outlet with the speed of gravitation. The far longer time required for threading the mazes of its new channel, would materially delay the appearance of the inundation in Egypt. Another effect would follow from the same cause. The quantity of water would be greatly diminished by this longer exposure to the burning sun of Ethiopia. This is the case at all seasons of the year. The Nile at the Barash, which is at the bifurcation of its two mouths, is a much less river than the Nile at Thebes or Philae, at the present day. The vast flats of Nile mud, covering thousands of square miles which, before the inundation of the previous year, had been the bottom of the lake, would also tend, in the year we are supposing, yet further to diminish the annual overflow. They had been for many months exposed to the sun and wind, and must have warped and cracked in a manner utterly inconceivable to those who have not actually witnessed the phenomenon. The mud has risen into huge blisters. It has sunk into deep hollows: it has cracked into yawning crevasses. We exactly describe the present appearance of the plain of Darfur, the locality in question. So much of the water of the inundation would be absorbed by these hollows, that we may safely assume that in an ordinary year, scarcely any of it would pass the foot of the lake; and, assuredly, after such a disturbance, it would be many years before the river would have so worked out the channels of its new course, that any thing like the usual overflow would reach Egypt. We are assuming here, that there should be no failure in the rains on the mountains: but in the seven years of famine there is every probability that such was not the case. "The famine was sore in all lands," and the want of rain which occasioned it, would extend to the mountains of Ethiopia: for modern observation has clearly established the fact that, as to its leading features, the weather spans the earth in great quadrants. In these circumstances, therefore, we submit, will be found a very satisfactory solution of the natural difficulties connected with the seven years of plenty and of famine. The geological evidence of the actual occurrence of a great disturbance of the annual overflow, and the monumental evidence that the time of its occurrence closely approximated to that of the reign of Aphophis, the patron of Joseph, we also present as collateral proofs of the verity of the inspired narrative, of no light or unimportant character.

We may perhaps here be permitted to answer an objection to such researches, which is often urged by excellent persons of devotional habits and contemplative and confiding temperaments. We want no confirmation to our own faith. We firmly believe that God is able to give seven years of plenty and of famine to Egypt, by a simple exercise of his own volition, and without the employment of natural phenomena at all. What good end is accomplished by such discoveries as these? The answer is not far to seek. The faith of these persons is not the faith which God demands of his people. It is a mere ignorant unreasoning assent to the dogma that God can do all things, leaving out the all-important limitation which the Bible applies to it: "He cannot deny himself." There is nothing more needful for man to know, than that these marvellous works in the days of old, were all subordinated to one rule or canon. There was no needless interference with the ordinary laws of nature. They were merely put into action at times before specified, in order that men might see God's mastery over them. We shall find this to be especially the case with all the supernatural interferences recorded in the history we have now to illustrate; and therefore it much concerns the consistency of the Divine procedure to discover, that the seven years of plenty and famine were likewise of the same character. There may in effect have been nothing supernatural in the entire transaction, beyond the prediction, and the divine wisdom imparted to Joseph in taking advantage of them. Yet is this no Neology, but Divinity in its best and loftiest sense.

" Now when Jacob saw that there was corn in Egypt, Jacob said unto his sons, Why do ye look one upon another? And he said, Behold! I have heard that there is corn in Egypt; get you down thither and buy for us from thence, that we may

"And Joseph's ten brethren went down to buy corn in Egypt. But Benjamin, Joseph's brother, Jacob sent not with his brethren; for he said, Lest peradventure mischief befal him. And the sons of Israel came to buy corn among those that came; for the famine was in the land of Canaan." Gen. xlii. 1—5.

The scene depicted in this concise narrative is a very animated one. The sandy paths across the desert of Suez are crowded with caravans of the inhabitants of Canaan, and their beasts of burden, laden with the valuable products of their country, and with silver and gold in rings, and all intent upon the purchase of corn. It was thus that the riches of Canaan flowed into Egypt. We are now in the first year of the famine only, and already the current has set in.

"And Joseph was ruling (exercising kingly power) over the land; and he it was that sold to all the people of the land: and Joseph's brethren came and bowed themselves down before him with their faces to the earth. . . . And Joseph remembered the dreams that he had dreamed of them." ver. 6, 9.

Twenty-one years had elapsed since the last interview of Joseph with his brethren. Then the hard features of the reckless hunters of the desert frowned fiercely upon a stripling bound and helpless, and their hands grasped their murderous weapons, so bitter was the envy that his prophetic dream had roused in them. They threw him into a pit to perish with hunger and thirst; they were debating as to the policy of drawing him up to despatch him, when the appearance of the Ishmaelite caravan and the avarice of Judah changed their determination into that which was even still more heartless and cruel. Now, a company of wrinkled and grey-bearded wayfaring men, they bowed themselves to the earth before the regal state of their former victim;—the very consummation at which the prophetic dreams that had exasperated their envy and rage against him had pointed; so that they had themselves fulfilled the divine intimation, and that, by the act of daring wickedness whereby they hoped to render it impossible. "There are many devices in a man's heart, nevertheless the counsel of the Lord, that shall stand." Prov. xix. 21. No wonder that "Joseph remembered the dreams that he had dreamed of them."

"And Joseph saw his brethren, and he knew them, but made himself strange unto them, and spake roughly unto them: and he said unto them, Whence come ye? And they said, From the land of Canaan to buy food. And Joseph knew his brethren, but they knew him not. . . .

"And Joseph said unto them, Ye are spies, to see the nakedness of the land ye are come. And they said unto him, Nay, my lord, but to buy food are thy servants come. We are all one man's sons; we are true men, thy servants are no spies. And he said unto them, Nay, but to see the nakedness of the land are ye come. And they said, Thy servants are twelve brethren, the sons of one man in the land of Canaan, and behold the youngest is this day with our father, and one is not. And Joseph said unto them, This is what I spake unto you, saying, Ye are spies. Hereby ye shall be proved; as Pharaoh lives ye shall not go hence, except your youngest brother come hither. Send one of you, and let him fetch your brother, and ye shall be kept in prison, that your words may be proved, whether there be any truth in you; or else, as Pharaoh lives, surely ye are spies. And he put them all together in ward for three days." Verses 7—19.

We have no regal monuments of the epoch now before us. Joseph evidently sate as a king in the gate, when his brethren were brought into his presence. It can therefore be only on monuments that discourse of the actions of kings that we can hope for any illustration of the passage. For these we must descend to a somewhat later period. A scene not uncommon in the civil wars that ended in the union of the two Egypts under one crown, represents the reception given to an embassy from the opposite faction. The ambassadors are called spies, and beaten, before they are admitted into the pre-

bitter was the envy that his prophetic dream had roused in them. They threw him into a pit to perish with hunger and thirst; they were debating as to the policy of drawing him up to despatch him, when the appearance of the Ishmaelite caravan and the avarice of Judah changed their determination into that which was even still more heartless and cruel. Now, a company of wrinkled and grey-bearded wayfaring men, they bowed themselves to the earth before the regal state of their former victim;—the very consummation at which the prophetic dreams that had exasperated their envy and rage against him had pointed; so that they had themselves fulfilled the divine intimation, and that, by the act of daring wickedness whereby they hoped to render it impossible. "There are many devices in a man's heart, nevertheless the counsel of the Lord, that shall stand." Prov. xix. 21. No wonder that " Joseph remembered the dreams that he had dreamed of them."

"And Joseph saw his brethren, and he knew them, but made himself strange unto them, and spake roughly unto them : and he said unto them, Whence come ye? And they said, From the land of Canaan to buy food. And Joseph knew his brethren, but they knew him not. . . .

" And Joseph said unto them, Ye are spies, to see the nakedness of the land ye are come. And they said unto him, Nay, my lord, but to buy food

JOSEPH IN EGYPT.

are thy servants come. We are all one man's sons; we are true men, thy servants are no spies. And he said unto them, Nay, but to see the nakedness of the land are ye come. And they said, Thy servants are twelve brethren, the sons of one man in the land of Canaan, and behold the youngest is this day with our father, and one is not. And Joseph said unto them, This is what I spake unto you, saying, Ye are spies. Hereby ye shall be proved; as Pharaoh lives ye shall not go hence, except your youngest brother come hither. Send one of you, and let him fetch your brother, and ye shall be kept in prison, that your words may be proved, whether there be any truth in you; or else, as Pharaoh lives, surely ye are spies. And he put them all together in ward for three days." Verses 7—19.

We have no regal monuments of the epoch now before us. Joseph evidently sate as a king in the gate, when his brethren were brought into his presence. It can therefore be only on monuments that discourse of the actions of kings that we can hope for any illustration of the passage. For these we must descend to a somewhat later period. A scene not uncommon in the civil wars that ended in the union of the two Egypts under one crown, represents the reception given to an embassy from the opposite faction. The ambassadors are called spies, and beaten, before they are admitted into the presence of the king. In Egypt every thing was prescriptive. There can hardly be a doubt that this was a point of court etiquette. If it were so, Joseph's brethren, we may be sure, were subjected to this discipline. In effect, it is not at all probable that a company, upon which such a charge was imputed as that made by Joseph against his brethren, would in the ancient world have escaped with no more grievous corporal inflictions than those of bonds and imprisonment. Even in the days of the Romans, the entire tone of society, and the collective mode of thought, would render it improbable that any individual, however exalted in rank, would be committed to prison upon a serious charge without being previously examined by scourging. When we call to mind the cruel wrong that Joseph had suffered from the unfeeling men who were now in his power, and also that he was utterly ignorant of the design of poor Reuben for his deliverance, we shall perceive that even if such were the case, his rigorous deportment would be amply justified by the circumstances. The precaution taken by Joseph on this memorable occasion would also be rendered needful by the political relations of the kingdom of Lower Egypt in the times of Aphophis. The Arvadites and Hittites were the two clans of the Canaanitish confederacy by whose aid the Mencherian Pharaohs had been expelled from Memphis.

But with the other Canaanitish nations they were frequently at war. The Canaanites in Egypt even confederated with the Egyptians for the purpose of invading Canaan. Of this fact we have the irrefragable evidence of the monuments. It was therefore highly important to the safety of the throne of Pharaoh that this vast tide of immigrants from Canaan should be closely watched, lest under the pretext of purchasing corn, some formidable force might be gradually introduced, and thus a double danger arise from within as well as from without. Under these circumstances, there would be nothing at all remarkable in the rough greeting wherewith Joseph challenged his brethren. It was the ordinary course with all large bodies of travellers from Canaan.

"And Joseph said to them the third day, This do, and live, for I fear God, If ye be true, let one of your brethren be bound in the house of your prison; go ye, carry corn for the famine of your houses. But bring your youngest brother unto me; so shall your words be verified, and ye shall not die. And they assented. And they said one to another, We are verily guilty concerning our brother, in that we saw the anguish of his soul when he besought us, and we would not hear; therefore is this distress come upon us. And Reuben answered them, saying, Spake I not unto you, saying, Do not sin against the child; and ye would not hear? Therefore behold also his blood is required. And they knew not that Joseph understood them: for he spake unto them by an interpreter. And he turned himself about from them and wept, and returned to them again, and spake unto them [repeating his decision], and took from them Simeon, and bound him before their eyes." Gen. xlii. 18—24.

The brethren of Joseph had now been for three days in prison, expecting hourly to be led forth to suffer an ignominious death at the hands of the public executioner. It was by this severe discipline that the compunctious visitings, (which all the anguish of their father, of which for so many years they had witnessed the daily proofs, had failed to awaken), first wrung their flinty hearts. It is quite clear from this passage that Reuben, as well as his father, had been completely deceived by the stratagem of the torn and bloody coat; nevertheless the conduct of this patriarch on the occasion, exactly squares with the general tone of his character (see Gen. xlix. 3, 4), and offers another internal evidence, if such be wanted, of the genuineness of the history before us. He did not (as was his clear duty) apprize his father of the lawless violence of his brethren towards Joseph, of which he himself was cognizant. Had he done so, it would have led to inquiries, whence doubtless the whole truth would have been elicited. It is a vain question to ask in reply, How then would the purposes of God have been fulfilled by Joseph? It is perfectly true that God was pleased to accomplish them by the moral infirmity of Reuben, as well as by the relentless cruelty of Simeon and the cold calculating avarice of Judah. Nevertheless Simeon and Judah, yea, and Reuben also, shall each bear his own sin. Man can incur God's displeasure, but he cannot counterwork his purposes.

It is sufficiently evident from the passage before us, that Joseph used the Egyptian language in this colloquy, and that it was unintelligible to his brethren. So clearly is this implied by the scope of the text, and so unanswerably is it demonstrated by the etymology of the word rightly translated "interpreter," and also by the comparison of the two languages, for which we have such ample materials, that we can only regret that an opposite statement, by commentators generally well entitled to the confidence of their readers, should have rendered this rectification needful.*

"Then Joseph commanded to fill their sacks with corn, and restore every man's money into his sack; and to give every man provision for the way: and thus did he unto them. And they laded their asses with corn and departed thence. And as one

* See, *inter alias*, Bagster's Comprehensive Bible on Gen. xlii. 23.

of them opened his sack to give his ass provender at the resting-place [in the desert] he saw his silver [in rings] for behold it was at his sack's mouth. And he said unto his brethren, My money is restored; and, lo, it is even in my sack: and their heart failed them, and they were afraid, saying one to another, What is this that God hath done unto us?

" And they came unto Jacob their father unto the land of Canaan, and told him all that befel unto them; saying, The man, who is the lord of the land, spake roughly to us, and took us for spies of the country. And we said unto him, We are true men; we are no spies: we be twelve brethren, sons of our father; one is not, and the youngest is this day with our father in the land of Canaan. And the man, the lord of the country, said unto us, Hereby shall I know that ye are true men; leave one of your brethren here with me, and take food for the famine of your households, and be gone: and bring your youngest brother unto me: then shall I know that ye are no spies, but ye are true men: so will I deliver you your brother, and ye shall traffic in the land.

" And it came to pass, as they emptied their sacks, that, behold, every man's bundle of money was in his sack: and when both they and their father saw the bundles of money, they were afraid. And Jacob their father said unto them, Me have ye bereaved of my children: Joseph is not, and Simeon is not, and ye will take Benjamin away: all these things are against me. And Reuben spake unto his father, saying, Slay my two sons, if I bring him not to thee: deliver him into my hand, and I will bring him to thee again. And he said, My son shall not go down with you; for his brother is dead, and he is left alone: if mischief befal him by the way in the which ye go, then shall ye bring down my grey hairs with sorrow to the grave.

"And the famine was sore in the land. And it came to pass, when they had eaten up the corn which they had brought up out of Egypt, their father said unto them, Go again, buy us a little food. And Judah spake unto him, saying, The man did solemnly protest unto us, saying, Ye shall not see my face, except your brother be with you. If thou wilt send our brother with us, we will go down and buy thee food: but if thou wilt not send him, we will not go down: for the man said unto us, Ye shall not see my face, except your brother be with you. And Israel said, Wherefore dealt ye so ill with me, as to tell the man whether ye had yet a brother? And they said, the man asked us straitly of our state, and of our kindred, saying, Is your father yet alive? have ye another brother? and we told him according to the tenor of these words: could we certainly know that he would say, Bring your brother down? And Judah said unto Israel his father, Send the lad with me, and we will arise and go; that we may live and not die, both we, and thou, and also our little ones. I will be surety for him; of my hand shalt thou require him: if I bring him not unto thee, and set him before thee, then let me bear the blame for ever. For except we had lingered, surely now we had returned this second time. And their father Israel said unto them, If it must be so now, do this; take of the best fruits of the land in your vessels, and carry down the man a present, a little balm, and a little honey, spices, and myrrh, nuts, and almonds: and take double money in your hand; and the money that was brought again in the mouth of your sacks, carry it again your hand: peradventure it was an oversight: take also your brother, and arise, go again unto the man: and God Almighty give you mercy before the man, that he may send away your other brother, and Benjamin. If I be bereaved of my children, I am bereaved." Gen. xlii. 25, to Gen. xliii. 14.

The inspired narrative now leaves the land of Egypt, we only quote it here for the sake of continuity. The workings of an evil conscience in the brethren of Joseph, found kindred feelings in the advanced age and infirmities of their father.

They were all afraid when they saw the linked rings of silver which they had taken down to Egypt to buy corn, returned at the mouth of their sacks. These chains of silver (Heb. צוררה " chains," "that which binds,") are frequently depicted in the tombs, and have even been found there. The custom of carrying the precious metals for the purposes of traffic in linked rings or chains was universal in ancient Egypt, where coined money was unknown until the days of the Ptolemies; and remained in occasional use throughout the world, until far into the middle ages.

The present prepared by Jacob and his sons for the ruler of Egypt, admits of so remarkable an illustration from the existing monuments of the latter kingdom, that it is not possible to pass them by on this occasion, even though they should lead us a little further into verbal criticism than comports exactly with our present design.

We will take the several articles enumerated in the order of their occurrence.—

1. Balm צרי. The resin or gum that exudes from the wounded bark of a tree: whence its Hebrew name, which means a wound or the issue (*ichor*) from a wound. Gums of many kinds, principally fragrant ones, are often found in the tombs of Egypt, both deposited in jars, and used in the embalming of mummies.

2. Honey. דְּבַשׁ (*debash*) It is well known that this word signified the thickened juice of grapes and dates, as well as the honey of bees. In the hieroglyphic account of the so-called expulsion of the shepherds from Egypt, a group appears in the catalogues of the spoils taken after each victory, which is evidently the same word. 𓏏𓃀𓐍 *tabkh** or 𓃀𓐍 *bkh*. In the latter form it is still read in the Coptic texts βυκκι "ripe dates." Many thousands of jars of this substance are enumerated among the spoils taken, or the tribute exacted from the Canaanites. We could not have a clearer proof that it was imported from Canaan into Egypt, where it was in great request.

3. Spices. נכאה. This is a Hebrew word, signifying, "that which is pounded small." The Egyptians were very particular in this branch of the apothecary's art. It was performed generally by female slaves, by grinding the substance to be triturated between two hard stones. So accurately was the process performed, that in the vast quantity of spices found in a mummy of a high class which was opened at Leeds twenty years ago, not a particle could be discovered larger than the rest, though diligent search was made for it. The substance here specified was prepared in Canaan.

4. Myrrh לט wrongly translated. It should have

* There was no *d* in the Egyptian language.

been rendered *Ladanum*, the λαδανον of the Greeks. It is the gum that exudes from the *Cistus Ladanifera*, a tree found in Canaan at this day. This perfume was in high esteem in ancient Egypt. There is now no occasion to appeal to learned authorities in proof of its frequent use there. It has frequently been found in the tombs, and its well-known odour was powerfully predominant in the mixture of spices with which the Leeds mummy was embalmed. Its appellative in hieroglyphics completes the proof. This will, we believe, be found in a group which is well ascertained to mean "perfume" of some sort, but to its assumed phonetic value, no equivalent has been hitherto found, either in Coptic or any other language. It is written ▨ *lt* or, ▨ *ntl*, or ▨ *lnt*. The initial character of this group resembles greatly one of the homophons of the letter *s*. ▨ ; so much so, that Champollion confounded the two, both in his copies and his readings;—nevertheless the comparison of many repetitions of this common group on the monuments themselves has convinced me, that it represents an object altogether different from that depicted by the character with which it has been supposed to be identical. I believe that its power was *l*, and that it was interpreted by the mouth ▨ at the end of the group. It was not possible to write them thus ▨, because then the mouth would be read as a mere grammatical form. Had the group been written thus ≋, that would have equivocated with another group of altogether different meaning. These are reasons amply sufficient for the metathesis which has changed *ltn* into *ntl*, 𓊛𓈖𓏌. We believe it therefore to be the hieroglyphic appellative of *Ladanum,* a word which the Greeks adopted without change. This perfume was largely used in the worship of the gods of Egypt, and vast quantities of it are repeatedly specified as part of the tribute exacted by Amosis from the Canaanites in the hieroglyphic record of his expulsion of the lower Egyptians from Memphis.*

5. Nuts בטנים. i. e. Pistacio nuts. These are not the produce of Egypt, but jars of them have repeatedly been found in the tombs.

6 Almonds. These are likewise in the same category. Their existence in the tombs, and the unfitness of the soil of Egypt for the growth of the trees that produce them, render it certain that both nuts and almonds were among the articles which ancient Egypt imported from Canaan.

" And the men took that present, and they took double money in their hands, [i. e., with them] and Benjamin ; and rose up and went down to Egypt, and stood before Joseph.

" And when Joseph saw Benjamin with them, he

* Generally called the granite sanctuary of Karnak. It is now in the Louvre at Paris.

said to *the steward of his house,* אֲשֶׁר, bring these men home and slay abundantly and prepare; for these men shall dine with me at noon. And the man did as Joseph bade, and brought the men into Joseph's house. And the men were afraid because they were brought into Joseph's house; and they said,— Because of the money that was returned in our sacks at the first time are we brought in; that he may *seek occasion against us* [lit. entangle us] and fall upon us, and take us for bondmen, and our asses." Gen. xliii. 15—18.

To detain one of the enemy upon a feigned civil charge has been a common stratagem of war at all times. The men evidently supposed themselves suspected by Joseph of belonging to some Canaanitish nation at war with Phiops, and that they had been trepanned by the *ruse* of the returned money. They now looked, on their arrival at Joseph's house, to be at once stripped of their garments and the rest of their property, and set to work with the other slaves and prisoners of war, that in the day-time performed the menial offices of the establishment, and at night were chained in oval brick dungeons, in the square enclosure that surrounded the palace. Such was doubtless the internal economy of Joseph's house, in common with the rest of the princes of Egypt.

A very mistaken notion in regard of the asses

mentioned in the text before us has taken possession of the minds of most scripture readers, mainly created by the attempts at pictorial illustrations made in the middle ages. It is assumed that ten men with ten asses only went into Egypt on this occasion, whereas, in all probability, the caravan of the Patriarchs consisted of many attendants besides themselves, and of some hundreds of asses. This animal was a valuable property in Egypt, and often appears among the properties of her ancient princes, as in the following, from the tomb of the prince *Hotp-ols* at *Sakkarah*.*

" And they came near to *him* that was *over the house* of Joseph and they spake with him at the door of the house." Gen. xliii. 19.

* No. 15 of the plan of Lepsius.

The present passage is adduced by some commentators, in proof that the languages of Egypt and Canaan were, in these remote times, so much alike, that the inhabitants of the two countries could understand each other. This is a mistake of inadvertency which a very superficial attention to the context would have sufficed to expose. The man with whom Joseph's brethren conversed, held in Joseph's house exactly the same office as Joseph himself had held in the house of Potiphar on his first arrival in Egypt; and if this office were held by a Canaanite slave in the one case, why not in the other also? Infidelity has found more pretexts in loose unsatisfactory glosses like this than in any other source of error that could be named.

"And [Joseph's brethren] said, O Sir, we came indeed down at the first time to buy food:—and it came to pass when we came to the inn, that we opened our sacks, and behold, every man's silver was at the mouth of his sack; our silver in full weight: and we have brought it again with us: and other silver have we brought with us to buy food: we cannot tell who put our silver in our sacks. And he said, Peace be unto you, fear not; your God and the God of your fathers hath given you treasure in your sacks; I had your silver. And he brought Simeon out to them." Gen. xliii. 19—23.

The weighing of silver in rings is a common subject in the tombs. The balance was the medium of adjustment of the entire traffic of the ancient world. The annexed design is from the tomb of Nahrai at Benihassan.

Simeon had been selected by Joseph to remain in prison as a hostage for the return of his brethren, because he was the originator and ringleader of the lawless violence through which Joseph had been sold into Egypt. That such was the case appears very evidently from the comparison of other passages, and from the general character of Simeon, which drew down upon him his father's curse. (See Gen. xlix. 5—7.) We are too apt to forget the extent to which we offend God when (under any pretext) we indulge the fierce and brutal passions of our natures against our fellow-men. This he has clearly proclaimed in his word. A thousand and a thousand times has he thundered the same truth in the unwilling ear of man by the terrors of his Providence. To how many slave-holders, to how many school-masters, yea, *proh pudor,* to how many parents, who, after the indulgence of their fierce passions upon their victims, " wipe their mouths and say, We have done no evil," does God address the cleaving malediction of the dying patriarch : " Cursed be their wrath, for it was fierce, and their anger for it was cruel ! "

" And the man brought the men into Joseph's house, and gave water, and they washed their feet; and he gave their asses provender.

" And they made ready the present against Joseph came at noon, for they heard that they should eat bread there.

" And when Joseph came home, they brought him the present which was in their hand into the house, and bowed themselves to him to the earth. And he asked them of their welfare, and said, Is your father well : the old man of whom ye spake ? Is he yet alive ? And they answered, Thy servant our father is in good health ; he is yet alive. And they bowed down their heads and made obeisance. And he lifted up his eyes and saw his brother Benjamin, his mother's son, and said, Is this your younger brother of whom ye spake unto me ? And he said, God be gracious unto thee, my son. And

Joseph went forth in haste, for his bowels did yearn upon his brother, and he sought where to weep, and he entered into his chamber and wept there." Gen. xliii. 24—30.

This passage needs no illustrative remarks. Its comment is written in the hearts of all men. It finds its interpretation in the bosom of every child of Adam. " One touch of nature makes the whole world kin ! "

" And [Joseph] washed his face, and went forth [from his chamber] and refrained himself. And he said, Set forth bread ; and they set forth for him by himself, and for them [his brethren] by themselves, and for the Egyptians which did eat with him by themselves." Ver. 31, 32.

The tombs of ancient Egypt fully illustrate the custom to which this passage alludes. Before the master and mistress of the house (when both sate down to the same banquet) was placed a table piled with bread in loaves and cakes, and in endless

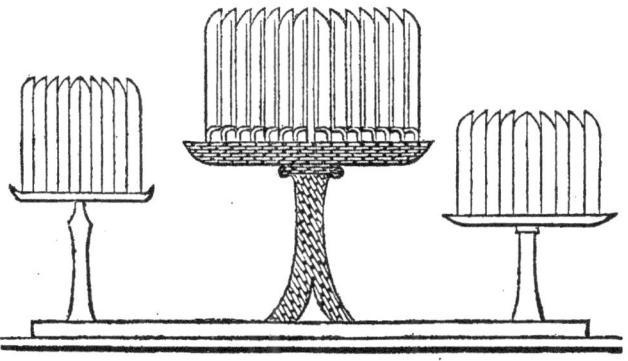

variety of forms. The baker's art was sedulously cultivated in Egypt, and, wonderful to tell, some of its productions remain to this day. Baskets of bread have been frequently found in the tombs. The preceding examples of tables of bread are all from tombs of the era of Joseph or somewhat earlier. The arrangement of the guests, according to our text, agrees also exactly with the indication of these pictures. The heads of the house and their children and dependents sate at separate tables.

" Because the Egyptians might not eat bread with the Hebrews ; for that is an abomination to the Egyptians." Verse 32.

For the illustration of this passage, there is no necessity to assume that the impurity of the Hebrews consisted in their being shepherds, by ordinary occupation, with the Chaldee, the Greek, and other ancient commentators. This gloss encumbers the narrative with a formidable difficulty, inasmuch as Pharaoh greatly favored the Canaanites, and admitted as his courtiers Canaanite shepherds, both by birth and descent. It was in religion only that the shepherd was unclean in Egypt. Foreigners generally were likewise accounted unclean and unfit for any intercourses beyond those of war and of traffic, by her utterly intolerant mythology. The name of a foreign nation, written in hieroglyphics, is always accompanied by some opprobrious epithet, and determined by a man in bonds. The following are examples: ⸺ "Arvad." ⸺ "the overthrown of Sheth," the Moabites. ⸺ "the wicked race of Cush," Ethiopia. All foreigners, and at all times, whether of peace or war, are thus written on the monuments. We may therefore clearly infer that it would be accounted pollution to sit at table with them.

" And they sate before him, the first-born according to his birthright, and the youngest according to his youth: and the men marvelled one at another. And he sent forth portions unto them from before him: but Benjamin's mess was five times so much as any of theirs. And they drank and were merry with him." Verses 33, 34.

The monumental illustrations of this custom also are as beautifully complete as any of those that have yet engaged our attention. The annexed engraving represents the tri-monthly banquet held in honor of the dead, in the noble hall of the tomb of the prince and chief physician Nahrai, at Beni Hassan. He was attached to the court of Pharaoh Amenemes II., who reigned in Egypt about a hundred years before the times of Joseph. The enormous quantity and variety of the viands are no exaggerations. Whole crowds of retainers waited without the hall to receive their portions of food at these banquets. The vaults underneath the hall

were of dimensions large enough for the mummies of all the retainers of the house of Nahrai; and all persons having relatives in the tomb were entitled to partake of the banquets. Within the hall the entire family of Nahrai attended upon their parents in the order of their primogeniture. The observance appears to have been—the youngest received the dish from the cooks and passed it to the child next in age. In this way it passed from hand to hand to the first-born, who stood before the father, and served the dish to him. The master of the house first cut off a portion for himself and the mother of the family, if she sate at the same table with him. In the banquets of Nahrai she sate at a separate table, and was attended in the same manner by her daughters, probably because she was a princess in her own right. The dish or joint was then placed by the first-born at the feet of his parents,

and the whole family remained standing until they had eaten. It was then once more presented by the first-born to the father, who cut from it, and placed upon slices or cakes of bread portions for each of his children, which being distributed, and another dish served to the father, the whole party sate down together—the children to eat of the first dish, the father of the second. The retainers of the house were afterwards served by the domestics, but always in the presence of Nahrai himself.* That similar state and ceremony were observed in the banquet which Joseph gave to his brethren, there cannot be a doubt. They handed the dishes to him and he sent them their portions on the bread which was piled before him. It will be noticed, that the bread on the table before Nahrai is cut in slices.

"And [Joseph] commanded him that was over his house, saying, Fill the men's sacks [pack-saddles] with provision as much as they can carry, and put every man's money in his sack's mouth. And put my cup, the silver cup, in the sack's mouth of the youngest, and his own money. And he did according to the word that Joseph had spoken. As soon as the morning was light, the men were sent

* In proof of the number of persons entitled to partake of these banquets, it may be mentioned, that in the tomb of Amenemes, which is in the immediate vicinity of that of Nahrai, 1000 mummies of soldiers who had fallen in the wars with Cush, were deposited in its vaults at one time.

away, they and their asses. And when they were gone out of the city and not yet far off—Gen. xliv. 1—4.

This must have been a city on the north-eastern border, adjacent to the desert which divides Egypt from Canaan. On, or Heliopolis, is so situated, and as it is the only city named in the inspired narrative, the proof that it was the scene of these transactions is as conclusive as if the fact had been formally stated.

" Joseph said unto his steward, Up, follow after the men; and when thou dost overtake them, say unto them, Wherefore have ye rewarded evil for good? Is not this it in which my lord drinketh, and whereby indeed he divineth? ye have done evil in so doing. And he overtook them, and he spake unto them these same words. And they said unto him, Wherefore saith my lord these words? God forbid that thy servants should do according to this thing: behold, the money, which we found in our sacks' mouths, we brought again unto thee out of the land of Canaan: how then should we steal out of thy Lord's house silver or gold? With whomsoever of thy servants it be found, both let him die, and we also will be my lord's bondmen. And he said, Now also let it be according unto your words: he with whom it is found shall be my servant; and ye shall be blameless. Then they speedily took down every man his sack to the ground, and opened every man his sack. And he searched, and began at the eldest, and left at the youngest: and the cup was found in Benjamin's sack. Then they rent their clothes, and laded every man his ass, and returned to the city. And Judah and his brethren came to Joseph's house; for he was yet there: and they fell before him on the ground. And Joseph said unto them, What deed is this that ye have done? wot ye not that such a man as I can certainly divine? And Judah said, What shall we say unto my lord? what shall we speak? or how shall we clear ourselves? God hath found out the iniquity of thy servants: behold, we are my lord's servants, both we, and he also with whom the cup is found. And he said, God forbid that I should do so: but the man in whose hand the cup is found, he shall be my servant; and as for you, get you up in peace unto your father. Then Judah came near unto him, and said, Oh my lord, let thy servant, I pray thee, speak a word in my lord's ears, and let not thine anger burn against thy servant: for thou art even as Pharaoh. My lord asked his servants, saying, Have ye a father or a brother? And we said unto my lord, We have a father, an old man, and a child of his old age, a little one; and his brother is dead, and he alone is left of his mother, and his father loveth him. And thou saidst unto thy servants, Bring him down unto me, that I may set mine eyes upon him. And we said unto my lord, The lad cannot leave his father: for if he should leave his father, his father would die. And thou saidst unto thy servants, Except your youngest brother come down with you, ye shall see my face no more. And it came to pass when we came up unto thy servant my father, we told him the words of my lord. And our father said, Go again, and buy us a little food. And we said, We cannot go down: if our youngest brother be with us, then will we go down: for we may not see the man's face, except our youngest brother be with us. And thy servant my father said unto us, Ye know that my wife bare me two sons: and the one went out from me, and I said, Surely he is torn in pieces; and I saw him not since: and if ye take this also from me, and mischief befal him, ye shall bring down my gray hairs with sorrow to the grave. Now therefore when I come to thy servant my father, and the lad be not with us; seeing that his life is bound up in the lad's life; it shall come to pass, when he seeth that the lad is not with us, that he will die: and thy servants shall bring down the grey hairs of thy servant our father with sorrow to the grave. For thy servant became surety for the lad unto my father, saying, If I bring him not unto thee, then I shall bear the blame to my father for ever. Now therefore, I pray thee, let thy servant abide instead of the lad, a bondman to my lord; and let the lad go up with his brethren. For how shall I go up to my father, and the lad be not with me? lest peradventure I shall see the evil that shall come on my father. Then Joseph could not refrain himself before all them that stood by him; and he cried, Cause every man to go out from me. And there stood no man with him, while Joseph made himself known unto his brethren. And he wept aloud: and the Egyptians and the house of Pharaoh heard. And Joseph said unto his brethren, I am Joseph: doth my father yet live." Gen. xliv. 4. to xlv. 3.

Here again we have no need of Archaic illustration or modern criticism. As long as man shall remain embodied on this earth, so long shall the simple unpretending truthfulness of this narrative touch his heart.

"And his brethren could not answer him, for they were troubled at his presence. And Joseph said unto his brethren, Come near to me, I pray you. And they came near. And he said, I am Joseph your brother, whom ye sold into Egypt. Now therefore be not grieved nor angry with yourselves, that ye sold me hither: for God did send me before you to preserve life. For these two years hath the famine been in the land: and yet there are five years, in which there shall be neither ploughing nor harvest." ver. 3—6.

This passage clearly points out the cause of the famine. The ploughing in Egypt takes place just as the waters of the inundation reach the field. In these disastrous years the river scarcely rose above its wonted level. There was no ploughing, because there was no water wherewith to irrigate. For the same reason, there was no harvest.

" And God sent me before you to preserve you a posterity in the earth, and to save your lives by a great deliverance. So now it was not you that sent me hither, but God: and he hath made me a father to Pharaoh, and lord of all his house, and a ruler throughout all the land of Egypt." ver. 7, 8.

These words are not the apologetic extenuation of the perpetrators of a foul wrong, when, after years of impunity they are suddenly confronted with the victim of their misdoings: they are addressed by the victim to his oppressors, as abashed and conscience-stricken they writhe in the grasp of his absolute power over them, and grovel in the dust before him. In the annals of Greece, of Rome, of the Middle Ages, of all Heathendom, Pagan and Christian, there is nothing so noble as this! Lord, what shall man be, when thy Holy Spirit hath through long discipline expelled from his soul the mist and taint of his birth-sin, and brought forth clearly and sharply the lineaments of Thine own image, wherein thou didst at first create him!

"Haste ye, and go up to my father, and say unto him, Thus saith thy son Joseph, God hath made me the lord of all Egypt: come down unto me, tarry not: and thou shalt dwell in the land of Goshen, and thou shalt be near unto me, thou and thy children, and thy children's children, and thy flocks, and thy herds, and all that thou hast; and there will I minister food unto thee (for yet there are five years of famine); lest thou, and thine household, and all that thou hast come to poverty." Gen. xlv. 9—11.

This was no chimerical fear. The same divine prescience in Joseph foresaw both the famine and its consequences. The impoverishment of the princes of Egypt, and of the petty kings of Canaan, by this fearful visitation, and the important consequences of both, are distinctly traceable, amid the dim shadows that conceal the history of mankind at these remote periods.

The word *Goshen* גֹּשֶׁן we have elsewhere ascertained to signify *a flower*,* and to be the epithet originally of the eastern portion of the Delta; but afterwards to have been applied to the whole of this division of Egypt, in exactly the same manner

* The Monumental History of Egypt, vol. ii. Binns and Goodwin, Bath.

as *Ramses,* which was the name of a city on the extreme western border of the Delta.

" And, behold, your eyes see, and the eyes of my brother Benjamin, that it is my mouth that speaketh unto you. And ye shall tell my father of all my glory in Egypt, and of all ye have seen ; and ye shall haste and bring down my father hither.

" And he fell upon his brother Benjamin's neck and wept, and Benjamin wept on his neck. Moreover he kissed all his brethren, and wept upon them: and after that his brethren talked with him." ver. 12—15.

This passage admits of no comment. " Lives there a man of soul so dead," as to read it without emotion? it is but vanity to attempt to excite it in him by any amplification.

" And the fame thereof was heard in Pharaoh's house, [even the] saying, Joseph's brethren are come: and it was good in the eyes of Pharaoh and of his servants." ver. 16.

" And Pharoah said unto Joseph, Say unto thy brethren, This do ye; lade your beasts, and go, get you unto the land of Canaan; and take your father and your households, and come unto me: and I will give you the good of the land of Egypt, and ye shall eat the fat of the land.

" Now thou [Joseph] art commanded, this do ye; take ye waggons out of the land of Egypt for your little ones, and for your wives, and bring your father, and come. Also regard not your stuff; for the good of all the land of Egypt is yours." ver. 17—20.

"And the children of Israel did so : and Joseph gave them waggons, according to the commandment of Pharaoh, and gave them provision for the way. To all of them he gave each man changes of raiment ; but to Benjamin he gave three hundred rings of silver and five changes of raiment.

"And to his father he sent thus : ten asses laden with the good things of Egypt, and ten she-asses laden with corn and bread, and prepared meat for his father by the way." ver. 23.

Our engraving of the banquet of Nahrai (above, p. 91), has already thrown light upon this passage : a further illustration would be supplied by one of the bills of fare of the feasts for the dead, which remain to this day inscribed on the walls of all the principal tombs of Egypt. In that of Eimei at Ghizeh, who was one of the princes of Suphis, no fewer than 98 dishes are directed to be set forth in the monthly and semi-monthly banquets.

Many more, equally striking, might also be collected from the same sources of knowledge, of the high perfection to which the culinary art had attained in Egypt in Joseph's days, giving entire verisimilitude and consistency to the present prepared by him for his aged father.

"So he sent his brethren away, and they departed: and he said unto them, See that ye fall not out by the way." ver. 24.

This caution would be greatly needed by the troop of rough, wild, impulsive men to whom it was addressed. Even to this day the governments of Egypt, Syria, and other countries bordering on the desert, are felt to be an intolerable restraint to the Arab rangers of the sand, and the return of a caravan of them to their native wastes is too often signalised by violent and sanguinary quarrels. Joseph's brethren had much to resent, and much to forbear, among themselves. In the absence of Joseph's caution, a bloody encounter would probably have been the issue of the bitter recriminations wherewith they would have wreaked on each other the resentful feelings that the recent exposure of their villanies had excited in them.

"And they went up out of Egypt, and came unto the land of Canaan unto Jacob their father, and told him, saying, Joseph is yet alive, and he is governor over all the land of Egypt. And his heart fainted, for he believed them not. And they told him all the words of Joseph which he had said unto them: and when he saw the waggons which Joseph sent to carry him, the spirit of Jacob their father revived. And Israel said, It is enough : Joseph my son is yet alive : I will go and see him before I die." Gen. xlv. 24—28.

" I had fainted unless I had believed to see the goodness of the Lord in the land of the living. Wait on the Lord ; be of good courage, and he shall strengthen thine heart : wait, I say, on the Lord ! ". Psalm xxxvii. 13, 14.

" And Israel took his journey, with all that he had, and came to Beer-sheba, and offered sacrifices unto the God of his father Isaac. And God spake unto Israel in the visions of the night, and said, Jacob, Jacob. And he said, Here am I. And he said, I am God, the God of thy father : fear not to go down into Egypt ; for I will there make of thee a great nation : I will go down before thee into Egypt ; and I will also surely bring thee up again ; and Joseph shall put his hand upon thine eyes." Gen. xlvi. 1—4.

It was at Beer-sheba that Abraham, after the ratification of his covenant with Abimelech, had, in token thereof, planted a tree by the well, which, from this circumstance, he named " the well of the oath," and " called upon the name of the Lord the everlasting God : the well by this token was confirmed to him and to his seed after him for a perpetual possession. Gen. xxi. 25—34. It was at Beer-sheba that the Lord appeared unto Isaac, and solemnly repeated to him the promise that he had at the first made to his father Abraham. In consequence Isaac also builded an altar there, and called upon the name of the Lord. Gen. xxvi. 23—25. Again, it was at Beersheba that Jacob himself had received from his father Isaac the parting prophetic benediction which conferred upon him, to the exclusion of Esau, the inheritance of the promise, to obtain which Abram their father had left Ur of the Chaldees. Gen. xxviii. 1—5, 10. The transaction therefore recorded in the passage before us was no light matter, neither was this explicit repetition of the promise in a place thus specially consecrated to its ratification, and under the wonderful circumstances in which Israel now sojourned at Beer-sheba, a common or insignificant event. It was on the last night of Jacob's sojourn in the land of promise, that God was pleased to repeat, for the last time, the promise made at the first to Abram, and in the place which Abram had especially consecrated to the God who had made that promise. These, we repeat it, are not circumstances to be superficially glossed over, in a book wherein not one word has been written in vain. That the importance nevertheless of this passage of Holy Writ should only fully appear now, that the sojourn of Israel in Egypt is receiving such large elucidation from the monuments that still exist in the valley of the Nile, is a special but not at all a singular circumstance, in the providential arrangements of God. He who hath addressed his word to man so long as man shall sojourn upon this earth, has also ordained, that with the lapse of time, the intelligence of man and the sphere of his knowledge shall advance likewise and continually : but the effect of this wider intellectual glance will only be, that the word of God will vindicate its verity more triumphantly, and more clearly demonstrate the adaptation of its teachings to the wants of man.

In order to make appear the great importance of the passage before us, we must call the attention of our readers to another portion of the Bible, which discourses of the points now under review.

" He that ministereth to you the Spirit and worketh miracles, doeth he it by the works of the law, or by the hearing of faith ? Even as Abraham believed God, and it was accounted to him for righteousness. Know ye therefore that they which are of faith, the same are the children of Abraham. And the Scripture foreseeing that God would justify the heathen through faith, declared before, the good news unto Abraham, *that is*, ' In thee and in thy seed shall all nations be blessed.' So then they which be of faith are blessed with faithful Abraham. For as many as are under the works of the law are under a curse : for it is written, Cursed is every one that continueth not in all things that are written in the book of the law to do them. But that no man is justified by the law in the sight of God is evident: for [it is written] the just shall live by faith; and the law is not of faith, but [it says] the man that doeth them shall live in them. Christ hath redeemed us from the curse of the law, being made a curse for us: for it is written, Cursed is every one that hangeth on a tree: that the blessing of Abraham might come on the Gentiles through Jesus Christ; that we might receive the promise of the Spirit through faith.

Brethren, I speak after the manner of men; though it be but a man's covenant, yet if it be confirmed, no man disannulleth, or addeth thereto. Now to Abraham and his seed were the promises made. He saith not, And to seeds, as of many; but as of one, And unto thy seed, which is Christ. And this I say, that the covenant, which was confirmed before of God in Christ, the law, which was four hundred and thirty years after, cannot disannul, that it should make the promise of none effect. For if the inheritance be of the law, it is no more of promise: but God gave it to Abraham by promise." Gal. iii. 5—18.

The scope of this passage, we need scarcely observe, is to prove that the Abrahamic promise was a matter superior to, and independent of, the Mosaic law ; and the proof of the position is found in the circumstance, that the promise was made to Abraham and to his *seed* as to one, not to his *seeds* or posterity generally, as to many ; (so the Jews interpret it ;) the one man, thus designated, being Christ. It follows, therefore, that it was to Christ in Abraham, and not to Abraham in person, that the promise, in its ultimate interpretation, was made. But, according to the Scripture doctrine of paternity, Christ was in Isaac, and Christ was in Jacob, quite as much as in Abraham. (See Hebrews vii. 9, 10.) It is therefore of no importance to which of the representatives and heads of the family of Abraham the promise is repeated. The same God speaks in it of the same Christ, and as long as the promise is repeated, so long the dispensation of the promise lasts. But in the passage before us, God orally declared the Abrahamic promise for the last time. It was never afterwards repeated to the chosen race by this mode of revelation. It is moreover wonderfully remarkable, that this last repetition took place on the last night of the sojourn of the Patriarchs in Canaan. On the day following the tribe of Israel crossed the borders of Egypt. We find, therefore, with admiration, but without surprise, that in this " covenant, well ordered in all things," the dispensation of the promise, (that is, of the divine utterance of the promise) which began with the call of Abram into Canaan, from Ur of the Chaldees, terminated on the last night of the sojourn in Canaan of Isaac his grandson.

Upon this view of the subject, another conclusion follows inevitably. It is from the end and not from the beginning of this dispensation of the promise that the interval between it and the law must be computed. To assume that in the passage we have quoted from the Galatians, St. Paul speaks only of the first enunciation of the promise to Abram is to ignore altogether the frequent subsequent repetitions of the same promise to himself and to Jacob. Whereas the entire argument of the apostle goes to show that God and his Christ were the only parties to the promise at any time, and consequently, that all the repetitions of the promise were of exactly the same value, inasmuch as they were all made by the same God of the same Christ. The four hundred and thirty years therefore mentioned by St. Paul, as the interval between the Abrahamic promise and the Mosaic law, dates from the last repetition of that promise to Jacob at Beer-sheba on the last night of his sojourn in the land of Canaan. This is very evident. Let us now turn to other passages of Holy Writ which mention the same interval.

"Now the sojourning of the children of Israel who dwelt in Egypt, was four hundred and thirty years. And it came to pass at the end of the four hundred and thirty years, even the self-same day it came to pass, that all the hosts of the Lord went out from the land of Egypt." Exodus xii. 10, 11.

It is not possible for language to be more explicit than this. The passage is found at the termination of the history of the bondage in Egypt; the duration of the sojourn of Israel there is a natural conclusion of the narrative. We are well aware of the interpolation which this text has suffered in the Samaritan Pentateuch, and some other authorities of the third and fourth centuries before the vulgar era, and whereby it is made to read " the sojourning of the children of Israel who dwelt *in Canaan and* in Egypt, &c." This gloss we apprehend, convicts itself of forgery, by the circumstance that it converts the passage into arrant nonsense. The natural termination of the history in the sojourn in Egypt, is the duration of that sojourn as we have already explained :—but thus interpolated, the passage does not give the duration of that sojourn at all; but the chronology of another event, altogether foreign and irrelevant to the matter in hand.

When we add to these that no copy of the Hebrew original has this reading, and that, as Bunsen has well observed, the very nature of the addition excites a strong suspicion of its falsehood, there is no occasion to detain the reader further with the well known motives of the interpolators. Enough has been advanced to establish the truth of the Hebrew reading. It is only the adoption of the gloss by many otherwise high authorities on Biblical criticism, which has rendered needful that which we have said upon it.

If the Bible is to decide this question, and not man's chronological and statistical speculations, the enquiry is at an end. This period of 400 years was distinctly prophesied to Abram, almost at the commencement of his sojourn in Canaan, Gen. xv. 13. The same period is also formally repeated in the inspired adoption of this prophecy by Stephen, Acts vii. 6, as well as by St. Paul in the passage already quoted from Galatians.

Thus clearly is it revealed in the word of God, that the children of Israel sojourned in Egypt for exactly four hundred and thirty years, and because it is thus revealed, and for no other reason, we at once assume it, and take our stand upon it boldly and decidedly. If it be objected to us, that by doing this we shall presently involve ourselves in inextricable difficulties, we reply, that we shall not for that reason tamper with the truth of God. We receive this fact as He has revealed it. We shall proceed, step by step, through the whole subject; and when the threatened difficulties arise, we will endeavour to deal with them. A tangible and precise fact like this, moreover, of times so remote from history is far too precious to be allowed to pass away before the chronological chimera of this critic, or the statistical spectre of that philosopher. We repeat that which we have already said before, that the writings of believers in revelation are the armoury whence its infidel assailants have drawn their deadliest weapons.

"And Jacob broke up [his encampment] at Beersheba : and the sons of Israel carried Jacob their father, and their little ones, and their wives, in the waggons which Pharaoh had sent to carry him," Gen. xlvi. 5.

The word here translated "waggon," עֲגָלָה meant originally, "young bullock," which being the universal beast of burden in the ancient world, afterwards gave its name to the vehicle to which it was yoked. The subject of draught-oxen is very common in the reliefs of Egypt, but the carriages are not on wheels, but on runners.

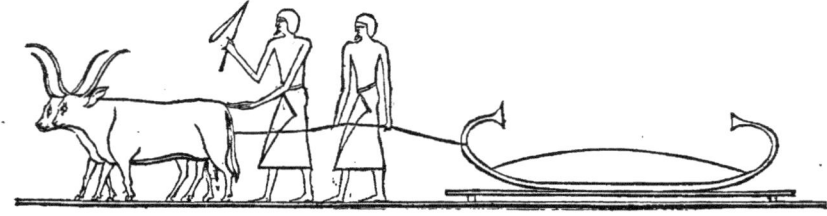

It was in such carriages, drawn by oxen, that the household stuff of the patriarchs was conveyed into

Egypt. Jacob, with the women and young children, went thither in palanquins, which were either drawn by men-slaves, or borne upon their shoulders.

FROM THE TOMB OF NAHRAI.

"And they took their cattle and their goods which they had gotten in the land of Canaan, and came into Egypt, Jacob and all his seed with him. His sons, and his sons' sons with him; his daughters and his sons' daughters, and all his seed brought he with him to Egypt. . . . . .

"All the souls that came with Jacob into Egypt of his issue, besides Jacob's sons' wives, all the souls were three-score and six. And the sons of Joseph which were born him in Egypt were two souls: all the souls of the house of Jacob which came into Egypt, were three-score and ten." Gen. xlvi. 6   26 2 .

The great precision after which the writer of this passage labours in the detail of these facts is very remarkable. It is impossible for a statement to be made more carefully. Now there are but two motives conceivable by which the penman can have been actuated in this writing. The one is his conviction, that the facts he had to state were deeply important to his history: the other his consciousness, that he was writing a falsehood which nevertheless he wished to impose upon his readers for truth. If in this or any other numerical statement the numbers thus formally recorded may be accepted in a vague indefinite sense, so that any one number may mean any other, (a mode of interpretation very much in vogue among certain critics of the present day) assuredly the passage before us was written for the purpose of deceiving and misleading the reader. This conclusion is inevitable.

"And he sent Judah before him unto Joseph, to direct his face unto Goshen; when they came into the land of Goshen.* And Joseph made ready his chariot, and went to meet Israel his father in Go-

* The city of On, or Heliopolis, was some miles to the southward of the Delta, of which (as we have already explained) Goshen was one of the ancient names. The circumstances here detailed, correspond very exactly both in time and place. The tribe of Jacob sought the grassy plains of the Delta for the pasturage of their cattle immediately on their arrival in Egypt. Judah, the first-born of Jacob, is sent to On, to announce to Joseph his father's arrival.

shen, and presented himself unto him, and he fell on his neck and wept on his neck a good while. And Israel said unto Joseph, now let me die, since I have seen thy face, because thou art yet alive." Gen. xlvi. 28—30.

It would be with the state and habiliments of a military chief that Joseph went forth on this occasion; by no other order of the community were horse-chariots, מוכבת, ever used.

"And Joseph said unto his brethren and unto his father's house, I will go up and shew Pharaoh, and say unto him, My brethren and my father's house, which were in the land of Canaan are come unto me. And the men are shepherds, they are also herdsmen, and their flocks and their herds, and all their possessions they have brought. And it shall come to pass when Pharaoh shall speak to you, and shall say, What is your occupation? that ye shall say, Thy servants have tended cattle from our youth, even until now, both we and also our fathers, that ye may dwell in the land of Goshen, for every shepherd is the abomination of Egypt." Gen. xxxi. 34.

So universally is the very well-known passage of Manetho preserved by Josephus in his first book against the sophist Apion, quoted as a comment upon this text, that we are absolutely compelled to follow a precedent so firmly established, and take here the question of the first shepherd-invasion of Egypt.

JOSEPH. 115

Having quoted this passage, commentators generally consider, that the abhorrence of the shepherd by the Egyptian is hereby fully accounted for. To this assumption we shall be compelled to demur.

It is as follows:—"There was a king [of Egypt] named Amountimæus. In his reign God was unpropitious, I do not know why; and unexpectedly, some men of ignoble race, rushing boldly from the East, made war upon the country and took it easily without a battle, and having made prisoners of the principal men in it, they burnt down the cities and overthrew the temples of the gods. They likewise used all the inhabitants as harshly as possible, slaying some, and selling others with their wives and children into slavery." Κατ, Απιον. I. 14.

This passage, which we have translated as closely as possible, convicts itself of intentional exaggeration by its phraseology. Nevertheless, that it is a genuine extract from the temple-records, there can be no doubt. We have already explained, that the men of ignoble race were the lower Egyptians, that they were the partizans of the older religion, and that the Canaanite settlers in the Delta took part with them in the schism that arose in Egypt upon the change made in her mythology by Mencheres. The monuments whence Manetho extracted this history being kept by the partizans of the opposite faction, we hereby fully explain both the application of the opprobrious nicknames of "shepherds" and "foreigners," to the Lower Egyptian Pharaohs, and the fearful picture which the account gives of the barbarities committed by the men from the east, who conquered Amountimæus, which the existing monuments of Egypt contradict *in toto*.

"At length they made one of themselves king, whose name was Salatis. He lived at Memphis, and put to tribute both the Upper and the Lower Country, and garrisoned the most important places. But he principally fortified the eastern parts, [of his dominion] fearing the growing desire of the Assyrians, who were then becoming very powerful, to invade his kingdom. So that, finding in the Setheoite nome a city very advantageously situated upon the eastern banks of the Bubastite branch [of the Nile] and called from some ancient myth, Avaris, he fortified it, making it very strong with walls, and garrisoned it with an immense force, amounting to 240,000 men. Here he held his court in the summer season, administering both the provisioning [of the garrison] and the collection of tribute, training [his troops] diligently in martial exercise through fear of a hostile attack from without. Having reigned for nineteen years, he died. After him another named Beon reigned for twenty-four years, and then another named Apachnas for forty-six years and seven months; then Aphophis for sixty-one years, and Jannas for fifty years and a month. After all these, Asses reigned also forty-nine years and two months. And these six were the first rulers over them, always at war with Egypt, and desiring principally to uproot it altogether."—*Ibid.*

These names of shepherd-kings are all opprobrious epithets, used as nicknames with punning allusions to the real names of the Lower Egyptian Pharaohs, to whom they were applied.

The passage itself is totally irreconcileable with the one that precedes it, whence it must have been inferred, that the shepherd invasion was a mere irruption of armed barbarians; but it agrees perfectly with the indirect testimony of the remaining monuments of this event, and with the scripture notices of Egypt under the shepherds, that is, the Lower Egyptian Pharaohs. Their kingdom was well ordered and peaceable; and a succession of the greatest and best that had ever ruled in Egypt, exercised the sovereign authority during reigns of long duration.

The expression, "these six were the *first* rulers over the shepherds," is well deserving of more attention than it has hitherto received; inasmuch as it distinctly alludes to a fact which the monuments have irrefragably established, namely, that the so-called shepherd-kingdom in Egypt, by no means ended with Asses, though he was probably expelled from

Memphis by the Mencherian Pharaóhs. To this point, which is of the last importance to the history of Israel in Egypt, we must return hereafter.

"This entire nation [that of the shepherds] was called *hyksōs*,—that is king-shepherds, for the word *hyk* signifies 'king,' in the sacred tongue, and *sōs* means 'a shepherd,' and 'shepherds' in the vulgar dialect; and the two united make *hyk-sōs*." Ibid.

This criticism is perfectly correct in every particular. The word *hyk* occurs in the sacred tongue, that is, in the hieroglyphics, with the meaning which Josephus assigns to it. ⟨glyph⟩ *hk* is a group of common occurrence in the texts; it means "king" of a foreign nation generally. The word *sōs* (σως) also is of equally common occurrence in the Coptic texts, which, being as we have explained, the Egyptian translation of the Bible and other Christian books, represents the vulgar dialect of ancient Egypt. It is written *shos*, and signifies "shepherd," also "ignominy," and, "one that is beaten." In the sacred tongue it is not read with this import; but the group which has been thus transcribed is of very common occurrence in the texts that explain the reliefs, representing wars with Lower Egypt—⟨glyph⟩ *shsu* or *shus*, which is evidently the same word. The determinative of the group shows us, however, that in hieroglyphics this word was not a common noun, but the proper name of some tribe or nation of foreigners, and enemies of Egypt. Sos, or Shos, was the name of a powerful tribe among the Canaanite auxiliaries of the Lower Egyptian Pharaohs, by whom the Mencherians were expelled from Memphis. So conspicuous a part did they take in this war, that their proper name in after ages had passed paræmiastically from the sacred to the vulgar dialect as the common appellative of " shepherd," and also of ignominy and " opprobrium " generally. The identification of the *shos* we will consider hereafter.

" Some say that these shepherds were Arabs. In another transcription ' king ' is not signified by the common noun *hyk,* but, on the contrary, it means ' captive : ' for the words *hyk* and *hak* in Egyptian signify literally ' captive,' ' prisoner of war.' This last [import] seems to me more credible, and in better agreement with ancient history." Ibid.

Josephus here is by no means equally happy. It is perfectly true that the words 𓉗𓃾𓌙 *hak Hierog.,* and HK *hak, Copt.* mean "to lead captive," " to take prisoner," though it is only by a pun that they can be brought into relation with the word *hyksos.* But our author was misled by an absurdity which, to the great detriment of the truth, he mixed up with his defence of the sacred books of the Jews. In order to magnify his own nation, he endeavours to prove throughout his work, that the Israelites were the shepherds who conquered Egypt. This at once accounts for his ready acceptance of this quibbling criticism, which, as he tells us afterwards, greatly favors his view, inasmuch as his forefathers were both shepherds by occupation and also captives in Egypt.

There is no subject in the entire compass of human knowledge which so imperatively demands from him that discusses it, a perfectly honest intention, or (we grieve to add) that so seldom obtains this its demand on any hand, as Biblical criticism.

" He (Manetho) says, that these before-named kings of the shepherds, as they were called, and those who were descended from them, ruled Egypt for 511 years. But after these things, he says, that there was an insurrection against the Shepherds, of the kings of the Thebaid and of the rest of Egypt, and there broke out against them a great war, and of long duration." Ibid.

The sum of the reigns of the Shepherd-kings he had before catalogued, is 259 years and ten months. So that, by the place before us, their kingdom lasted 251 years after Asses, who was expelled from Memphis. But the lists of kings which profess to be the compend or digest of Manetho's history, put down the whole duration of the Shepherd-kingdom in

Egypt at 953 years. We have elsewhere expressed our conviction that this kingdom in the Delta had been founded long before the conquest of Memphis by Salatis or Saites, in the reign of Amun-Timæus. The scriptural and monumental grounds upon which this opinion has been formed, we have already detailed in part, and they will appear further in the course of our present undertaking.

Most unwilling as we are to add needlessly to our already sufficiently copious subject, it seems incumbent on us to remark on the present passage from Josephus, that a very large and influential school of modern investigators have been entirely mistaken in their interpretation of it: and that their mistake has led to chronological assumptions altogether incompatible with the truth of the Bible. They read Josephus as though he had said, that the Shepherd kings ruled Egypt for 511 years after the taking of Memphis by Salatis, and then the insurrection of the Theban kings arose: whereas, in the original, Josephus says no such thing. He merely tells us that in Manetho's narrative the account of the duration of the Shepherd-kingdom is followed by that of the insurrection which ultimately overthrew it. It was not his intention to state at all in this place the chronological connection between the two events, —for, assuredly, he never could have meant to say that the Shepherds ruled in Egypt for 511 years, and then waged a long war which ended in their expulsion,—because thereby he would have overthrown entirely the theory he was just about to enounce, that the Shepherds were the Israelites: inasmuch as his own books, which he knew intimately, declared authoritatively that the sojourn of Israel in Egypt was exactly 430 years. As we proceed with our subject, we shall find other occasions whereon more conveniently to discuss the time of the capture of Memphis.

It will have sufficiently appeared from what we have stated, that the so-called Shepherd invasion of Egypt, which was merely a civil war between two native pretenders to the crown, was not the reason why " every shepherd was an abomination to the Egyptians," as is assumed by Biblical critics. This antagonism between the husbandman and the herdsman had a far earlier origin. It began with Cain and Abel: and in Egypt, where the one pursuit was agriculture, and where every thing was prescriptive, it was a doctrine of religion that every shepherd by occupation was unclean, and inadmissible within the precincts of her temples. All this we have before explained (p. 19). The Lower Egyptian ascendancy then did not make every shepherd an abomination to the Egyptians, but the Lower Egyptians were afterwards called " Shepherds," that is " abominable," by the Upper Egyptians, because of their victories over them.

" Then Joseph came and told Pharaoh, and said, my father, and my brethren, and their flocks, and their herds, and all that they have, are come out of the land of Canaan, and, behold, they are in the land of Goshen. And he took some of his brethren, even five men, and presented them unto Pharaoh. And Pharaoh said unto his brethren, What is your occupation? And they said unto Pharaoh, Thy servants are shepherds, both we and also our fathers. They said moreover unto Pharaoh, For to sojourn in the land are we come; for thy servants have no pasture for their flocks: for the famine is sore in the land of Canaan; now therefore, we pray thee, let thy servants dwell in the land of Goshen." Gen. xlvii. 1—4.

This passage puts the cause of the famine out of the reach of a doubt. It was not a blight on the corn. It was not an excess of rain in the time of harvest. It was a drought upon the whole earth. At the same time that the pastures of Canaan were as arid and as dusty as the waste wilderness that surrounds them, the thick forests that clothe the mountains of Ethiopia were also drooping for lack of moisture, and the Nile " was smitten in its seven streams, so that men went over dry shod:" even as it shall be again at some future period, and for some similar display of the goodness and severity of God towards his people Israel. Is. xi. 15, 16.

"And Pharaoh spake unto Joseph, saying, Thy father and thy brethren are come unto thee: the land of Egypt is before thee; in the best of the land make thy father and brethren to dwell: in the land of Goshen let them dwell: and if thou knowest any men of fitness [for the office] among them, set them over my cattle." ver. 5, 6.

The office proposed by Pharaoh for the acceptance of Joseph's brethren was one frequently held by the princes of Egypt. 𓌞 "Superintendent of the king's cattle," is one of the titles of a prince, whose funeral tablet is in the *Museo de bei arti*, at Florence. It has been there ever since the days of the Medici, and was doubtless found in Lower Egypt. The title is also often written thus: 𓌞 "royal scribe (or enumerator) of the *bodies* of cattle," or as we should say, "*heads* of cattle." This was an office evidently sought after and highly esteemed in Ancient Egypt, a circumstance strongly confirmatory of our explanation of the sense in which "every shepherd (or cattle-feeder—רוֹעֶה means both) was an abomination to the Egyptians." They were religiously unclean, and not allowed to dwell in the cities of Egypt, which were all accounted the precincts of the temples of their tutelary gods, that invariably stood in the midst of them. This restriction seems to have gone no further than those who immediately attended upon the cattle.

"And Joseph brought in Jacob his father, and set him before Pharaoh : and Jacob blessed Pharaoh. And Pharaoh said unto Jacob, How old art thou ? And Jacob said unto Pharaoh, The days of the years of my pilgrimage are an hundred and thirty years; few and evil have the days of the years of my life been, and have not attained unto the days of the years of the life of my fathers in the days of their pilgrimage. And Jacob blessed Pharaoh, and went out from before Pharaoh." Gen. xlvii. 7—10.

In this passage is contained the only formal statement of the fact, that the life of man had undergone a considerable abbreviation in the course of the period that had then elapsed since the creation and the deluge. The recorded length of the lives of the men of these still earlier times had already made apparent this same fact. It is moreover to be noted, that in the times of Jacob human life had a much longer average duration than afterwards. This is a fact which will presently demand our attention. It was not until later, that the days of the years of man's life had dwindled down " to three-score years and ten." Ps. xc. 10. These are truths revealed so clearly and obviously, that it is hard to conceive how a distinct denial of them, or even such an explanation of them, as shall make the names of the earlier patriarchs not those of individuals, but of tribes, and the Scripture numbers generally the metaphorical representations of vague, undefined, and undefineable lapses of time, can nevertheless consist with expressions of boundless respect for the Old Testament. Such is the case nevertheless, and with more than one writer of high authority on our subject.

" And Joseph placed his father and his brethren, and gave them a possession in the land of Egypt, in the best of the land, in the land of Rameses, as Pharaoh had commanded. And Joseph nourished his father and his brethren, and all his father's household with bread, according to their families." ver. 12, 13.

This is the narrative of the inspired historian. He applies to the part of Goshen in which Joseph located his father and his tribe, the name which it obtained long afterwards in the days of the captivity (see Exod. i. 11). It is almost needless to remark, that Rameses must have been either another name for Goshen, or a part of Goshen. This appears very evidently from the text and context. Its locality we shall find hereafter.

Thus have we subjected the whole of the inspired narrative of the circumstances which led to the location in Egypt of the tribe or sept of Jacob, in every single particular, to the most trying ordeal, by which it is possible to test the genuineness of any professed history of the past. We have minutely compared its incidental allusions, those unimportant accessories, in which all feigned narratives invariably betray themselves by blunders and anachronisms, with the yet existing monuments of the time and country of which it purports to relate the history. How the Mosaic narrative comes forth from the torture-chamber, wherein this crucial question has been administered to it,—whether its genuineness or imposture have appeared in the process, we, without one impulse of fear, without one shadow of mistrust, leave to the judgment of the reader the most hostile to its authenticity, that may cast his eye upon our pages.

These contemporary monuments have corrected the mistakes and misapprehensions of twenty-five hundred years. They have restored to significance and perfect harmony with the context, words which, in the days of Ptolemy Epiphanes and the Septuagint, were mere cabalisms. Their import had been long forgotten, and they were only to be represented in the new version by the transcription of their Hebrew characters into Greek.

We have repeatedly remarked, in the course of our investigation, that not one word in the Bible was written in vain: we have now another and similar proposition to lay down. Not one event in Providence has happened in vain. It has not been in vain that the monuments of Ancient Egypt have remained until now deeply hidden beneath the sand of the desert. Neither has their present disclosure taken place for no higher purpose than to supply materials for huge unreadable volumes, in which the writers may display their learning, their philosophic rejection of the Bible, and their implicit faith in Eratosthenes, Censorinus, and other ancient Greek authorities. That it is for the illustration of the Bible that these materials for the history of Ancient Egypt have been kept by a miracle in Providence, we have long felt convinced. Our purpose in the present work is to demonstrate the truth of this our conviction.

CHAPTER III.

THE FAMINE.

"AND there was no bread in all the land; for the famine was very sore, so that the land of Egypt and the land of Canaan fainted by reason of the famine. And Joseph gathered up all the money that was found in the land of Egypt, and in the land of Canaan, for the corn which they bought: and Joseph brought the money into Pharaoh's house. And when the money failed in the land of Egypt and in the land of Canaan, all the Egyptians came unto Joseph and said, Give us bread, for why should we die before thee, for the money faileth? And Joseph said, Give me your cattle; and I will give you for your cattle, if money fail. And they brought their cattle unto Joseph: and Joseph gave them bread for horses, for flocks, for herds, and for asses: and he brought them through that year with [the] bread [he gave them]." Gen. xlvii. 13—17.

This was but the third year of the famine. At

its conclusion, the whole of the moveable property of Egypt and Canaan is Pharaoh's. The rings of silver and gold are in his treasure-houses. The cattle of all kinds feed on the grassy plains of the Delta, under the supervision of the king's servants.

The enumeration of the several kinds of cattle mentioned here, is illustrated by the tombs of the princes of Egypt of the times of Joseph. Cattle of several sorts formed an important part of their wealth. They are represented on the walls of their tombs with minute accuracy : so much so, that each separate head has the appearance of a portrait. It would convey a wrong impression were we to assume that the flocks and herds of Egypt were like those that now graze the pastures of England. They consisted of collections of many different species of bovine and caprine animals. The princes were in the habit of going forth to the mountains on hunting expeditions, at the head of long trains of attendants, for the purpose of taking them alive in toils. It is not until the times immediately preceding those of Joseph that they are ever represented hunting with deadly weapons. The experiment which ultimately issued in the present breeds of tame cattle was then in progress. Gazelles, antelopes, and wild goats of various species constituted the flocks of the princes of Egypt. Zebus, yaks, brahmin-bulls, as well as the wild cattle, both of Western Asia and

Eastern Africa, were their herds. Even in the days of Joseph's immediate predecessors, a highly-valued possession of one of the princes of the twelfth dynasty, Nahrai,* consisted in a tame breed of the oryx, the gnou, or some other species of the colossal antelopes that to this day bound in herds over the vast plains of interior Africa.

The concentration of the cattle of vast districts in one place, and under one hand and management, which is implied by the inspired narrative, would have the effect of greatly settling the tame breeds which were afterwards in use. This effect certainly followed: for of the cattle depicted in the tombs of Egypt, which belong to later times than those of Joseph, the flocks are all goats, and the herds are all oxen, of three or four breeds only.

The ass was always the beast of burden of Egypt, from the very earliest period of which we have any monumental record. He still strays wild in herds, and browses the oases of the desert tracts that hem in Egypt on all sides. The Zebra, the Twaggai, and the other striped asses of interior Africa do not appear ever to have reached Egypt. Had they been seen there, doubtless they would have been highly valued.

The horse was unknown in Egypt in the times

* His tomb is at Beni-hassan, in Middle Egypt.

that preceded the Lower Egyptian or shepherd kingdom. He constantly appears, and as a property in the highest possible estimation, on the monuments of the times that followed that kingdom. It is well worthy of note that, in exact accordance with this monumental indication, the horse is not mentioned among the possessions acquired by Abram during his sojourn in Egypt. Gen. xii. 15. Whereas, in the passage before us, the horse stands first of all among the cattle of the princes of Egypt. The political changes which have taken place in the interval between the times of Abram, and those of Joseph, satisfactorily account for this discrepancy which prevails alike in the texts and on the monuments. Doubtless with the great influx of eastern strangers into Lower Egypt which they promoted, the horse was introduced from his native wilds of Arabia.

The camel, which was one of Abram's possessions in Egypt, formed no part of the live stock of Egypt in Joseph's time. It is not represented in the pictures, nor mentioned in the inscriptions of one monument of Egypt of any epoch whatever. It was doubtless an unclean animal there, and not permitted under any circumstances to enter the precincts of the kingdom. We have already explained, that in Abram's times the tenure of the Delta was very uncertain and precarious, and that it seems to have been well nigh common ground to the Egyptians and Canaanites: whereas, under the Lower Egyptian kingdom it became a part of Egypt, where the laws and usages of the realm were rigidly enforced. So fully does this comparison of the inspired text with the existing monuments, bring out its truth to the minutest particular.

The domestic animals of ancient Egypt, as depicted on the monuments, and traceable in their existing remains, would form a deeply interesting subject of investigation.

"When that year was ended, they came to him the second year and said unto him, We will not hide from our lord how that our money is spent; my lord also hath our herds of cattle; there is not ought left in the sight of my lord, but our bodies, and our lands: Wherefore shall we die before thine eyes, both we and our lands? buy us and our land for bread, and we and our land will be servants unto Pharaoh: and give us seed, that we may live and not die, that the land be not desolate.

"And Joseph bought all the land of Egypt for Pharaoh; for the Egyptians sold every man his field, because the famine prevailed over them: so the land became Pharaoh's. And as for the people, he removed them to cities from one end of the borders of Egypt, even to the other end thereof." Gen. xlvii. 18—21.

A great and momentous change in the social condition of the entire population of Lower Egypt is assuredly implied by the passage before us to have originated in these governmental acts of Joseph, and to have been still prevalent in the times of the writer of the present narrative. The change thus effected is the one which, in every case, clearly marks the transition of a people from the state of semi-barbarism to that of civilization. It consists in the reclamation of the mass of the inhabitants of a country from a wandering life passed in tents to a fixed life passed in cities and villages. It was in all other ancient countries a process so slow and gradual as altogether to escape historical notice, save in some myth or religious fable wherein the priesthood conferred the honour of originating it upon some noted benefactor of their temples and worship. In the land into the ancient history of which we are now enquiring, where nothing perishes, the period, the occasion, and the man by whom it was accomplished, are all preserved.

It was in the fourth year of the famine that the Divine wisdom in Joseph laid the foundation of laws and institutions in Egypt, upon which she flourished as an independent state for nearly 2000 years afterwards. A duration which surpasses more than threefold that of any other ancient monarchy.

The monumental indications of the occurrence of

such a political change about the time when the Bible informs us it took place, are neither few nor unimportant. The Greek lists hint obscurely, but intelligibly, at the great disorders and irregularities of government that afflicted Egypt at the commencement of the monarchy. Changes of dynasty, anarchies, and civil wars, are noted as common occurrences. The monuments speak of a state of things in the infancy of the monarchy, which was sure to produce these effects. The princes of Egypt had possessions so vast, and laid claim to powers so unlimited, that it is really not easy to comprehend what power was left for Pharaoh to exercise. In these times he must have been in the position of our kings in the Middle Ages, the mere slave and vassal of the haughty nobles that surrounded him. The effect, as well as the cause, is clearly chronicled in this wonderful stone-history. The early kings of Egypt seem to have been as uncertain in their dwelling-place as their subjects. The immediate successors of the founder of Memphis, the first metropolis of Egypt, administered the affairs of the kingdom there for a few generations only. Then comes an interval of 200 years, in which no royal name, save of an obscure king or two, occurs in her cemeteries. The successors of these primitive kings have left their memorials higher up the valley; and the Greek lists, in strict harmony with this monumental indication, tells us that the successors of the builders of the pyramids had for their capital, Abydos, far in Middle Egypt, on its extreme southern limit, and 200 miles from Memphis.* Then follows a religious civil war, and an anarchy which is filled up in the lists as usual, with hundreds of anonymous kings reigning for one or two millennia, and with about half a dozen names of obscure kings on the monuments. It was thus that the priests of Egypt ever wrote history! Then, once more, a new family reigning still at Abydos, or Coptos, exercised dominion over the whole of Egypt, and the monuments and the lists are again in accordance: but in little more than a century, Amun Timæus, the last of this dynasty, is dispossessed of Memphis by the Lower Egyptian king, Saitis, and Egypt is divided into at least two distinct monarchies. Of what is all this the indication, but of that which has hitherto taken place in the infancy of all the monarchies of the world? An insufficient modicum of authority unwillingly conceded to the reigning monarch by a factious oligarchy of haughty nobles. It is scarcely needful for us to explain how exactly the measures with which the Divine Wisdom inspired Joseph on the occasion of the famine, struck at the root of this evil, and laid the foundation of the absolute, yet

* This city is called in the lists, Elephantine. I have elsewhere dealt with this mistake, History of Egypt, vol. i.

well-ordered monarchy which, in the infancy of states, and in ages of semi-barbarism, is the only possible form of government under which prosperity and justice to the ruled are reciprocated by tranquillity and permanence to the rulers.

The monuments of Egypt of the ages that followed the times of Joseph, present a very remarkable contrast in this particular, to those that precede him. In these earlier periods, the only remaining memorial of Pharaoh is the pyramid in which he was buried. The great works were all executed by the princes and potentates that surrounded him. He is only named, while living, on the occasion of conferring some tract of land on one of his nobles. After his death they made an idol of him, worshipped him in his pyramid, and constituted themselves his priests and ministering attendants: offices which of course were well endowed both with revenues and political power. This is the occasion on which the names of the kings of primitive Egypt appear far more frequently than on any other.

Nothing can be more striking than the contrast to this state of things which is presented by the monuments of the times that succeeded the epoch of Joseph. Now Pharaoh is every thing: whereas before, he had been a mere pageant, next to nothing. The princes of Egypt, who had been supreme in the earlier period, become, in their turn, insignificant and powerless, save through Pharaoh, in these later times. The titles of *Abrach, Saris, Rapha-he,* and other distinctions, which were all but universal in the court of the early Pharaohs, fell into utter desuetude in the times of their successors. The nobles of Egypt, in the *post-pastoral* period of her history, were contented with the offices of generals, admirals, superintendents of estates, judges, and other functions, all entirely subordinate to the royal power of Pharaoh; and date the great transactions of their lives by the year of Pharaoh's reign—a practice of which there is not a single example in the preceding times. The name of the reigning king is, in short, recorded every where, and nothing is done in Egypt, either in peace or war, but Pharaoh is at the head of the movement. Even in the tombs of the princes this contrast to the earlier epoch prevails as every where else. The princes of the pyramids were petty kings nearly independent of Pharaoh. The nobles of Thebes were as much the dependents on the will of Pharaoh as the slaves that ground his corn. The contrast in this particular of the two epochs, is as perfect as possible; and the institutions of Joseph, embodied in the passage of the inspired narrative before us, most satisfactorily account for it.

The institutions of Joseph extended over all Egypt. His patron was a most magnificent monarch. The memorials of his reign have been carefully defaced every where by the fanatic bigotry of his successors. His memory has likewise been reviled by them as a shepherd and a foreigner. But the few remains that have escaped them, betray their falsehood and their barbarism.

At Shech Said, Sowet-al Misdan, El Bircheh, and some other localities in the south of Middle Egypt, there are many tombs of the nobles who wrote his name [hieroglyph]. He was evidently a rich and munificent king. The arts of design attained in his age a perfection certainly not surpassed, probably not equalled in any other epoch. Like the most eminent of his predecessors, he built a palace which must have been of magnificent dimensions, and richly endowed; for the princes of his court were all ambitious to fill offices connected with its construction or economy. [hieroglyph] This monarch was the Phiops or Aphophis of the lists, and the patron of Joseph; for there was but one Pharaoh of the name.

The institutions of Joseph, then, were coextensive with the kingdom of Aphophis; that is, with Egypt Proper; and the changes he here introduced affected the entire monarchy, and were not confined to the Delta. It was on this account that they became permanent, and have left their traces upon the yet existing monuments of the country, which, at every step of our enquiry, seems more strongly to vindicate its claim to be entitled the land of wonders. All these questions we shall presently consider.

"Only the land of the priests bought he (Joseph) not: for the priests had a portion from Pharaoh, and ate the portion that Pharaoh gave them: wherefore Joseph bought not their lands." Gen. xlvii. 22.

If our identification of Pharaoh Aphophis on the monuments be correct, this is exactly the measure we should have anticipated from a monarch of his piety and munificence. He himself undertook the victualling of the temples during the famine, from the drafts which, as Pharaoh, he drew upon the magazines of Joseph. So that the land of the priests Joseph did not purchase, for it was never brought to market. The nobles and the priests of Egypt therefore were placed by the events of the famine in two entirely distinct categories. In the preceding times they had stood in the same position as landowners. This is the clear import of the sacred text, not one word of which, we repeat, has been written in vain.

"Then Joseph said unto the people: Behold, I have bought you this day and your land for Pharaoh. There shall be seed for you [when the famine is past] and ye shall sow the land. And it shall be [the law] that ye shall give a fifth part of the yield to Pharaoh, and four parts shall be your own, for seed of the field and for your food, and for them of your households, and for food for your little ones. And they said, Thou hast saved our lives : let us find grace in the sight of my lord, and we will be the servants [slaves] of Pharaoh. And Joseph made it law over the land of Egypt unto this day, the fifth to Pharaoh, save the land of the priests alone, for that was not Pharaoh's." Gen. xlvii. 23—26.

The wisdom with which Joseph was endowed from God is very conspicuous throughout the whole record of his administration, and perhaps appears no where more clearly than in this the last transaction thereof, which has been preserved in the inspired narrative. He does not dispossess the princes of Egypt of their land unconditionally, notwithstanding their avowed willingness so to surrender it. This would have left the entire population of the country in the grasp of an autocrat; which would have infallibly ended in one of those iron tyrannies that afflict a nation for a few years, and then are swept away by the mercy of God. But with infinite sagacity he took advantage of the occasion accurately to adjust the question between the sovereign and his nobles, so that the authority of the one, and the privileges of the other, were both clearly defined. The expenses of the government of Egypt were defrayed by the impost; and then the proprietorship of the land reverted to the original possessors. The power of Pharaoh was hereby increased, so as to enable him to maintain the rights of the crown against the daring ambition of his nobles, but not so as to constitute him an irresponsible autocrat or tyrant. The nobles also were no longer in position to assume the titles and prerogatives of kings,* as they constantly do on the walls of their banquet-halls, in the times that preceded Joseph, and to trouble Egypt with incessant civil wars of pretension; but neither were they deprived of their just rights and properties by this most sagacious adjustment. Joseph accepted of their full acknowledgment of the supremacy of Pharaoh, and the fifth part of the future produce of their lands, in compensation for their nourishment for that year, and the three following years during which the famine was to last. Afterwards he gave them seed from his garners, wherewith to sow their fields, which were once more overflowed by the fertilizing waters of the Nile. Even to this particular he had already bound himself and the government of Pharaoh, by express stipulation in the original contract; thereby guarding, as far as possible, against any advantage being taken of the forlorn condition of the princes of Egypt, for further exactions on the part of Pharaoh, in case of his own demise.

* Though they never pretended to the crown; which, by the fundamental law of the kin dom was hereditar in the famil of Menes.

The principle of this most equitable adjustment, seems to have remained the law of Egypt up to the extinction of the monarchy. The terms of it were far too honest and moderate not to be intrenched upon by the dominant party in after-ages. In the days of Diodorus Siculus, who visited Egypt about the time of the birth of our Saviour, the king's share in the produce had grown to one-third, and been commuted by the cession to the crown of that proportion of the land itself.*

The relative position of the priesthood in Egypt likewise underwent a considerable modification by those institutions of Joseph, the monumental evidence of which it will now be incumbent upon us to examine. These, as we trust to show, are neither few nor dubious. In primitive Egypt, as its history stands written on its coeval monuments, the father of the family who was even then a prince, was also the priest. All the higher offices connected with religion mingle with military and naval commands in the long lists of titles and dignities of these petty kings. The individuals actually ministrant in the various offices of the worship of the gods and kings, scarcely appear in their tombs, and when they are represented there, it is merely as members of the prince's household. They were, in fact, the servants or slaves of nobles, as much so as

* Historiarum, lib. i. c. 73.

the keepers of their cattle, or their agricultural labourers.* It would seem from the inspired narrative, that a similar state of things with the Egyptian priesthood prevailed in Joseph's days. The embalmers, who are said to be his servants, Gen. 1. 2, were an order of the priesthood, as we shall find hereafter.

The monumental history of the times that followed those of Joseph, present to us the Egyptian priesthood under an aspect as remarkably contrasted with their former condition, as we have found to have been that of the princes of the same two epochs. The priest and his function have risen wonderfully in position and importance among the institutions of Egypt. The only remains of præ-pastoral Egypt, are tombs, palaces, and pyramids. These last, with their precincts, were the only temples; for all their gods were dead men, so that it was fitting that all their temples should be sepulchres. The temples of Athom (that is, Adam, the first man, identified with the sun) at Heliopolis, and of Pthah (that is, Phut, the son of Ham, at Memphis) were enclosures surrounding pyramids. In that at Heliopolis, was most probably deposited some so-

---

* The monumental evidence of this state of things under the Old Kingdom is very ample. The copious details both in reliefs and hieroglyphics, of which it is composed, pertain rather to an entire monumental History of Egypt, than to the present work.

called relic of the father of mankind. It is not certain that a single temple, properly so called, existed in the old kingdom.

In wonderful contrast to this, the remains of the new kingdom are all templar. In addition to the ruins of temples, which are by far the most frequent of all memorials of post-pastoral Egypt, the palaces of the Pharaohs, and the houses of the nobles, were covered within and without with reliefs representing shrines of gods, trains of priests, and pomps of worship. In the sepulchral vaults of the nobles themselves, the adamantine chain of prescription is gradually loosened, and the exemplar of the tombs of their forefathers of Old Egypt, where every thing was secular life, its arts and acts, and where, save in proper names and titles, the gods were never mentioned, is somewhat departed from at the very commencement of the war with the Lower Egyptians or Shepherds. Even at this period, (about the time of the death of Joseph,) the ceremonies of the great man's funeral intermix with the labours of his slaves; and the enumeration of his flocks and herds, in the decorations of the tombs of the princes of Egypt. The examples of this first step in the transition occur at Elethya in Upper Egypt, and in the oldest of the sepulchral vaults at Gournou in Western Thebes. As we proceed downwards with the stream of history, the secular progressively recedes, to give place to the ecclesiastical, in the tombs and sepulchral monuments of the nobles of Egypt, until, at the last periods of the monarchy, the former entirely disappears, and nothing but religious processions and mystic devices surround the embalmed corpse in the coffin.

The tombs of the later Pharaohs seem to have set the example or fashion of this change. Their decorations were from the commencement of this epoch, mythic and ecclesiastical only. On the temples built by these Pharaohs, the more ancient ones mingled the pictures of their wars with the Shepherds and the negroes, with the processions of worship and the pictures of gods : but from the works of their successors they entirely disappear, and through a long succession of inglorious reigns, the priesthood advanced continually in wealth and influence, until at length it mounted the throne of Pharaoh; and the summit of the power of the Egyptian mythology, and the lowest abyss of political and national degradation into which Egypt ever fell, during the long period that she existed as a kingdom under native Pharaohs, is marked by a dynasty of priests.*

---

* It is supposed by Bunsen to be the 21st dynasty. They have left but few remains of their sovereignty, and these of vile execution, testifying to great decay in the arts of design. They reigned in Egypt about the times of Samuel the Prophet.

THE FAMINE. 147

The Greek tradition is consentaneous to these monumental indications of the great increase of the power of the priesthood during the later periods of the Egyptian monarchy. The passage we have just quoted from Diodorus Siculus informs us, that in the days of his visit to Egypt one-third of the entire surface belonged to them.

Thus have we ascertained that in that interval of the history of ancient Egypt during which Joseph administered the affairs of the kingdom, her institutions had undergone a great and momentous change, affecting very seriously the relative positions of Pharaoh, his nobles, and the priesthood. So marked and unmistakeable is this social revolution, that it clearly appears upon the comparison of the coeval monuments of the two epochs.

The ordinances of Joseph, which form our present text, professedly dealt with all these three conditions of men in ancient Egypt; and the changes in society which those ordinances would inevitably have produced in after-times, are precisely those which the coeval monuments of these after-times so loudly and plainly declare to have taken place.

We have not the slightest hope that either this or any other similar consideration will for one moment relax the serene smile of dignified incredulity with which modern philosophy eyes askance the pages of the books of Moses, or that she will condescend any other reply than the reiteration of her wonted oracular response, "Joseph, his name, his history, and his ordinances are all metaphor." To those, however, who still believe the Bible to be the word of God, it may be some consolation to find that God's truth has not quite so much to fear from man's researches as some well-meaning but ill-informed preachers and writers have endeavoured to persuade them.

"And Israel dwelt in the land of Egypt and in the country of Goshen, and they had possessions therein, and grew and multiplied exceedingly." Gen. xlvii. 27.

This clause again opens the question of the duration of the sojourn of Israel in Egypt. We submit that the entire passage, and especially the phrase in it, "and they had possessions therein," that is, they possessed lands, is altogether incompatible with so inconsiderable a lapse of time as the 215 years of the vulgar computation.

The deeply interesting circumstances that attended the death of Jacob we pass over, only because they do not admit of illustration from the monuments or history of Ancient Egypt.

"And Joseph fell upon his father's face, and wept upon him, and kissed him. And Joseph commanded his servants, the רפאים *raphaim*, to embalm his father: and the raphaim embalmed Israel." Gen.

THE FAMINE. 149

The office or function which the inspired historian has transcribed from the Egyptian in the sacred text, is very frequently noted among the titles of honour borne by the princes of Egypt of the times of Joseph. The group which represents it 〖𓂋𓏤𓐍𓂝〗 reproduced letter for letter the Hebrew transcription רפא, which is rightly translated "physician" in the English Bible. The root, which was common to both Egyptian and Hebrew, meant " to heal," and from thence arose the subsidiary senses " to amend," " to mend," " to sew ; " but its primary import was " to heal," The healing art in Egypt, as in all other nations in the earlier stages of civilization, was in the highest possible repute. So much so that the title 〖𓍹𓂋〗 " chief physician" was the summit of the ambition of the haughty nobles of the old kingdom : and the fortunate possessor of it invariably places it at the head of his blazon. It even precedes the title " royal prince," *saris*. The circumstance that the direct practitioners of the healing art formed part of the household of Joseph, points out clearly that this honour also had not been withheld from him by his bountiful and grateful benefactor.

According to the tenets of the Egyptian mythology, the embalmment of the dead was the highest and noblest exercise of the healing art. It was the triumph over the grand disease to which all other ailments tended, and in which they terminated. The embalmer's duties once completed, the man was dead no longer. His body, perfectly pure, shining, and beautiful without, and innate with divinity, reposed in its gorgeous temple, the consecrated image of a god, worshipped and imparting blessings. His soul, alternately performing acts of worship to the gods, of prowess against their enemies, and reposing in the Elysian fields on the banks of the celestial Nile (the course of the sun in heaven), awaited nevertheless with impatience the revolution of the cycle of years after which it would return, bearing life and breath, to its former tenement. Then the resuscitated man would step forth from his tomb, once more to dwell in his beloved Egypt. Heavily as it is encumbered with coarse symbols and mythic absurdities, the fable betrays nevertheless the deep conviction which possessed the minds of its inventors, that man was not made to die, neither the image of God impressed upon his external form to see corruption!

We have already stated that the healing art was always sacred in Egypt. It passed altogether into the hands of the priesthood, in the changes in society which originated with the ordinances of Joseph. In the Later Kingdom the title of "chief physician" is scarcely assumed by any secular prince, before the times of Psammetichus, when the monarchy was on the verge of extinction, B.C. 600. A *dilettante* taste for archæology seems then to have brought these old titles once more into vogue.

The physicians of the New Kingdom, however, like the scribes, did not disdain to associate secular offices with their sacred functions ; but the art itself was in these later times completely identified with religion. So much so, that the translators of the Egyptian Bible rejected the word *rapha* altogether. It however remains in the Coptic texts, as the appellative of a heathen temple, which being the residence of the physicians, would naturally enough be named in common discourse, " the doctor's house," *erpee* [ЄРПНЄ]. The same word is retained in Egypt to this day. The ruins of a temple are still named in the vernacular Arabic *birbé*.

The well-known passages of Herodotus ii. 85—89, and Diodorus Siculus i. 91, which describe the modes of embalming practised by the Egyptians, have been so often quoted at length, in illustration of this text, and therefore so familiar to most readers, and so easily accessible to all, that we are spared the necessity of more than a casual reference to them, in the brief sketch of the art ; as it appears, from the mummies themselves, to have been actually in practice, with which we propose to comment upon it.

Unless we assume that the remains discovered in the chamber of the third pyramid, by Colonel Howard Vyse, are those of the mummy of King Mencheres (which we are free to confess is very doubtful), no human bodies have been found in Egypt, of which we have evidence that they are so old as the times of Joseph. The tomb of Menthotp, the courtier of a Pharaoh of the 11th dynasty, which was opened twenty years ago by Passalaqua at Gournou, is the oldest that ever was discovered intact. There the body, its swathing, and the case had all mouldered to black dust, so that not even the bones were distinguishable. We believe the earliest known mummy to be that of the priest Sa-amun, which was found by the same excavator in the same burial-place. He lived in the reign of Ramses IX., about 1000 B.C. His mummy has been opened, and its accessories minutely and carefully examined. The comparison of the results of this examination, with the accounts of the Greek authors to which we have referred, utterly dispels the assumption of the French savans that nothing changed in Egypt, from the foundation of the monarchy to its extinction. In Egypt, as everywhere else, the art of embalming, like every thing human, was greatly modified by the varying circumstances of the long succession of ages during which it continued to be practised; so that a mummy of the ordinary age of those now existing, that is, of the Greek and Roman periods, or thereabouts, gives no illustration to the embalming of the body of Jacob, beyond the fact that the practice prevailed in Egypt at both epochs.

According to our Greek authorities, the first process in the embalming, after the body had been disembowelled, was to steep it for thirty days in a solution of the salt called natron. This was the practice in the times of both Diodorus and Herodotus, 450 B.C. It had also prevailed at an earlier period: for the flesh of the mummy of Sa-amun, 1000 B.C., is saturated with this salt. But to judge by the effects, some change in the mode of application had taken place, even in that interval. The flesh of Sa-amun is entirely adipocire, which suggests the inference, that at the earlier epoch the mummy was not steeped as in the days of Herodotus, but the natronized fluid was incessantly poured over it by attendants. The flesh of the priestess *Asrui*, " the porteress," at Manchester, is in the same state. She lived in the days of Sesonchis, about a century later than Sa-amun. Here then is a change in a custom of embalming, which prepares us for the inference to which we have been driven by the facts which have been presented to us. So powerful an antiseptic is this solution of natron, so perfectly imperishable does it make the body, that had it been earlier known, the whole of the mummies of all epochs alike would have come down to this time. This conviction first occurred to us as we were standing ankle deep in the black dust, to which all the mummies of the old kingdom have mouldered away, in one of the pits of Ghizeh. Gems, rings, amulets, all of the remotest periods are constantly found among the dust. The articles of wood, the baskets of bread and fruits in these tombs are scarcely altered, but the bodies, their swathings, and their coffins, are all dust. The conclusion seems inevitable. The art of embalming was then in its infancy; so that the bodies have decayed, and communicated their rottenness to the wood and linen that were in contact with them. This process we conceive, would in the climate of Egypt have been impossible, had the practice of applying to the body the natron so universal in the deserts around Egypt then existed.

The next process in the embalmer's art consists, according to our Greek authorities, in anointing the body with palm wine and oil of cedar, and filling up all its cavities with a mixture of fragrant gums, resins and woods. Myrrh, and cassia, or cinnamon, are specified, with other spices not named, as entering into the compound which was used for this purpose.

These practises likewise prevailed in Egypt more that 500 years before the times of Herodotus, the earliest of our written authorities. The linen cloths next to the body of Sa-amun are deeply stained with some strong astringent like palm wine or oil of cedar. We have already mentioned, that cassia, or cinnamon, and myrrh, were most distinctly perceptible in the spicery that filled the cavities of the body, as well as *ladanum*, which is mentioned along with them in the Scripture account of the imports of spices from Canaan.

The examination of this mummy also brought to light the circumstance, that the mode of applying the spices underwent considerable modification in the time that thence elapsed before the visit of Herodotus, like the use of the natron. In his days, the spice was only put into the cavities of the body : such is actually the case with mummies cotemporary with Herodotus. But when Sa-amun was embalmed, not only were the cavities filled, but the whole surface of the body was embedded in a mass of spicery. The impossibility of replacing it in its present state when once the linen that bound it to the body had been removed, suggested the conclusion, that some of the ingredients of which it was compounded had been viscid or semi-fluid, and that it had at first been applied to the body in the form of a paste. The average depth of this layer of spicery was at least two inches, so that the quantity must have been enormous. Were we upon the history of Egypt, it would be easy to discover, in the changed political circumstances of Egypt and the world at the two epochs in question, an abundant reason why the embalmers of the later period used some cheaper expedient, for the preservation of the body, than these costly compounds.

We find therefore that no mummies now existing come within 1000 years of the epoch of Joseph, and also that the embalmer's art in Egypt underwent considerable modifications with the lapse of time. We conclude from hence, that the only certain and tangible illustration which the embalming of Jacob receives from the passages of Herodotus and Diodorus, is the establishment of the fact, that the art of embalming the dead was practised in Egypt in the days of these writers, as well as at the epoch of Joseph.

"And forty days were fulfilled for him [Jacob]; for so are fulfilled the days of those that are embalmed. And the Egyptians wept for him seventy days." Gen. l. 3.

The time occupied in the embalming and the attendant funeral ceremonies underwent, as might have been anticipated, far less change than the art itself, in the vast interval that separates the epoch of Joseph from that of Herodotus and Diodorus.— To the passage before us, therefore, these writers furnish a highly valuable illustration. According to Herodotus, the period assigned by religion, and on no account to be departed from, for the embalming, was seventy days, *u.s.* Diodorus says, that the time occupied by the process was upwards of thirty days. Our text by reconciling these two passages, seems to indicate, that the same prescription prevailed at both epochs. The forty days were occupied in the actual process, the remaining thirty in the swathing and decoration of the mummy, and the weeping lasted for the whole seventy days.

The customs that prevailed at this seventy days weeping for the dead, are so particularly specified by both authors, and are so remarkably illustrated by the paintings in the tomb of Sa-amun, at Gournou, that there can scarcely be a doubt, that in them we have the counterpart of that which took place on the death of Jacob.

Herodotus says, that on the death of an Egyptian, the females of the household covered their heads and faces with mud, and leaving the house, went about the streets uncinctured, and howling, and beating themselves. The men also beat themselves, but did not defile their persons nor wear their garments unbound. Lib. ii. 83. Diodorus repeats all these particulars, with the addition, that the family of the deceased neither used the bath, nor drank wine, nor changed their garments during this ceremony, which lasted the whole time that the body was in the embalmer's hands.

The mourning for the father of Sa-amun which

is represented on the wall of the tomb at Gournou, where his body was found, so remarkably illustrates these particulars, that we have great pleasure in introducing it. *See Plate I.*

The occurrence here depicted, must have taken place betwen six and seven hundred years before the times of Herodotus. So that it is not easy to conceive of any ancient fact receiving a more perfect illustration than is supplied by these ancient authorities to the mourning of the Egyptians for Jacob.

" And when the days of weeping for him [lit. his weeping] were past, Joseph spake unto the house of Pharaoh saying :" Gen. 1. 4.

By the house of Pharaoh we are to understand Pharaoh in council, that is, Pharaoh and the estates of Egypt. The word " house," had in Egyptian a meaning very similar to that which we apply to it in the phrase " houses of Parliament," i. e., parliament. Thus the hieroglyphic group for a banquet or festal assemblage is ⌷ litt, " a good house or apartment," i. e., a room well garnished for the guests. In the same manner the group which exactly translates the expression before us, ⌷ lit. "the king's house" is frequently used in the texts with the sense of " council," and even of " acts of council." These figurative uses of the word ⌷ or ⌷ " house or dwelling," are of importance in the interpretation of the hieroglyphic texts. Our remarks upon them in this place are rendered necessary by the circumstance, that the phrase בית פרעה with the import of "council, or *entourage*, of Pharaoh" is scarcely Hebrew, though (as we have seen) it was a very common mode of expression in ancient Egypt.

"If now I have found grace in your eyes, speak, I pray you, in the ears of Pharaoh, saying, My father made me swear, saying, Lo, I die: in the grave which I have digged for me in the land of Canaan, there shalt thou bury me. Now therefore let me go up, I pray thee, and bury my father, and I will come again. And Pharaoh said, Go up, and bury thy father, according as he made thee swear. And Joseph went up to bury his father, and with him went up all the court of Pharaoh, even the nobles of his palace, and all the nobles of the land of Egypt. And all the household of Joseph, and of his brethren, and his father's household. Only their little ones, their flocks and their herds, they left in the land of Goshen. And there went up with him both chariots and horsemen: and it was a very great company. And they came to the plain of Atad, which is beyond Jordan, and there they lamented a great lamentation, and a heavy. And Joseph made the funeral *abel* אָבֶל of his father for seven days. And when the inhabitants of the land, the Canaanites, saw the mourning in the plain of Atad, they said, This is a great funeral from Egypt. Therefore the name of it was called Abel Mizraim, "the funeral of Egypt." Gen. l. 4—11.

Egypt mourned for Jacob with the mourning of a king. No more solemn pomp, no higher or more regal state could have followed the bier on which the mummy of Pharaoh journeyed to its long home. The sons of Pharaoh, the princes and the nobles, the commanders of the armies, the judges, all were there. The chariots and horses of Pharaoh and of the great ones of Egypt swelled the pomp of the procession. The scene before us was no ordinary one. It was not an event of frequent or even occasional occurrence, like the funeral of one of the kings or nobles of the country. The funeral rites which were celebrated for seven successive days on the plains of Atad, were sufficiently removed from either of these categories, to be recorded in the traditions of Canaan, and to give to the place where they were celebrated, a name commemorative of them, which it still retained in the days when Moses wrote, and long afterwards.

We can scarcely review the life of this patriarch thus associated with its closing scene, without calling to remembrance the promise of Him whom Jacob had served so perseveringly and so faithfully: "Them that honour me, I will honour." 1 Sam. ii. 30.

THE FAMINE.

The existing monuments of Ancient Egypt do not fail us here, any more than on those former occasions on which we have appealed to them. The word we render "noble," is, in the original, the literal translation of a title whereby the collective nobility of Egypt is signified on monuments of all epochs. This epithet was long ago detected by Champollion in the Greek transcription of the name of one of the gods of Egypt, Haroeris, i. e. "Hor," (Horus)—Oeris "the greater," "the elder." As a title of honor, it is of constant occurrence in the inscriptions on the tombs and coffins of princes. It was supposed to have vanished altogether from the Coptic texts, save in the reflex shadow of it, adumbrated by the interrogative pronoun ⲞⲨⲈⲠ, "how great," *quantus?* It was the sagacity of Samuel Birch, of the British Museum, that first pointed out its existence there, under the reduplicated form of *hello* "old." This was the primitive sense of the group which the inspired writer followed, translating it by זָקֵן "elder." Its determinative is a man bearing the staff with which age supports its tottering steps :

—pedibus me
Porto meis et manu nullo subeunte bacillo.
—Juvenal. Sat. III.

This staff had become a symbol of office in Egypt altogether irrespective of age, long before the time of Joseph. In that time, and afterwards, the use

of this group in the texts to express nobility is so frequent, that it almost becomes pronominal.

The word אבל *abel*, with the sense of "mourning," "funeral rite," occurs in the Egyptian texts of all transcriptions, with the elision of the moveable letter *l* or *r* final. In the Coptic texts *hebi* means "to mourn;" in hieroglyphics 𓊵𓏏𓏛 *hb* or *ub* means funeral ceremonies generally, like its Hebrew counterpart. The initial 𓉐 which is interpreted by 𓎛 h or u, is the picture of the banquet-hall with pillars of a tomb, like those at Beni Hassan, Essiout, and other localities in Middle Egypt. They are noble vaults, excavated in the solid rock, and supported by columns which have been left when the surrounding solid was removed. In those halls were held the appointed periodical banquets for the dead. Square pits of great depth were hewn in the floors, and in these the mummies were deposited. The Egyptian artists, who knew nothing of perspective, represented these pits by the lozenge in the centre of the base. ☐ The name of this hall has been *eb,* or *hebi,** which thence came to be also the appellative of the ceremonies observed in it.

" And his (Jacob's) sons did unto him according as he commanded them : for his sons carried him into the land of Canaan, and buried him in the cave of the field of Machpelah, which Abraham bought with the field for a possession of a burying-place of Ephron the Hittite, before Mamre." Gen. l. 12, 13.

The funeral ceremonies, according to the ritual of Egypt, having been completed at Atad, the sons of Israel alone proceed to the cave of Machpelah, bearing to its final resting-place the embalmed body of their father. Of the observances which took place on the burial of the dead with the clan or sept of Abraham at this time, we know nothing. The few practices on such occasions mentioned any where in the inspired narrative, are those natural expressions of grief which are common to all mankind. We can only infer from the very peculiar circumstances of their sojourn in Canaan, that they were perfectly free from all admixture with the

* The אבל *ebel* of the Hebrew text.

idolatries of Canaan and of Egypt. Yet, in order to the right understanding of that narrative, it is very needful to keep in mind, that the chosen seed of Abraham was not at this particular period commissioned to make any especial protest, either direct or indirect, against these idolatries, beyond that of not immediately participating in their acts of worship. They were as yet very few in number, and they dwelt in the midst of nations who were engaged in corrupting the truth regarding God and the future state, by overlaying it with coarse earthly symbols: but much that was true still remained in the religions both of Egypt and Canaan, and this truth the Israelites of course held in common with them. Four hundred years afterwards, at the time of the Exodus, the case was very different. We make no greater mistake, than when, following the guidance of the vain, fruitless speculations of the so-called learning of the last two centuries, we assume that the idolatries of Egypt and Canaan were already venerable and well-established superstitions in the patriarchal times. The Bible declares the direct opposite to this. There was much right acquaintance with the true God in these times both in Egypt (Gen. xii. 17—20, &c.) and Canaan. (Gen. xx. 1—7; xxvi. 6—11.) It is, moreover, expressly declared in the same inspired narrative, of one of the most offensive members of the Canaanite confederation, the Amorites, (Gen. xv. 16,) that at the time of the call of Abram their idolatrous perversion of the truth עון was not yet completed, and therefore the judgments against them were delayed for 600 years. The general definitions of idolatry, moreover, embodied in God's revelation to man, declare it to be a corruption of the truth regarding religion; (Rom. i. 20—23, &c.) but corruption is a gradual and progressive change: and to assume that at so early a period as the one before us, that change had already been completely undergone by the religious opinions both of Egypt and Canaan, is also to assume that mankind had already existed on the earth, as it then was, for some millennia of years,—a position which the Bible contradicts, which the traditive history of all nations contradicts, and which the existing monuments of Egypt contradict likewise, and no less emphatically than either of the other two witnesses. This is the question really in debate between the believer and the infidel at this moment,—the length of time during which man has been upon the earth as it now is,—in other words, the number of years that have elapsed since the deluge; for this reason we state our convictions upon it at length.

The rites which took place on the plains of Atad, at which the armies of Egypt and the flower of her nobility assisted, would admit of a very ample comment from the tombs. But as thereby we should illustrate the customs, not of Israel, but of Egypt, it will suffice to mention here, that they consisted principally of banquets and of games of strength and agility. In these last the funeral games of Greece had, doubtless, their origin. The very few notices of the Hebrew funeral customs, which are to be found in the Bible, do not justify us in assuming that either of these practices ever obtained among the descendants of Abraham.

" And Joseph returned into Egypt, he and his brethren, and all that went up with him, to bury his father, after he had buried his father.

" And when Joseph's brethren saw that their father was dead, they said, Joseph will peradventure hate us, and will certainly requite us all the evil that we did to him. And they charged Joseph (as his elder brothers) saying, Thy father did command before he died, saying, So shall ye say unto Joseph, Forgive, I pray thee now the trespass of thy brethren and their sin : for they did unto thee evil : and now we pray thee, forgive the trespass of the servants of the God of thy father. And Joseph wept when they spake unto him. And his brethren also went up and fell down before his face ; and they said, Behold, we are thy servants ! And Joseph said unto them, Fear not : am I in the place of God ? For though ye thought evil against me, God meant it unto good, that what is done this day might come to pass, even the saving alive of much people. Now, therefore, fear ye not, I will nourish you and your little ones. And he comforted them and spake to their hearts." Gen. l. 14—21.

This is the last recorded transaction in the life of Joseph. Like so many of his former acts, it needs no ethical comment: for, " thereby he being dead yet speaketh," and to the heart of every man who is privileged to peruse his history.

" And Joseph dwelt in Egypt, he and his father's house; and Joseph lived an hundred and ten years. And Joseph saw Ephraim's children of the third *descent:* the children also of Machir the son of Manasseh were brought up on Joseph's knees.

" And Joseph said unto his brethren, I die, and God will surely visit you and bring you out of this land, which he sware to Abraham, to Isaac, and to Jacob. And Joseph took an oath of the children of Israel, saying, God will surely visit you, and ye shall carry up my bones from hence. So Joseph died the son of a hundred and ten years." Verses 22—26.

" Mark the perfect man, and behold the upright; for the end of that man is peace." Psalm xxxvii. 37.

We must now ascertain the year of the sojourn of Israel in Egypt, wherein Joseph's death took place. He was thirty years old when he first stood before Pharaoh (Gen. xli. 36). The immigration into Egypt took place in the second year of the famine, (cxlv. 6,) which, at the utmost, cannot have been more than ten years afterwards. It follows, therefore, that when Joseph died, Israel had been in Egypt for seventy years.

"And they embalmed him (Joseph) and he was put into a coffin in Egypt." Verse 26.

The imperfect mode of embalming (in use at this time) upon which the practitioners of the art so greatly improved afterwards, would abundantly suffice to keep the mummy in perfect beauty and fragrance for the 400 years that elapsed before Joseph was committed to his tomb in Canaan. It is for ten times that duration that it has proved unequal to rescue the flesh of man from corruption.

The mortal remains of Joseph were not buried in Egypt. His coffin, upon the lid of which was moulded with plaster and coloured, as exact a likeness of his countenance, (which, doubtless, called up vividly the remembrance of him to his immediate survivors) as art in Egypt could accomplish, occupied a very conspicuous and most honorable place in the house of Ephraim his first-born. Mummies in Ancient Egypt were heir-looms highly valued, and upon certain occasions pledges for loans of money. The fragrant odour emitted by the spices in which they were embalmed, made them welcome inmates in halls of entertainment ; so much so, that the sepulture was often deferred for centuries, so that many successive generations were frequently ranged upright against the walls of the grand hall of entertainment in the family mansion. They were, in short, exactly as the family portraits of our great houses in modern times.

This very strange custom, which renders so perfectly natural and in order the dying request of Joseph, is minutely described by Diodorus Siculus (lib. i. c. 91). Its existence also at a time absolutely cotemporary with that of Joseph is recorded in the tomb of the chief physician Nahrai at Beni Hassan. The noble vault which was the banquet-hall of this tomb is thirty feet square, and of an elevation which harmonizes admirably with this dimension. The roof is triple arched, and the two groinings are supported by four square fluted massives. A long hieroglyphic inscription, in 222 short columns, runs round the surbase of this hall : the rest of the walls being decorated with pictures of the arts of common life and the funeral banquet, according to the rigid prescription of religion for all the tombs of Egypt. The inscription embodies the names of six successive representatives of the family to which its deep mummy-pits (one of which is open and plundered in the floor of the hall) served as a place of sepulture. Nahrai the excavator commemorates the gifts in land and canals of irrigation presented to his father and grandfather by the two first monarchs of the twelfth dynasty. We have already explained that the reign of the former of these Pharaohs (Amenemes I.) commenced during the sojourn of Abram in Egypt.

The son of Nahrai, En-sha, continues the inscription on the death of his father, and on his death his son Nuhotph again proceeds with it. Nuhotph was cotemporary with Amuntimœus the fifth king of this dynasty, whom Saites the Lower Egyptian dispossessed of Memphis.

This disaster to the Theban Pharaohs is silently but most significantly commemorated in the inscription before us. At the end of Nuhotph's contribution to it is a votive tablet, representing a man sitting at a table of shew-bread in the act of presenting it. The style of art which prevailed when this tablet was executed, was altogether different from that of the rest of the tomb. It calls to mind the execution of the tombs at Elythya in Upper Egypt, which were excavated in the times of the eighteenth dynasty, about 200 years after those of Nuhotph. The inscription that follows it exactly fills up the entire surbase of the hall. It was added by a representative of the family named *Souk-enh* "the living crocodile:" but the paintings which cover the rest of the walls of this gorgeous vault enable us to state distinctly that he was neither his son, his grandson, nor even his great-grandson. All the house of Nahrai to that degree, and to the number of more than a hundred individuals, are represented there, and no one of them bears the name of Sukenes. It was therefore in the sense of remote descendant that Sukenes wrote himself the son of Nahrai, whose family he represented. The name tells the disastrous history of the descendants of these heros of Upper Egypt, whose glories had been shared by the ancestors of Sukenes. The inscription itself records the fallen fortunes of his house.

After the loss of Memphis, Amun-timæus seems to have left the especial service of the gods of that city, who (in his notion doubtless) had forsaken him, and to have put himself under the tutelage of the god of the city nearest Memphis that still remained in his hands, which was Crocodilopolis in the Faium. Here he built the temple and palace which, in the days of Herodotus, was one of the wonders of Egypt, under the name of *the Labyrinth*, and the remains of which, bearing the name of Amun-timæus everywhere, were cleared from the sand about seven years ago by Lepsius. This temple was dedicated to the local god of the place, *Sevek* or *Souk*, the crocodile. Herodotus expressly mentions this fact.* The two or three ill-fated individuals that succeeded Amun-timæus on the tottering throne of the Mencherian Pharaohs all took the crocodile in the second ring of their royal names. And when the Lower Egyptians, or the famine, or both, drove them from the Faium and Middle Egypt, they instituted the worship of the crocodile in the two cities they founded in the Upper country, Elethya and Ombos.

The name Sukenes, therefore, plainly indicates that the family of Nahrai had remained faithful to the royal house of their patrons. The inscription

PORCH OF THE TOMB OF NAHRAI.

* Lib. ii. c. 148.

he has engraven on the wall tells as plainly that it had shared in their disasters also. It was probably inscribed after the expulsion of the Lower Egyptians from this part of Middle Egypt, late in the eighteenth dynasty. Sukenes tells us in it, that he had put up a door of wood to the banquet-hall, and a fence of wood to the porch of the tomb, which remains to this day, one of the most beautiful objects in Egypt. Both closures had originally been of metal, as the scratches on the rock still show visibly. He also commemorates certain other repairs that he had made, so that the tomb had been plundered by the conquerors. He concludes with an address to the mummy of Nahrai the excavator of the tomb, inviting him to come in and lie down in the resting-place which the piety of his descendant had thus made ready for him.

Here then was the mummy of a man who had died almost two centuries before the times of Joseph, but was not interred until more than two centuries afterwards.

So pregnant is this illustration, that we presume it will be an apology for the long historical detail which has been required to introduce it.

We have already explained the extraordinary notions and customs that prevailed in Egypt regarding the body after death, its embalming, and its final resting-place. Their prevalence may possibly have prepared the reader in some measure for a statement we are very reluctant to make, so little does it seem to comport with the spirit of truth and soberness in which it is our earnest desire to carry on the present inquiry. There are at Sacchara, immediately over against Memphis, the ruins of the tomb of a prince in Egypt, whose name was that of Joseph, written in hieroglyphics. It is in the close vicinity of the largest pyramid of that group, which, from other circumstances, we assume to have been that of Aphophis and his father Meris. The titles and offices held by this personage were also those of Joseph. He was "chief *ab-rech*,"* and "director of the granaries of all Egypt," as well as the possessor of several other offices. The name has been assimilated to an Egyptian phrase expressive of Joseph's function in Egypt, *i-suph*, " he came to save ; " Copt. " he will save." The letters are so exactly those of Joseph's name— יוסף—that the identity does not seem to admit of question. It may have been that, as in other cases, his tomb was carried on at the public expense, as a mark of public respect and esteem; but we must confess we incline to the opinion, that at a late period in the life of Joseph, the Egyptian successor to his offices had also assumed his name, and that he was the excavator of the tomb. We give here his portrait and his titles.

* Gen xli. 4, 5. See above, p. 55.

CHAPTER IV.

EGYPT DURING THE SOJOURN—RISE OF THE NEW KING.

We do not here discuss the question of the duration of the sojourn. It will soon appear that if the Greek lists of the kings of Egypt gave us reliable chronology, it must have lasted 430 years. But such was by no means the case. The question therefore still remains an open one, notwithstanding their testimony.

From our historical authorities, we obtain two certainties regarding this period. The one is, that the patron of Joseph was the shepherd king Aphophis. This (as we have already explained) is the concurrent testimony of all the Egyptian records translated by the Greeks. The other certainty appears upon the monuments, and their testimony is equally clear and irresistible. It is the name of the king that knew not Joseph.

The time of the rise of the new king is our first question. We have ascertained that Aaron was born eighty-three years, and Moses eighty years before the Exodus. It further appears from the inspired narrative, that the infanticidal decree of the new king (Exod. i. 22.) had been issued in the interval between the two births: for on the birth of Aaron (Exod. vi. 20.) no concealment was required, such as took place on that of Moses, chap. ii. 1—7. Seven years being allowed for the former attempts to keep down the numbers of Israel, (which is probable enough, chap. i. 8—21,) would give us ninety years before the Exodus for the rise of the new king.

The cotemporary monuments of this epoch are numerous, but their testimony is obscure and hard to understand. The histories collected by the curiosity of the later Greeks, about the time of our Saviour, from the temple records of Egypt, are the other source of our knowledge. They exactly resemble all other histories written in similar circumstances. A vast mass of fable, often incoherent, has accumulated upon a skeleton or frame-work of truth. The very laborious collation of these two, has done something to expose the fables of the one, and to unravel the perplexities of the other. It is with this something, and with this alone, that we intend to trouble our readers.

We must of necessity commence with a brief summary of the previous history of Egypt.

The temple records open with the statement that when Menes the human founder of the kingdom ascended the throne, Egypt had been governed by the gods for more than 17,000 years. The monuments disclose the origin of this manifest fiction. The first gods of Egypt were the patriarchs of the Old World, who were made in some cases local gods of cities founded by their descendants. In other instances they were themselves the founders of the cities wherein they were worshipped after their death. It was the well-known long lives of men before the flood, and immediately after it, that originated the fable of the 17,000 years.

In order to prove this point, namely, that the first gods of Egypt were dead men, and the patriarchs of the Bible, we take the opportunity of giving here the few notices of this false religion which are required to illustrate the text before us.

𓁹𓏏𓅓 *atm*, i. e. אדם Adam, the father of mankind. He was the local god of the city of On, or Heliopolis, the capital of Aphophis, and at all times one of the capitals of Egypt. He was the human impersonation of the sun, which was "the father of all the gods" of Egypt. All idolatry seems to have began with the notion that the sun was God.

𓉿𓃀𓀭 or 𓉿𓈖𓃀𓀭 or 𓉿𓃀𓇳𓀭 *nu* or *nuh*, נוח Noah, the god of the annual overflow, and of water generally. The city in which he was first worshipped we shall find presently. He was afterwards made local at any new point to the southward of former settlements in the valley in which a city was built. He was often named 𓉿𓃀𓏌 *nu-mu*, that is "No or Noah of the waters." He was also named " father of the gods," in allusion, doubtless, to the post-diluvian origin of mankind.

𓊨𓏥 *os-iri*, Osiris, called afterwards Mizraim, מצרים. He was first named יצר " the potter." It was changed to Mizraim, " two cities," when Menes founded Memphis. Other names were also changed for like purposes. This father of ancient Egypt most probably died and was buried at Busiris in the Delta, where he was afterwards local god. In this circumstance originated a number of myths or fables, wherein he was made king of the dead;— being, as we have elsewhere explained, the rightful king of all Egyptians, as the father of the race. The changes in the religion of Egypt introduced by King Mencheres, in which began the civil broils which Abram is said to have composed during his sojourn in Egypt, were all of them connected with the worship of Osiris.

𓅭𓂦 *sb*, i. e. סְבָא, Seba the son of Cush. Gen. x. 7. He is the youngest of all the deified men in the system. For this reason he is entitled 𓅭𓏭𓀭 " youngest of the gods." The city in which he was local was Crocodilopolis in Middle Egypt, which was near Abydos. This was one reason why, very long afterwards, he was feigned to be the father of Osiris.

𓊪𓏏𓎛 *Phtha* or *pth*, i. e. פוּט Phut, the brother of Mizraim. Gen. x. 6. Menes, the founder of the monarchy, was the first of the clan of Mizraim to cross the Nile and colonize the western bank. Phut has given its Egyptian name to the bow, (Copt. *phit* hieroglyphic *pt*,) either because he was its inventor, or because he greatly excelled in the use of it. The Nile seems to have been the limit of the territories of Mizraim and Phut on the first peopling of North-East Africa. When Menes crossed the Nile, he made the patriarch of the district the local god of his new city. All pictures of the idol Phtha (i. e. Phut deified) have a green skin; which denotes conventionally the sallow hue acquired by light-complexioned races when first exposed to the sun of the desert. The family of Phut is not given in the Bible. He had probably nine sons; for his descendants, the negroes of the Lybian desert, were named in hieroglyphics 𓐂 i. e. the nine nations of the Phutim.

𓃭𓏥𓀀 *amn* or *hmn*, the patriarch חם Ham. In one dialect of Egyptian every final *m* took an *n* after it. He was first deified at Peremoun in the Delta. The introducer of Ham into Upper Egypt has left the record of it in his own name. He was the king who founded the twelfth dynasty of the lists. He seems to have colonized Eastern Thebes, and to have made Ham or Amoun the local god of his new city. For this reason he named himself 〔cartouche〕 or 〔cartouche〕 i. e. "the beginner or bringer-in of Amun." In later times Amun became one of the greatest gods in Egypt, as the tutelary of the race of kings by whom the shepherds were expelled. Many of the great revolutions that shook the monarchy during the period now before us, originated in the pretensions of Amun to rule over the gods of other cities.

These will sufficiently prove the truth of our statement, that the gods of Egypt were dead men. They were demons (δαιμονες) only in the sense of "the souls of dead men," and not in that of "fallen spirits" or "devils," as is generally supposed. The inventors of this mythology were well acquainted with the truth regarding this mysterious subject, as it was taught by the patriarchal tradition. Of this the following group affords us a perfectly satisfactory evidence.

⌐◧𒀭 *st-oni*,* (Σεθωνις, *Plutarch de Iside,*) "Seth or Sethonis," "the Author of Evil." *Book of the Dead, Part II.* The evil principle of the Egyptian mythology. *Hebrew* שטן, SATAN.

The goddesses were probably the deified wives of the primitive patriarchs. As their names have not been preserved in Scripture, they of course cannot be identified.† Some of the early gods are also in the same position. Month or Mars, Thoth, the god of wisdom, Anubis, the guardian of the tomb, and others, are doubtless deifications of cotemporaries and relatives of Ham and Mizraim, whose names do not appear in the Bible.

These deified men were regarded at first as mere

---

* The character ▨ is a block of stone. It is fully written thus ⌐◠ *on*, in the Coptic texts "a stone." The last character is a man wearing a mask representing the head of an ass, which is the conventional determinative of all groups expressing the names of foreign gods and evil spirits. The use of the block of stone to express the sound of the syllables *oni*, exemplifies a not unfrequent application of pictures in writing foreign words in hieroglyphics. The name Osiris is thus written ⌐┐ *oshe*, Copt. "a throne." ◁▷ *iri*, Copt. "an eye." *osh-iri.*— There are many other instances.

† We are only able to give one exception. It is the name of the wife of Athom or Adam. She was the Venus of the Mythology. Her name was written by the Greeks ἀθωρ *Hathor*. It stood thus in hieroglyphics, ◨ *eit-hor*, "the house or habitation of Horus," i. e. of the filial deity from whom also descended the rest of the gods. ☐ *ei* or *ev* "a house," seems to be the transcription of הוה EVE, the mother of mankind.

city gods: having no particular attribute of divinity beyond that of the protection of the district in which they were worshipped. Even Adam is scarcely identified with the sun in the tombs of Ghizeh. Noah is the only exception. He is connected with the overflow, and the waters of the Nile from the beginning.

The consciousness of their worshippers that the gods had once been men, is remarkably exemplified by the circumstance that the first kings of Egypt were also made gods on their death, and were worshipped in their pyramids as in temples. In the tombs of the princes of Egypt of the most remote epoch, the deceased kings are at the least on a level with the gods; and an office connected with the worship of Suphis, for example, in the Great Pyramid, is named before the priesthood of Phtha in the list of a prince's titles. The reform of Mencheres seems to have been especially directed against this multiplication of gods; for this king-worship does not appear in the tombs of his adherents. It must nevertheless be understood that the gods entirely lost all their human relations, save their names, when they were once enshrined. Whatever were the motives of the first introducers of them, they afterwards formed combinations and connexions altogether independent of their former earthly positions. Mizraim, for example, was made the son of Sebah his nephew, and Phut was the first-born of Adam. When these myths were invented, the memory of the men had perished altogether.

This man-worship exhibited, very soon after its invention, its tendency to go downwards in the scale of existence. Cechous, the second king of the second dynasty, is said in the Greek lists to have introduced into Egypt the worship of animals. This worship is noted on the earliest Egyptian monuments that exist, as well as on the latest. The motives which at first induced the inventors of this most degraded idolatry to assign certain animals to certain gods, were various, and do not appear to have followed any particular rule. The animal in which Nu or Noah was worshipped was the ram or goat; for there is scarcely a distinction between the two animals in hot countries. The circumstance that the goat under the name of Mendes was the sacred animal of a city in the eastern Delta, to which it gave its name, (see above) decides that Noah was the local god of the nome of Mendes. It is very supposeable that the traditive memory of the circumstance that an animal so serviceable to man had been saved in the ark, would suggest this association. The bull was the animal impersonation of Adam at Heliopolis. It was named *Mnevis*. We know nothing of the reason why. Ptha at Memphis had also a bull for his sacred animal.

His name was Apis. The comparison of the names of the god and his bull in hieroglyphics throws a little light upon the notions which were in the minds of the inventors. ▢ *pth* has been altered from Phut ▢ by the addition of a letter, to assimilate it in sound to the word פתח *pth* "to open," "disclose," (in Egyptian *phōth* "to write in hieroglyphics.") Apis is written ⌐ *hp* which is merely the god's name inverted, and with a direct inversion of its meaning also. The initial ⌐ is the pent-house or screen, whence oracular responses were given in the temples of Egypt. The word *hp,* signifies "to hide," "to cover," in Egyptian and also in Hebrew חפה. So that the man was the god manifest, and the beast the god concealed. We can give a rather better account of the sacred animal of Anubis, which was the dog or jackal, because he was the local god of Lycopolis in the Busiritic nome,* which was situated on the extreme north-eastern border of the Delta, where, being constantly exposed to the attacks of foreign enemies, great vigilance was required. The dog, we need not explain, denoted vigilance †

Such was the religion of Egypt when Israel sojourned there, and partook in its idol ceremonies.

* This city is mentioned in the Rosetta inscr. (*line* 28, Gr.) as having been attacked by the Syrians in that day.

† See Note at the end of this Chapter.

It was the worship of dead men and live animals, and nothing more. All the mysticism, symbols, and combinations which somewhat veiled its grossness in after times, had not then been invented. The system was in its naked absurdity. For the regular succession of times and seasons, without disastrous interruptions like the seven years' famine,—for aid in the various changes and chances in man's affairs, which he always feels to be out of his own control,—nay more, for all the hopes of the life to come, in which Egypt from the first most firmly believed, they were taught to betake themselves to these most ridiculous and impotent gods ; whose worshippers nevertheless, Egyptian as well as Israelite, fully acknowledge the truth that God is One. We might express our astonishment at this fatuity, were it not also exemplified in the present day, and by millions of living men.

The process by which these local gods became afterwards, at different periods, gods in all Egypt, is easy to apprehend. Noah was apparently always so, for very obvious reasons. The Sun was also god everywhere, from the first : but whether Adam was always associated with him is not so clear. Anubis guarded all tombs, and therefore was wanted in every city. In other instances some signal success or good fortune befalling a city was placed to the credit of a local god, and crowds of worshippers from other parts of Egypt flocked to his shrine. The benefits of this intercourse would form another item in his favour; his reputation would continue to advance, and shortly a shrine for his worship would appear in the temple of some neighbouring city. The jealousy which this intruder awoke in the original holder of the fane was allayed by another expedient. One of the seers beheld in vision, or an oracle proclaimed from beneath the pent-house, that the two gods were in fact nearly connected, and that the new-comer was heartily welcomed by his affectionate relative. Thus originated the family ties among the gods of Egypt. On the other hand, when a calamity befel a city or district, the local god bore the blame, and his shrine was neglected for that of some more propitious or powerful divinity. There is no greater mistake than to assume, with most writers on this subject, that the idolatry of Egypt was a system complete from the first, and never undergoing any change afterwards. Three great political revolutions befel Egypt in the interval which is now before us. Every one of them was a religious war, and resulted in great and radical changes in her mythology: so that the present explanation is imperatively required for the right understanding of the history we have to relate.

The history of the gods in Egypt is thus linked

with that of the men who ruled there after them. The gods taught mankind the common arts of life, and made men fit to govern themselves. They then left the earth. We now understand this. The gods of Egypt were men;—the first settlers and their ancestors. This is the framework of the fable. It is itself a reconstruction most shapeless and unsightly, of that oldest of all traditions, that knowledge of every kind came at first from God.

The first settlers, we now find, formed encampments, and built cities along the eastern bank of the easternmost mouth of the Nile—the Phathmetic branch. They made their capital Heliopolis. In this city the hieroglyphic system of writing was invented, and for this reason it always remained the seat of learning in Egypt. Here also the first stone temple seems to have been built to Adam, as the human impersonation of the sun: for one of the invariable epithets of Athom is "god of the great temple." The temples of the other cities of the first settlers were built with bricks of Nile mud.

Very shortly after the first settlement—certainly within a hundred years, Menes crossed the Nile and built Memphis. With him begins the human history of Egypt. Five dynasties of kings are enumerated in the Greek lists as having reigned after him. Some of these now turn out to be cotemporary. We also know from the monuments that the power of these successors of Menes was confined to Memphis and its neighbourhood, and that the valley to the southward was still waste and uninhabited, save at certain points, of which Abydos, (about a hundred miles from Memphis on the southern border of Middle Egypt) was the extreme limit to the southward.

This epoch was brought to a close by the religious changes, and the wars consequent upon them, of Menes, the last monarch of the fifth dynasty, as he appears to have been on the monuments. Its duration seems to have been about 300 years.

Hitherto the Greek lists and the monuments are in tolerable harmony, but we now enter upon an epoch when they are in utterly hopeless disagreement. Six dynasties of all but nameless kings in the lists, reigning for nearly a thousand years, are represented on the monuments by six successive monarchs only. The study of these combined documents shows clearly that advantage was taken in later times, of anarchies and civil broils, when the records of Egypt were imperfectly kept, to insert therein fabulous reigns and centuries, for the purpose of exaggerating the antiquity of Egypt. Such a commotion did take place at this time; for the capital of the successors of Mencheres was no longer Memphis. It, however, did not last long, for the arts underwent no degradation in the interval of its occurrence. It was in this interval that Abram sojourned in Egypt, and is said to have composed the religious feuds in which the civil war originated.

The succession afterwards is a very intricate question, belonging to the history of Egypt, and not to that of Israel. It appears that while the six monarchs, who as adherents to the reforms of Mencheres are recorded in the monuments, reigned at Abydos, another succession of weak and inglorious kings still maintained the old pyramid worship in some cities in the eastern Delta.

The cessation of this civil war is denoted by the sudden return of the Greek lists to exact harmony with the hieroglyphic pedigrees of the kings of Egypt. The names of seven kings, reigning for about a century and a half, are recorded with wonderfully little variation in both documents. This is the twelfth dynasty of the lists. The monuments show that the crowns of Egypt were hereditary during these seven descents. They also show that Egypt enjoyed great material prosperity under the monarchs of the twelfth dynasty. These kings wrote their names in two rings or shields, which shows them to have been the adherents in religion to the reforms of Mencheres, as we have before explained. The second of these illustrious kings, (Sesortosis I.) made an addition to the temple of Adam at Heliopolis:

but the names of none of his successors have been found either in that city or in any other locality of the Delta. The history suggested by this circumstance is important, and will hereafter require consideration. The monuments show that, except at one or two isolated points, the rule of the monarchs of this dynasty was principally confined to Middle Egypt, on the western bank of the Nile. The founder of it opened in person the great canal or river of the Faium, which remains to this day under the name of the Bahr Iussuf. This fact is related in hieroglyphics in the tomb of Nahrai at Beni-hassan. The object of this canal was the irrigation of the singular valley that branches off from the Nile, about fifty miles south of Memphis, far into the western desert. It is at this day the province of the Faium. The wealth of the monarchy would be greatly increased by this noble work. During the reigns of the five last monarchs of the twelfth dynasty, the capitals of Egypt appear to have been, Memphis in the north, and in the south Abydos or Coptos, both cities close upon the southern limit of Middle Egypt. The grand object which this entire dynasty had in view, appears clearly from the monuments to have been, the extension of their dominions up the valley of the Nile to the southward. They colonized Upper Egypt. Before their times, Eilethya was the furthest point in this district, of which the Pharaohs had possession. They also conquered Nubia, and added it to Egypt, up to the very borders of Ethiopia; driving out from both districts the descendants of Cush, who, though as far advanced in civilization as the Egyptians, were, from their numerous divisions into petty kingdoms, unable to contend with them. The monuments of the twelfth dynasty are the unerring witnesses of these historical facts.

The inevitable consequence of this concentration of the efforts of the kings of Upper Egypt to the southward of their dominions, would be the neglect of their northern border. To the condition of northern Egypt in these remote epochs, we have already frequently alluded. The Delta was common ground to Egypt and Canaan. Even in the palmiest days of the successors of Menes, the shepherds of Canaan not only ranged undisturbed over the grassy plains of the Delta, but also depastured their flocks beneath the very walls of Memphis, and were evidently acknowledged as the allies or subjects of the monarchy.* This state of things shortly before the visit of Abram to Egypt, renders perfectly harmonious and intelligible, all the particulars of it recorded in the inspired narrative. Attached by the fertility of

* The shepherd Philitis was said by the priests to have been the builder of the pyramid of Suphis. He doubtless assisted in its construction. It was through hatred of the memory of Suphis that this legend was preserved. Suphis, then, was more hateful than the shepherds. *Herod.* ii. 28.

the soil, vast multitudes of Canaanites had settled in the Delta in cities and encampments. They had adopted the religion of Egypt. This was inevitable, for the doctrine of local gods was universal in all ancient idolatries. They likewise adopted the manners, the language, the dress of Egypt, as well as its religion. They were, in a word, Egyptians in every thing but descent. This, however, was a point which, at this remote epoch, when the memories of the first dispersion were yet fresh in the minds of all men, would never be for a moment forgotten. This difference of race in ancient Egypt would operate in exactly the same manner as the tinge of colour in modern colonies.* Notwithstanding the exactitude of his outward conformity, notwithstanding his useful, or social, or amiable qualities, the Canaanite would always remain a shepherd, an unclean person, an abomination, in the eyes of the pure Egyptian. Such we apprehend to have been the state of things in the Delta during the period which the reforms of Mencheres brought to a termination.

The high praise which the priesthood of Egypt was never weary of pouring upon the name and memory of Mencheres, render it quite certain that the reforms in religion introduced by him, had for

* The *misethiopism* of all European colonists is an infatuation, the fearful consequences of which are not yet developed.

one especial object the increase of the power and influence of their order. In closer connection therewith, both the mythology and the ritual of worship were likewise settled by them, rendering the religion more exclusively Egyptian, and therefore more intolerant of all foreigners; so that their very nature, and probably enough design also, would be to exclude the Egypto-Canaanites in a body from their communion. This very powerful cause would combine with the alliance and friendship they had so long enjoyed with the old kings, to keep the shepherds true to the religion of the pyramids. It does not, however, appear that they took any part in the civil war that followed. They seem rather to have retired to their fastnesses amid the swamps of the Delta, and received there as refugees their co-religionists from the cities of Middle Egypt, whence they were expelled by the Mencherian reformers. Their force would thus be concentrated and increased.

The peace between the two factions does not appear to have been of any long duration. The monumental facts of Heliopolis leave us to infer that this city was lost to the successors of Sesortosis I. So that either the civil war broke out again during his life-time, and Heliopolis was surprised and taken by the king-worshippers of the Delta, or it was ceded by treaty; the Nile being made by mutual consent the boundary of the territories of two cotemporary and rival Pharaohs; for with the single exception of the grottoes of Benihassan, there is not a locality in Egypt Proper on the eastern bank where any remains of the twelfth dynasty have been found.

During the reigns of the three successors of Sesortosis I. there appears to have been between the two Pharaohs an armed truce. It was nothing more; for the monuments show that both successions always pretended to the sovereignty of all Egypt. This lasted for about a century. The period corresponds with the declining years of Abraham, and the youth and manhood of Isaac. During this interval, while the western Pharaohs pursued their triumphs over the southern Cushites, the kings of the Delta, and of eastern Middle Egypt, seem to have been developing the fertility of the soil, planting cities and cultivating commerce with their eastern neighbours in the Desert and in Canaan. The only evidence of this fact is negative, but very strong. The arts flourished greatly in their reigns; and at the termination of the period, they were in force enough to cross the Nile and to take Memphis by a *coup de main* from their western neighbours. The cause of this revival of hostilities had been forgotten in the times of Josephus, and there is nothing yet found in the monuments whence it could be inferred. They do however make it evident that Amun-Timæus made no strenuous efforts to dispossess his rival Saites of the possession of Memphis. On the other hand, he evidently submitted to it as a divine dispensation: a token of the anger of the gods. This was precisely the account of the fall of Memphis, which Manetho found written in the temple-records. The proceedings of Amun-Timæus, on the loss of his capital, are highly characteristic of ancient idolatry, and of the modes of thought that it produced. He made peace with the victor, pursued his conquests over Cush in the south, and with the spoils built, at the point nearest to Memphis which remained in his possession, a stately palace-temple, which he dedicated to the local divinity, —Sevek, " the crocodile," or Seba. He adopted this god as the tutelary of his own family, naming all his sons and daughters after him. This change of gods was doubtless suggested by the loss of Memphis. Nevertheless Amun-Timæus showed his respect for, or fear of, the religion which had dispossessed him of his capital, by building a pyramid for his own tomb close by his new palace: a form of sepulchre so strictly peculiar to the old religion, that it seems on this account to have been unanimously rejected by all the other royal adherents to the reforms of Mencheres.

The city in which Amun-Timæus built his palace was situated in the Faium, to the fertility of which district his ancestors had so largely contributed by their works of engineering. The ruins of both palace and pyramid remain to this day. They were discovered very recently by Dr. Lepsius. The city was afterwards named by the Greeks, Crocodilopolis.

Aphophis, the patron of Joseph, appears on the monuments as the third successor of Säites the conqueror of Memphis, and founder of the city of Sais in the eastern Delta, whom the priesthood named Salatis in derision. The same unerring records of the past also disclose the wonderful fact, that these monarchs were not shepherds by descent, but sons and heirs in the direct line, of Menes and the old Pharaohs; so that the narrative of Moses is true to the jot and tittle. They were termed shepherd-kings, and their names were converted into nicknames,—because of the religious tenets they professed, and because of their tolerant and enlightened policy towards the Canaanites,—by the priests who kept the archives of Egypt in after ages. On the monuments, the greatest of the Pharaohs were proud to enrol them in their pedigrees, among their ancestors. This point belongs to the history of Egypt.*

Aphophis, Phiops or Apappus (for by all these several names in the lists, the same individual is really designated) was one of the most magnificent of the Pharaohs. He is said to have ascended the

* History of Egypt, Vol. ii.

throne at six years of age, and to have been king of Egypt for a hundred years. The monuments give countenance to this tradition. He is repeatedly represented there as co-regent with his father and grandfather. The latter was the captor of Memphis. The known monuments of Aphophis are few hitherto: for the remains of Memphis and Heliopolis are still covered with sand. When they shall be disinterred we shall probably be in a position to say more upon the transactions of his long reign. Those however that remain tell unmistakeably of victory, prosperity, and the perfection of the fine arts.

The only exploit of Aphophis, of which a monumental record remains, is the defeat of the Egyptians of the opposite faction. The deed of arms is commemorated in a superb tablet sculptured on the face of one of the granite cliffs of the Wady Meghara, in the Sinaitic peninsula. The tablet was engraved in the 18th year of the reign of his father, on the 6th day of the month Mesore, the last month of the year. It is in two compartments. In the first of them Aphophis wears the crown of Lower Egypt, and is represented in the act of rushing hastily towards the south, bearing in his right hand the flagellum, and holding forth with his left a roll of papyrus, whereon was written his claim to the sovereignty of Upper Egypt. Some aggression on the part of the descendant of Amun-Timæus had therefore been the occasion of the war. In the next compartment he has assumed the crown of Upper Egypt, and is grasping with his left hand the hair of his vanquished enemy, while the right hand is raised in the act of striking him with a battle-axe. The enemy is an Egyptian in countenance, wearing the long hair which distinguished afterwards the Upper from the Lower Egyptians. His weakness and cowardice are most significantly symbolised. The figure is androgynous. It has the beard of a man and the breast of a woman. This defeat is said in the accompanying hieroglyphics to have taken place in the mountains of Western Thebes. One of the results of the victory was doubtless the cession to the Shepherds of the valuable copper-mines of Wady Meghara, which we find from other tablets also sculptured on its cliffs to have been in the possession of the kings of the 12th dynasty up to Amun-Timæus. In the hieroglyphic genealogy of the kings of Egypt in the chamber of Karnak, Aphophis is declared to be king of Lower Egypt at the time that Sebachon the successor of Amun-Timæus was king in Upper Egypt. Twenty-four officers of the army of Aphophis have had their names inscribed at the foot of this tablet. The force they commanded had doubtless come to take possession of the mines. They were moreover commissioned to bring from thence metal for bronze colossi of the victor and his associates in the monarchy.

We give here a copy of this beautiful tablet, principally because, as may be observed, in the two figures of Aphophis, however rigid, and metallic, and unlifelike, the features are nevertheless the same. They may be taken, therefore to be *portraits* of the patron of Joseph!

The power of the kingdom of the Mencherian reformers on the western bank of the Nile was rapidly declining throughout the entire reign of Aphophis: so much so that his successor penetrated Upper Egypt as far as Assuan on its extreme southern border, and inscribed himself on the rocks there as king of the Lower country and conqueror of the Upper. In the genealogy of Karnak also, to which we have just referred, he is written by his descendant, king of Lower Egypt, governing Upper Egypt by a viceroy, even as the Pharaohs of the 12th dynasty had governed Memphis.

These favourable circumstances for the development of the foreign policy of Aphophis, (which was too liberal and enlightened for his generation), were largely taken advantage of by him for the encouragement of the fine arts. He built for himself a magnificent palace on the eastern bank of the Nile, almost directly opposite to the labyrinth of Amun-Timæus and in obvious rivalry of it. The revenues of this palace-temple must have been immense. The offices attached to it formed the summit of the ambition of all the princes of his court. The tombs of these princes are the most beautiful in Egypt. The following design is from that of the *Saris Shusen,* mayor of the Aphophœum, 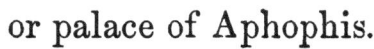 or palace of Aphophis.

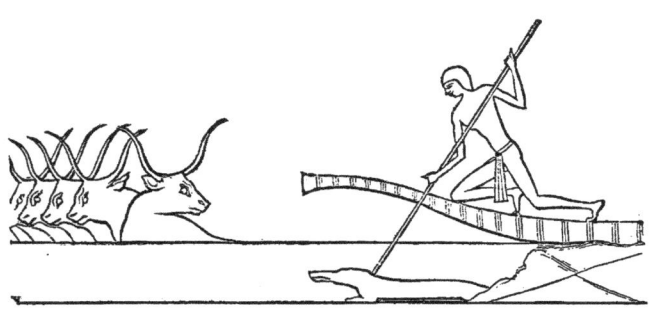

This picture tells its own story. The great cattle

of *Shusen* are in the waters of the yearly overflow. The bull which heads the herd perceives a crocodile approaching, and his alarm is pourtrayed with much truth to nature. One of the cattle-keepers however is there in his boat or launch of papyrus reeds, and spears the assailant. The intention of this beautiful design is twofold. It commends the vigilance of the herdsmen of Shushen. It also expresses contempt and abhorrence of the crocodile-god of the royal rival of Aphophis on the other bank of the river.

There are many other tombs of extreme beauty, and all of the princes of Pharaoh Aphophis, in the same mountain, which is at Suadé in Middle Egypt, over against the modern city of Nineveh. At other places also tombs of the courtiers of Aphophis have been found; Shech Said, for example, about fifty miles to the southward,—Chenoboscion, which is still further south, and many intermediate points. They everywhere bear uniform testimony to the high perfection which art in Egypt attained in the days of Pharaoh Aphophis.

The quarry-marks which the kings of Egypt were wont to inscribe upon the rocks and mountains, whence they hewed the materials for the construction of their temples and palaces, now furnish very important and historical notices of the events of their reigns. The granites and porphyries of the mountains of the Gulf of Suez were in large demand for works of art and ornament during the reign of Pharaoh Aphophis. At the ancient quarry now called Hamamat on the desert road from Keneh on the Nile, to Kossayr on the Red Sea, the inscriptions inform us that a considerable force was stationed there to superintend the workmen in the days of Aphophis and his co-regents. The officers of this force inscribe their names on the festival of opening the temple of Ptha or Phut at Memphis, for several successive years. It would seem to have been principally for the decoration of this temple and Memphis, that the quarry was wrought. The high reputation of Aphophis and his father, for the beautiful works of architecture and art with which Memphis was adorned by them, was very gracefully commemorated. The name of the pyramid in which they were both interred, was made in after ages the trivial or vulgar name of Memphis.* It stood in the immediate vicinity of the city, and took, like other royal pyramids,† one of the titles of the kings who built it. "[of] Aphophis the fair constructor the pyramid," or "[of] Meris‡ the fair constructor the pyramid,"

---

* The name of Memphis in religion was "the house," or "Temple of Ptha."

† History of Egypt, Vol. ii.

‡ The name of the father of Aphophis. I found these names of the pyramids in a tomb at Chenoboscion.

was its name at length. In common speech the king's name was omitted (as with all other pyramids) and it was called 𓏞𓏤𓉴. " the pyramid of the fair constructors," which also was made ever afterwards the name of the city. It was pronounced *man-nufi.* The Coptic transcription preserves it unchanged. The Greeks changed it slightly for the sake of euphony, to Μεμφις. The Hebrews about the time of the captivity in Babylon abbreviated it to נֹף Noph, and מֹף Moph. (Jer. ii. 14; Hos. ix. 6, &c.) The name Memphis, then, was to all who read hieroglyphics in Ancient Egypt during the whole period that they remained legible, the commemoration of the fair constructions wherewith the patron of Joseph had adorned the glorious city that bore it. Several other interesting facts of history also appear in these quarry marks at Hamamat.

On the death of Salatis, Meris (whose name was long afterwards punned, or rhymed, or gingled into Benis or *Benois*, " a dirty fellow," by the Alexandrians*) divided the monarchy with his son; and on the first day of the great festival of Ptha at Memphis, Meris was crowned king of Upper Egypt, and Aphophis, or Apappus, of Lower Egypt. The coronation took place in the temple of Ptha, and

---

* The names of the Shepherd-kings in the Greek lists are a piece of wit, for which the Alexandrians were always famous.

both assumed the dress and attributes of that god, thereby declaring themselves his votaries. This event was commemorated by a shrine of porphyry hewn from the quarry of Hamamat.

Another tablet in the same quarry tells us in further illustration of the history of Egypt in the days of Joseph, that Meris the father of his patron, took Coptos on the western bank near Thebes, from the Mencherians, and made it the capital of Upper Egypt. About a hundred years earlier, Coptos was the capital of the Mencherian king Sesortosis I, of the 12th dynasty. This fact is stated in the tomb of Amenemes, one of his sons at Benihassan.

Thus clearly does it appear, that all Egypt was under the government to which Joseph was minister, and that his institutions applied to the entire monarchy!

The 18th of Meris is a year commemorated in the annals of the quarries of Hamamat as well as in those of the mines of Meghara. On the 27th day of Ephip, that is nine days before his arrival at Meghara, the son of Meris passed through Hamamat, doubtless on his way thither, and ordered the garrison there to commence very extensive operations connected with the decoration of the temple of Ptha at Memphis.

The fact so important to the Mosaic history, that Aphophis the patron of Joseph ruled over all Egypt, is confirmed still more triumphantly by the quarry marks in the red sandstone of Eilethya (called by the Arabs El Kab) which is situated in Upper Egypt, about twenty miles to the south of Thebes, and within thirty miles of Assonan, the extreme limit of all that ever was Egypt. Building stones and blocks for colossal statues were repeatedly cut from thence; both in the life-time of Meris, and afterwards his son Aphophis cut blocks from thence for colossal sitting figures of his entire ancestry. There cannot be a doubt, therefore, that on the death of his father, Aphophis, or Phiops, or Apappus, (for by these latter names alone he was really known in the annals of Egypt) was sole king both of Upper and Lower Egypt, from its extreme southern limit to the Mediterranean on the north.

These very clear monumental indications of the highly flourishing condition of Egypt under the Pharaoh to whom Joseph was minister, receive a confirmation from the Greek traditions, the force of which appears never yet to have been perceived. The Alexandrian chronologers are perfectly unanimous in ascribing to the shepherd-kings all the reforms in the Egyptian calendar, whereby the vague year of 360 days was restored to harmony with the actual seasons. Salatis, or Saites, the grandfather of Apappus, is said to have added to the year the five days of the epoch.* Asses, his descendant, improved upon this expedient, by making the addition to consist of half a day or twelve hours to each month.* No Greek authority ascribes this reform to any other line of monarchs in Egypt but the shepherd-kings. Thus clearly does the Greek tradition convict of absurdity its own fable regarding the barbarism of the shepherds. For it will be observed, that the reform is begun by Saites, the first of the shepherd-kings, and perfected to a degree upon which we in the present day, have scarcely been able to advance by the last of them. This circumstance denotes a progressive civilization of a character very foreign to any thing that appears in the manners of ancient Egypt in later times, where all was as stationary as in China or Japan. The same tendency shews itself also in the foreign policy of this illustrious line of kings, upon which we have already remarked, and which procured for them the opprobrious epithet of shepherds in the annals of the priesthood of after-ages.

Egypt was then a great, a prosperous, and a flourishing kingdom, when Joseph was minister to Pharaoh. So says the Bible: and the truth of its statement is abundantly confirmed, both by the Greek tradition, and by the cotemporary monuments that still exist in Egypt.

We have at length brought up to one point the

* Seol. in Plat. Tim. Bekker, i. 424.

histories of Egypt and Israel. Whether Joseph survived Apappus, his master, and was minister to his son and successor, or died during the long reign of the former, the Greek lists afford us no means of determining. They are a mere mass of confusion. The Egyptian kings before us figure in them in double and triple entry. In the history of Egypt to which it belongs, we have given the full discussion of this question. The result of that discussion is all that belongs to this place.

The son of Apappus was named ▢ *mrnra*, which the Greeks would probably have hellenized into *Melaneris*. He does not however appear in their lists at all. The fame of Melaneris is purely monumental. Whoever was his minister, he was a great and prosperous monarch. In his reign the depression of the Mencherian faction reached its lowest point. They were expelled from all Egypt. No dated monuments of the reign of Melaneris have been discovered. We can therefore know nothing of the length of it.

On the death of Melaneris a war of succession most probably took place. It is certain that afterwards, Upper and Lower Egypt had each its dynasty of shepherd-kings, and that the kingdom of Apappus was never re-constructed.

The king who succeeded Melaneris at Memphis and Heliopolis was named Jannes by the Alexandrians, which was a pun upon his real name ⟨cartouche⟩ *Unas*. A single quarry mark at Hamamat records his name; and the tomb of one of his princes exists at Sakkara, which was the cemetery of Memphis.

The same obscurity besets the monumental record of the author of this line of kings. His name is scarcely found, except on quarry-marks ⟨cartouche⟩ *Othoes*. Not impossibly he was one of the obscure predecessors of Saites.

The last of them was Asses ⟨cartouche⟩ whose monumental fame is equally slight, and in whose reign Memphis was lost to the shepherd kingdom. As we have the ample record of this event, both in the Greek traditions and in hieroglyphics, our narrative will now return to something more like history.

The Greek tradition of this event is a quotation from the Egyptian history written in that language, at the command of Ptolemy Philadelphus, in the third century before Christ, by a priest of the temple of the city of Sebenne in the Delta named Manetho. So very turbid and perplexed is the language of this quotation, that it throws considerable doubt upon the fluency and accuracy of Manetho's Greek, whatever may have been his proficiency in deciphering his native hieroglyphics. With the unravelling of the knots and intricacies of this his narrative, which has been effected with much labour by the comparison of it with the testimony of the monuments, we have nothing to do here.* The result, which is all that belongs to our present undertaking, is as follows:—" In the reign of Asses, a king of the Thebaid, [i.e., Upper Egypt] named Amosis, confederated with the kings of other parts of Egypt, and expelled the shepherds from Memphis. After this defeat they retired from the rest of Egypt, to a district about 10,000 arouræ [that is 300 miles] in circumference, which they fortified with a wall very great and strong. In this enclosure they kept all their goods and plunder. Thothmosis, the son of Amosis, besieged them in this their strong hold with 480,000 men;—but at length he gave up the siege, and made a treaty with the besieged, wherein it was stipulated that the shepherds should leave Egypt unmolested, with all their property, and go where they would. They did so depart from Egypt, and to the number of not less than 2,400,000. They went into the desert, taking the road that leads to Syria." †

This our version of Manetho does a good deal to clear his narrative of some of its grosser intricacies and inconsequences. Nevertheless we must acknow-

---

* See History of Egypt, Vol. ii. p.

† Josephus Cont. Apion. i. 14. A floating number of 511 years for the Shepherd rule in Egypt, also occurs in this narrative; but the two events at each extremity of it do not appear.

ledge that it egregiously fails to commend itself to the understanding, as sober, credible history. The following appear to be the certainties which it embodies.

I. Memphis was lost to the shepherd-kingdom in the reign of Asses.

II. The king who dispossessed him of it was named Amosis. In the lists he appears as the first king of the 18th dynasty.

III. Amosis was confederate with other kings of Upper Egypt, when he made this successful attack upon Memphis.

IV. After the loss of Memphis, the shepherds retired to a district 300 miles in circuit. Three hundred miles being just about the circumference of the district traversed by the mouths of the Nile, which the Greeks called the Delta, we conclude that it was into the Delta that the shepherds retreated.

V. The great and very strong wall is now intelligible. The defeated king fortified Heliopolis his capital, at the crown or head of the Delta. He likewise built forts to defend the river and its approaches at the point where it first branches into mouths, now called the Barash. The mode in which this history is narrated is very instructive as to the spirit in which it was written.

This is the whole of the history which it seems possible safely to infer from Manetho's narrative, without the further assistance of the monuments. To them, therefore, we now return.

The hieroglyphic name of Amosis repeatedly occurs both on cotemporary monuments and in the genealogies of his royal descendants. He wrote his name in two rings [hieroglyphs] which shows him to have been an adherent of the Mencherian faction. He is also placed in the genealogies as the immediate descendant of Amun-timœus, who was expelled from Memphis by Saites.* These facts might have been inferred from the narrative of Manetho.

Amosis certainly had possession of Memphis; for in the twenty-second year of his reign he made additions to the temple of Ptha in that city, and in the same year he built a temple in it to his god Amoun. These facts are recorded by the quarry marks on the rock of Toorah, which is immediately over against the ruins of Memphis. The formal hieroglyphic statement of the capture of Memphis, we shall presently have to consider.

The loose uncertainty of Manetho's narrative is still more strikingly illustrated by the monumental identification of Thothmosis whom he calls the son of Amosis. Thothmosis was the descendant of Amosis, but there were at least six removes and more than a century of time between them. It is

---

* Tablet of Abydos, &c.

from the monuments constructed by this Thothmosis that we shall be able to continue the history of the shepherds in Upper Egypt, from the times of Melaneris where we left it; and also that of the Mencherian kings, up to the period of the capture of Memphis, so as to trace this event to its probable cause.

The expulsion from Egypt of the shepherds by Thothmosis [cartouche] has no other monumental foundation, than that Heliopolis was ceded to him by treaty with the Pharaoh then at the head of the shepherd kingdom, and that he colonized the extreme north-western angle of the Delta, founding there the city now called Alexandria. Thothmosis was at peace with the shepherds, and traded largely with them during the whole of his reign. The representatives of the kingdom of Apappus seem on the cession of Heliopolis to have made their capital Xois in the centre of the Delta. In the Greek lists they are the seventy-six Xoite kings who reigned for 184 years. They were the contemporaries of the 18th and 19th dynasties of the same lists. The only name with which the monuments have made us certainly acquainted is that of the last of them, who ceded the miserable remnant of the dominions of Apappus, to the king that knew not Joseph, and became the husband of his daughter. This transaction we shall find to have taken place at Heliopolis.

The emigration therefore in Manetho's history of 2,400,000 shepherds is a mere blundering anticipation of the events of the Exodus.

The causes of the decline of the kingdom of Apappus, we must now endeavour to trace on the monuments of Thothmosis.

This monarch was most probably the son by incest * of Queen Amenses and her father Mesphres his predecessor. They were all three magnificent monarchs. Their constructions, especially at Thebes, which Amosis their ancestor had made his capital, were of great beauty. They founded the palace of Karnak in the portion of that city on the eastern bank of the Nile. Amongst other remains in this palace was a side chamber, or cloister, in which is represented the worship of sixty-one of the royal and vice-regal ancestors of Thothmosis. This most important monument yet exists at Paris in a mutilated state. It has hitherto contributed but little to the illustration of Egyptian history. The study however of the monuments locally in other parts of Egypt has thrown considerable light upon it. An examination of all the royal names that are legible in this monument we have given elsewhere. The result stands thus :—

* The Egyptians certainly never had the sense of the enormity of these offences, which prevailed so universally among the Semitic and Japhetian races in the ancient world. The extinction of the aboriginal Mizraites, in the days of the Ptolemies, had probably resulted from this cause princi all . Histor f F t Vol. i. ch. i. . 14.

31 kings face left.

16 kings of Lower Egypt.

D	C	B	A
Saites who took Memphis.	Menes.	6 Theban kings, 12th dynasty.	8 Theban kings, 11th and 12th dynasties.
	Viceroy of Memphis.		
7 Memphite kings of the first 6 dynasties.	Viceroy.		
	Amenemes III.		
	Viceroy.		
	Othoes.		
	Aphophis.	Viceroy of Thebes.	
	Melaneris.		
8 Xoite kings, 14th dynasty.	2 Xoites, 6 Shepherds in Upper Egypt.	7 Theban kings, 13th dynasty.	6 Theban kings, 17th dynasty.
			Amosis.
H	G	F	E

16 kings of Lower Egypt or Shepherds.

15 kings of Upper Egypt.

14 kings of Upper Egypt.

It will be observed that the thrones of the kings are arranged on the walls of the chamber in four rows.

In the two upper rows are 32 kings.
In the two lower rows are 29 kings.
—
61

The names of the kings in the two upper rows are all those of kings in Lower Egypt, writing their names in one ring only.

The names of the kings in the two lower rows are all those of kings in Upper Egypt, who wrote their names in two rings.

At the extremities of the two side-walls next the door of the entrance to the chamber, are the remains of pictures of Thothmosis doing sacrifice to the two lower rows of kings;—that is of kings in Upper Egypt. We know him to have been a lineal descendant of Amosis, and accordingly Amosis appears at the head in the lowest row to the right of the entrance. The name is mutilated, save the first character, and a portion of the second.

The pictures of the worshipper of the two upper rows of kings have entirely perished. It cannot have been Thothmosis, as has been conjectured.* In

---

* Or if it was Thothmosis, as he worships the kings of Upper Egypt under his name in Lower Egypt, so he worshipped the Lower Egyptians under his name in the Upper country. We have so restored him in our diagram.

this case his figure would have occupied the space of all the four rows: as appears in innumerable examples of Egyptian art, the rules of which admitted of no variation. We believe that the worshipper of these kings in Lower Egypt was his queen, and that the monument commemorated an act of pacification between the two factions that had so long divided Egypt. Thothmosis seems to have married the daughter of the king of Heliopolis, perhaps the heiress to the throne. Probably enough, it was in her right that this capital was added to his dominions, and the war which in all the previous reigns had raged between the two factions, ended in a permanent peace. The chamber of Karnak now becomes significant. In token of this pacification the king and queen worship each their respective royal ancestry in the same shrine. This act of worship would be an important concession on the part of Thothmosis to the religion of his queen and her subjects; inasmuch as king-worship had certainly been abolished by the Mencherian reforms.

From this monument we now derive a very important fact connected with the fall of Memphis and of the kingdom of Apappus. The kings of Upper Egypt, of the line of the Shepherds, confederated with the Mencherian reformers in Nubia; for in this genealogy they appear as kings in Lower

Egypt, and contemporary with these their rivals in Upper Egypt. There had been peace and amity between the two factions for some successions when Amosis came to the throne. What more probable, then, than that he himself had set the example which his descendant Thothmosis appears to have imitated, by espousing the daughter of the Shepherd-king of Upper Egypt, and thereby becoming the rightful heir to both pretensions. This circumstance, in itself perfectly natural and usual, removes entirely the historical difficulty as to the causes of the fall of Memphis. The force of Upper Egypt and Nubia was confederated under Amosis. By common consent they made Amun, the god of eastern Thebes, the patron of the war. The priesthood, doubtless, fanned the flame of enthusiasm, and they would rush to the assault of the strongholds of the polluters of the sacred soil of Egypt, the allies of impure foreigners, with all the ardor of a crusade.

Thothmosis wrote in hieroglyphics the chronicle of this capture of Memphis by Amosis, on the exterior of a magnificent shrine of red granite, which formed part of the same palace of Karnak. Of this most valuable record nothing but a fragment remains. It consists of fifty-four lines of hieroglyphics, all greatly mutilated. We have already translated the whole of them.* They embody the follow-

* History of Egypt, Vol. ii.

ing historical facts: Amosis took Memphis when he was twenty-nine years old. Its name is written 𓏠𓈖 "the land of *Noph*." We have already seen that this was the habitual abbreviation of the name of Memphis with the Hebrews. It is spoken of in this inscription invariably as a Canaanite city. This is the case with all other cities of Egypt in the hands of foreigners, and in all hieroglyphic inscriptions. Their names are spelt according to the foreign pronunciation of them, and are written as those of strange cities. It is highly probable, moreover, that the liberal policy of the Aphophean Pharaohs would be far in advance of the prepossessions of their own Egyptian subjects, and as well as of the rest of the inhabitants of Egypt. The cousequence of this would be both large defections to the banner of Amosis, and also revolts within the territories of the Memphite king. These would again tend to drive him to more dependence upon the immigrants from Canaan, and also to alliances with the kings of their confederacy in Canaan itself; so that in every succeeding year, the war would more and more lose its civil, and acquire an international complexion. These considerations divest of all inconsistency with the facts already ascertained—the circumstance that in this chronicle the war of Amosis against Memphis is spoken of as a war with the Canaanite nations of Arvad and

Heth, and the hereditary and native Pharaoh of Lower Egypt as the king of Arvad.

The war lasted for seven years certain : probably much longer. In the latter years of it Amosis seems to have abandoned all further attack upon the territory of the Memphite Pharaohs, and to have even confederated with them against the Canaanites and Assyrians, who were threatening Egypt with an invasion across the desert of Suez.

Thus clearly does it appear from both the monumental and traditive records of the event, that the fall of Memphis exercised no adverse influence whatever upon the position of Israel in Egypt. The Delta entire still remained, by the declaration of both authorities, under the rule of the descendants of the patron of Joseph.

In the year after the capture of Memphis, Amosis crossed the desert and took by storm the strong hold of Adasa, in the south of Canaan. Doubtless the strong defences with which, as Manetho records, the Shepherds fortified their northern border, would deter him from further aggressions upon their territories. There was also another motive for this diversion of the war, at least equally powerful in ancient times. Enormous booty fell into the hands of the conqueror, on the capture of Memphis. But a still larger prey escaped the conquerors, and was carried across the desert by the Canaanite confederates of the Memphite king. It was in pursuit of this, that Amosis marched upon Adasa. It would appear, that upon the loss of Memphis the Aphopean Pharaoh had purchased peace by the further cession of Hermopolis in Middle Egypt; retiring, altogether to the Delta, as Manetho writes : for the wars of the six following years of the reign of Amosis are all foreign wars with Arvad, Heth, and Naharaim, the spoil whereof he embarks on the Nile at the cities of Tanis and Athribis in the eastern Delta : both cities being at the time in the hands of the Shepherds, as the mode of writing their names in hieroglyphics plainly indicates.

The immediate successors of Amosis (the Theban Pharaohs, as we may now call them) seem to have principally occupied themselves with the prosecution of the conquests begun by their ancestors over Cush to the southward. Mesphres, the father of Thothmosis, is the first of them who has recorded his name on any monument in the Delta. He founded the city of Alexandria on its north-western point, but apparently as a colony, not as a conquest.

The cession of Heliopolis to Thothmosis was the first event adverse to Israel, that had yet occurred in the history of Egypt. In his reign a gang of captive Israelites is represented making bricks in the tomb of *Ris-share,* the superintendent of his constructions at Thebes; but in all probability they were Simeonites or Levites, and misdemeanants against the laws of Egypt. The Delta still acknowledged the sovereignty of the Xoite kings, the descendants of Apappus.

Events adverse to Egypt were never related to strangers by the Egyptian priesthood, whatever record of them may have existed in the temple muniments. It was only the wide circulation in Egypt in the days of the Ptolemaic kings [B. C. 304 to B. C. 19] of the Jewish account of the Exodus, and its undeniable truth, that extorted from them the mutilated and falsified story of the Shepherd invasion, which we have just quoted. Great misfortunes befel the kingdom of the Theban Pharaohs in the days of the successors of Thothmosis; but not a word or hint of them appears in the Greek tradition. Their history is altogether monumental.

ARMAIS, the grandson and second successor of Thothmosis, experienced in the seventh year of his reign a disastrous defeat from the Phutim of the Sahara, in the immediate neighbourhood of the island of Philœ, close to the southern border of Egypt. Armais fled northward before his enemies, who pursued him, and entered Thebes his capital in triumph. There they were joined by a faction in Egypt, headed by the half-brother of Armais, a very dark mulatto, whom they placed on the throne, giving him to wife a Phutite princess. Headed by this pretender, they continued the pursuit of Armais, who fled to Memphis, where he seems to have purchased the assistance of the Apophean Pharaoh at Xois by the cession of Heliopolis, and by this aid to have been able to make some stand against his negro conquerors. He remained at Memphis and Alexandria long enough to inscribe his name on temples, the ruins of which exist to this day. At the former city he dedicated a temple to the Sphinx of Sephres, the builder of the second pyramid of Ghizeh. This huge colossus, which is a hewn rock in its place, remains to this day. The Xoite or Aphophean Pharaohs whose alliance he was then seeking, were especially devoted to the worship of Sephres, and named themselves after this ancient king. The Greek lists say that the brother of Armais finally expelled him from all Egypt.

The consequence of these events to Upper Egypt was a disputed succession to the throne of Thebes. For several descents, a line of Negro kings, on the eastern bank of the Nile, contended for the sovereignty of Egypt with the sons of Amosis on the western bank. The war was of course a religious war: for such was the nature of all civil wars in Egypt at all periods of her history. It seems to have been the attempt to identify Amun with the sun (of which Nesteres of the 11th dynasty had been the author) that was the cause of the discontent in Egypt, in which the success of the Negroes originated. The new sectaries worshipped the disc of the sun only, renouncing most scrupulously all other idols. They however erased the names and pictures of Amun alone from the temples.* Amenophis Memnon, the son and successor of Armais, ended this schism at Thebes in the usual way. He married the Negro princess at the head of the other pretension. In Middle Egypt, nevertheless, these black sectaries continued for two or three descents longer to claim the sovereignty of Egypt.

These disasters to the rival throne would leave the southern frontier of the Xoite Pharaohs unmolested, and enable them once more to develope the policy of the great Apappus.† To this course they would, moreover, now be driven by another cause. The children of Israel had now greatly increased both in numbers, wealth, and influence in their kingdom. They had not adopted the language of Egypt, though they seem to have conformed gen-

---

* History of Egypt, Vol. ii.
† The remains of a temple of the Negro disc-worshippers is said to exist at Tanis, on the north-east of the Delta. The style of their constructions, which is extremely beautiful, yielding in artistic merit to the works of no other race or time in Egypt, is, nevertheless, so peculiar, that they are readily distinguished. Trans. R. S. L. Vol. i. pp. 76—92, 140—148. This is a further illustration of the tolerant policy of the Shepherd-Pharaohs.

erally to its customs and institutions. Their sympathies would therefore naturally flow out towards the people across the desert, inhabiting the country to which they were one day to return, and speaking the same language with themselves: and in the councils of Pharaoh the voices of the princes of Israel would be in favour of alliances with the kings of Canaan; so that the general policy of the government of the Delta would be to encourage the settlement of the Canaanites in the cities and pasturages on its eastern border.

The same state of things continued during the reigns of the two remaining Theban Pharaohs, which brought the dynasty (the 18th of the lists) of which Amosis was the founder to its termination. Throughout them the Pharaohs of Thebes and the Delta were at peace.

The 18th dynasty consisted of ten successive monarchs, reigning at Thebes for about 200 years.

The short reign of Rameses [cartouche] the founder of the following Theban dynasty seems to have been occupied with the expulsion of the Negro disc-worshippers from the eastern bank of the Nile. This was probably the benefit conferred on Egypt, which procured for him from the priesthood the honour of being placed at the head of a new dynasty, though in fact he was the son of his predecessor.

Sethos [hieroglyphs] the son and successor of Rameses, was, like his father, a fierce fanatic against the Negro disc-worshippers. He built the propyla of his palace-temple, at Karnak in Eastern Thebes, with the stones of one of their temples which had stood in the vicinity, and which he razed to the ground.* In the first year of his reign he boasts of a great and successful war against the Shepherds of Canaan, five actions of which he had recorded on the north external wall of the same palace-temple. The minute analysis of this vast picture we have given elsewhere.† The epitome of the history it embodies is all that belongs to this place.

The dominions of the Xoite Pharaoh are named here the land of Arvad, as on the granite shrine of Thothmosis: but the epithet Upper or Southern ([hieroglyphs] *rtn-hr*, the Upper Arvadites") is added to distinguish Arvad in Egypt, from Arvad in Canaan, which Sethos also visited, and which is named [hieroglyphs] " the lower (northern) Arvadites."

As we have already stated, the bulk of the Canaanite settlers in the Delta were of the tribes of Arvad and Heth. No admixture, however, took place between the two tribes, even after they had embraced the religion of their new country, and

---

* Trans. Roy. Soc. Lit., *U.S.*
† History of Egypt, Vol. ii.

were located in the cities of Middle Egypt and the Delta. They still remained Arvadites and Hittites. They dwelt in separate cities, and the national distinctions were as strictly kept up in Egypt as in Canaan. This was the universal custom in ancient times. It prevails to a considerable extent among the inhabitants of the East to the present day. In our western parts of the world, it is peculiar to one tribe only—the Jews. A very natural consequence of this distinction had evidently befallen Arvad and Heth in Egypt, during the interval between the reigns of Amosis and Sethos. There had been a war between them. Heth had been worsted and expelled from Egypt. The Xoite kings had taken the part of Arvad. The Hittites crossed the desert, and the story of their wrongs roused the vindictive passions of their brethren in Canaan. They confederated with other tribes, made war upon Arvad, and invaded his territory in Canaan, and those also of his ally the Xoite king of Egypt, under whom Arvad held possessions in suzereignty. In this emergency the king of Xois sought the aid of the Theban Pharaoh, Sethos I. These were the causes of the war, the results of which are embodied in the vast picture which surrounds the side portal in the north external wall of the palace of Karnak.

The belligerents in this war were Sethos I. of

Thebes, confederate with the Xoite king (or Upper Arvad, as his co-regent in Upper Egypt, who "bears no rival next the throne," names him by a haughty and insolent taunt), also with Lower Arvad (that is Arvad in Canaan) and Naharaim or Mesopotamia. On the other side Heth, with whose pretensions to possessions in Egypt the war had originated, was in league with the Amorites, the Zuzim of Kanah, Moab and Ammon, and the Jebusites, and had invaded the territories of the Xoite Pharaoh. The Zuzim and Moab were also claimants of strong-holds in Egypt as well as Heth. This was (as we have seen) the motive of the war, which, according to the picture of it, was wonderfully successful. After repelling the invaders from Egypt, Sethos pursues them into Canaan, dislodges them from Adasa in the mountains of Judea, routs them in battle after battle, and overruns the entire land as far as the foot of Hermon, which being then the name of the whole southern face of the mountain-ranges both of Libanus and Anti-Libanus, means of course that he marched through all Canaan or Phenicia. He then vindicates the claims of Arvad in Canaan, i. e. Lower Arvad, to the right of felling timber in the forests of Hermon for the supply of Egypt, where no timber grows. Having accomplished this, he receives an embassy of congratulation, with rich presents, from Tyre, the chief city of Arvad in Canaan; then defeats the Zuzim, sacking Canaan or Kanah their chief city, and returns to Egypt on the eastern bank of Jordan, through the territories of the Jebusite and of Moab.

If the averments of this pictorial rhodomontade are to be literally received, the Xoite king purchased the aid of his Theban brother at a very costly price. Six cities or strongholds in the Delta were ceded by him to Sethos. The names of four of them are still legible: the other two have suffered mutilation. The legible names consist of Tanis, Bubastis, and Heliopolis, on the eastern border of the Delta, and Sais on its western boundary. Five stations in the desert of Suez are also included in the concessions of the Xoite king to Sethos. Of their three numutilated names, one only (namely, Kadesh-Barnea in the Wilderness) is mentioned in the Bible.

This ancient war, the cotemporaneous record of which remains extant to this day, is important to the history of Israel in Egypt. The contingent of Israel to the army of the Xoite king would be very considerable; and when the war was carried into Canaan, doubtless they formed part of the invading force. This circumstance exactly harmonizes with the single fact which alone stands recorded in the inspired narrative, during this long interval which we are now endeavouring to fill up from the monuments of Ancient Egypt. It is the defeat of the

Ephraimites by the Philistines of Gath, which is mentioned in the pedigree of Joshua. 1 Chron. vii. 20, 21. The clear inference from hence, that in this interval there were frequent wars with Canaan, is thus established by the monuments of Egypt.

Sethos I. reigned at Thebes for fifty-five years. There is no record of any war of his on the northern frontier of his kingdom afterwards. The beautiful obelisk now standing in the Piazza del Popolo at Rome informs us, in the hieroglyphic inscription engraven upon it, that it was erected by Sethos before the temple of Re-Athom at Heliopolis. Thus is the cession of this capital to Sethos, which is recorded at Thebes, confirmed by its own monuments. This, in common with the tomb of Sethos and all other monuments of his reign, which are very numerous, tell us unmistakeably that it was long, peaceful, and prosperous.

The son and successor of Sethos was for five years co-regent with his father. He is named in the stories related to the Greeks by the Egyptian priesthood, Sesostris. In the lists and on the monuments his name is Ramses. In the fifth year of his accession, (the first of his sole reign) there was again a war on the north-eastern frontier of Egypt. As we have three picture-records of this war on three of the greatest temples now remaining in Egypt, the details of it are very amply chronicled. The motive of it was precisely the same as that of the former war. The pretensions of the Hittites and of Moab to possessions in Egypt had been revived. They confederated with other tribes of Canaan, and the dominions of the Xoite king in the Delta again suffered an invasion. He applied once more for aid to his haughty brother at Thebes. An alliance was formed between them, and the repulse of the invaders by their combined armies is the subject commemorated in these boastful pictures. Notwithstanding the amplitude of the space occupied by its details on the walls of the temples, the war of Ramses with Canaan was a very inferior affair, both in its prosecution and its results to Egypt, to that of Sethos his father.

The very intricate details of this war we have given elsewhere. They are neither important to the history of Israel, nor to any other history, because they are not true—save in one or two circumstances. The war issued in the cession of Hadasha and Phenne, or Punon in the peninsula of Sinai, to the Canaanites, whereby probably the claims of Heth to possessions in Egypt were compromised. In the war of Sethos, Hadasha had remained with the Xoite dynasty, and Phenne with the Theban at its termination. Both crowns therefore contributed to the concession by which the peace was purchased.

Throughout the pictures of this war, the Xoite Pharaoh is invariably spoken of as Upper Arvad in the explanatory text that accompanies them, and his soldiers are represented as fighting in the ranks of Egypt, but with the helmet, arms, and costume of Tyre or Arvad, though in the cast of their countenances and their complexions they are decided Egyptians. The fact we have now ascertained, that the Upper Arvad of the hieroglyphics is a taunting epithet for the kingdom of the Xoites in the Delta, satisfactorily explains all these circumstances.

The copy from Ipsambul in Nubia, of the picture of one of these soldiers, will, we trust, not be without interest, now that it is understood that they represent the armies of the kings in whose dominions Israel sojourned in Egypt; and under whose banners the fighting men of Israel marched.

There is a tablet of Ramses, in which he is represented smiting his enemies, on a rock on the northern bank of the Nahr el Kelb, the ancient river Lycus, which was the boundary of Arvad in Canaan to the northward. This, however, must have been executed by his allies the Arvadites of Canaan, and at his command, for it does not appear from the hieroglyphics that he ever penetrated beyond Hadasha in the mountains of the Dead Sea, which is separated from the valley of the Lycus by the whole extent of the land.

How little this war, of which the hieroglyphics boast so loudly, really availed for the pacification of Egypt, appears abundantly in the sequel. Only four years afterwards, the Xoite kingdom was again invaded, and by the very Canaanite nation whose utter discomfiture is paraded in the temple-picture, namely, Sheth, or Moab and Ammon. The principal cities in the Delta were in the hands of Moab when Ramses arrived there. This is the evident tenor of the narrative of the war which still exists.* Israel, now very powerful in the Delta, would certainly take no part in a war against their kindred, the descendants of Lot :—a circumstance which amply accounts for the success of the invasion. Ramses came as a pacificator. One of the terms of it was, all but certainly, the marriage of the heir to the Xoite throne with a princess of Moab. This sufficiently appears in the hieroglyphic record of the next transaction, in which the Xoite king is no longer entitled King of Upper Arvad, but Prince of Moab.

This transaction is a memorable one in the annals, both of Israel and Egypt. It took place in the twenty-first year of the reign of Ramses.

* It is a Papyrus in the British Museum. The Salier Papyrus.

The record of it is a long hieroglyphic inscription on the south external wall of Karnak, in Eastern Thebes. The mode of inscribing this event differs entirely from that of those we have hitherto examined. The history of a war was a picture. It was to commemorate civil and peaceable communications with foreigners, that the present mode was applied. This explanation is required by the style of this singular inscription, which is as grandiloquent against the foreigners, and breathes bloodshed and slaughter as furiously as any battle-piece in Egypt. It was, nevertheless, a treaty of pacification and alliance, offensive and defensive, between Ramses and the kings of *Ar Moab* and *Aroer* ערער , probably at this period the capital cities of the two members of the warlike confederacy of Moab and Ammon. Its name in Egypt was that of its country: *shtin*, "the mountains of Sheth or Siddim." *

The interview between the contracting parties took place at Heliopolis, The terms of the treaty are hinted at in this obscurely-worded document, which is also greatly mutilated. They are confirmed by other cœval monuments. They stand thus:

Egypt conceded to Moab all claim upon any pos-

---

* In Appendix A will be found a synopsis of the principal Canaanite names, written in hieroglyphics, with their identification. Israel had at this time no national name.

session to the eastward of the Phathmetic branch of the Nile. Moab in return conceded to Egypt her pretension to all cities and lands to the westward of this boundary. The names of four of these ceded cities are yet legible. They are Sais in the western Delta, Xois in the central Delta, and Phelbis and Sebennytus in the eastern portion of the same division of Egypt. The gods of both parties sanction the treaty. Athom-ra [i. e. Adam the sun] the god of Heliopolis, appears for Ramses. Ashtoreth, the goddess of Moab, and Astar, the god of Heth, meet him on the other part. An annual interchange of presents between the two powers was also stipulated in token of perpetual amity.

The ratification of this treaty has perished from the inscription, but it appears upon other monuments. It is that of which we have had so many former examples, and which seems to have been universal in ancient Egypt. The king of Ar Moab, who was the Xoite Pharaoh, Si-Phtha, married Thouoris, the daughter of Ramses, and consented to govern in the Delta, his present dominions, as *viceroy*, on the condition, that on the death of his father-in-law he should succeed him as Pharaoh in all Egypt.

The acceptance of these terms evidently implies that the Xoite kingdom was greatly depressed in the days of Si Phtha. In the absence of direct history, we may be sure that the occasion of it would be the close union and sympathy between Israel and Moab, which had reduced the power of the Xoite Pharaoh to a mere shadow, so that he sought the aid of Ramses to save his throne from destruction and the Delta from being made a province of the Moabites. The date of this treaty is therefore beyond doubt that also of the rise of the new king that knew not Joseph; inasmuch as thereby the kingdom of Aphophis was finally merged in that of the Theban Pharaohs.

The back-reckoning which synchronises the histories of Egypt and Israel for the period we have considered, is all that now remains.

In the 21st year of Ramses, he had reigned alone for 16 years.
  The reign of Sethos . . . . . 55 ,,
  Ramses I. . . . . $1\frac{1}{2}$,,
  The ten kings of the 18th dynasty . . 205 ,,
             $277\frac{1}{2}$ years.

This was the interval that had elapsed from the capture of Memphis by Amosis, to the rise of the new king. If we add to this number the 90 years which we assume for the proximate interval between this event and the Exodus, and deduct the sum from 430, the whole duration of the sojourn, it will give us the 64th year of the sojourn for the date of the fall of Memphis, which is 6 years only before the death of Joseph. When we further consider that the durations of the reigns of these Pharaohs are taken from the Greek lists, which are by no means certainties, frequently err, and always in excess, it follows that the death of Joseph and the fall of Memphis (the first great blow to the kingdom of his patron) are very nearly synchronous : which is exactly what the ancient history of the whole world would have led us to anticipate, where the personal character of the ruler had so much to do with the prosperous or adverse circumstances of his kingdom.

NOTE—The single trait of the manners and customs of Israel in Egypt at this epoch, which the Bible has recorded, is their association with the pure worship of the patriarchal tradition, that of these idols of Egypt. This fact is hinted at in the book of Deuteronomy xxix. 16, 17. It is stated distinctly in general terms by the prophet Ezekiel xx. 7, 8. The traces of this their false worship also appear in other passages. They worshipped the steer or ox עֵגֶל. Exod. xxxii. 4, &c. This would doubtless be the bull Mnevis, the sacred animal of On or Heliopolis. The goat likewise was one of the gods of their idolatry שָׂעִיר Leviticus xvii. 7, in which we recognise the sacred animal of the Mendesian nome.

That the worship of Israel should be thus assimilated with that of Egypt, was a natural consequence of their present circumstances. They were the prosperous and thriving subjects of a settled, well-ordered, and tranquil state. They therefore adopted in a measure its religion.

CHAPTER V.

THE KING THAT KNEW NOT JOSEPH.

"AND Joseph died, and all his brethren, and all that generation. And the children of Israel were fruitful and multiplied, and waxed exceeding mighty; and the land was filled with them." Exod. i. 6.

We once more bring the text upon which we are engaged before the reader's eye, in order that he may perceive how exactly and to the minutest particular, all that we have found upon the monuments regarding the last days of the Xoite kingdom in the Delta corresponds with the terms of it. "Israel waxed exceeding mighty:" therefore first Heth is expelled from Egypt. Soon afterwards Arvad also loses his influence there. The circumstances that both tribes had been among the first settlers in the Delta, had assisted Saites in the taking of Memphis, and had also been among the first to make peace with the conqueror after its re-capture by Amosis, availed nothing. They were the hereditary enemies of Israel. They were of another race, and therefore they must depart to make room for the kindred of the reigning tribe, the children of Lot. This result of our inquiry furnishes, we submit, a proof neither wire-drawn nor weak, that we have interpreted aright, both the sacred text and the hieroglyphic inscriptions.

" And the land was filled with them." The entire extent of the kingdom in which Israel sojourned, is the obvious import of this phrase. We shall find no difficulty in demonstrating that Israel was scattered over the whole Delta, and that this district " was filled with them," when we come to consider the events of the Exodus.

" Now there arose up a new king over Egypt, which knew not Joseph.

" And he said unto his people, Behold, the people of the children of Israel are more and mightier than we! Come on, let us deal subtilly with them, lest they multiply; and it come to pass, that when there falleth out any war, he also [Israel] be among those that hate us, and fight against us, and so get the ascendancy over the land." Ver. 8—10.

Israel has now acquired great political influence in the Xoite kingdom. We have already detected the clearly visible traces of it on the cotemporary monuments of Egypt. The present text would suggest the probability that it was the fear of the rapid increase of this influence, that had induced Si-phtha, or his council, to seek the alliance of the Theban Pharaoh, and to submit to the conditions of it.

When Ramses had annexed the Delta to his own monarchy, he found the process going on there, of which the annals of modern colonization furnish us with so many parallel examples. One of the two races that inhabited it was extinguishing the other. The sons of Mizraim were rapidly disappearing before the Abrahamic immigrants that thronged the Delta. Ramses dealt with both the intruding races. Moab, as we have seen, left Egypt under treaty. With Israel his mode of dealing was suggested by the antipathy of races in himself and in his subjects; a perfect hallucination of the mind, and one of all others the least under the control of reason, and the most difficult to assign to any rational cause. Yet has it been a most powerful motive at all periods of the history of man. Sparta and Messene is a familiar example of its prevalence in the days of old; and, not to multiply modern instances, negro slavery in the present day.

"Therefore they did set over them taskmasters to afflict them with their tasks. And they built for

Pharaoh magazines, [fortresses] even Pithom and Rameses." Ver. 11.

This was the beginning of the captivity. The children of Israel have no more in Egypt the immunities which had been granted them by Aphophis in consideration of the counsels and services of Joseph, and which placed them exactly on a level with the native Egyptians. The decree of the 21st of Rameses, deprives them of all these, and places them in the position of sojourners there, as strangers within or without the gates of the cities; thereby rendering them liable to the forced services which were exacted of tribes so situated, according to the practice of the ancient world. The universality of this custom is so perfectly established by another place in the subsequent history of Israel, that we give the passage at length.

" And Hiram the king of Tyre answered in writing, which he sent to Solomon, * * * We will cut wood out of Lebanon, according to all thy need: and we will bring it to thee in floats by sea to Joppa; and thou shalt carry it up to Jerusalem.

" And Solomon numbered all the strangers in the land of Israel, after the numbering wherewith David his father had numbered them; and they were found 153,600.

" And he set 70,000 of them to be bearers of burdens, and 80,000 to be hewers in the mountains,

and 3600 overseers to set the people a work."
2 Chron. ii. 11, 16—18.

It is surprising that the illustration of the bondage in Egypt afforded by this remarkable passage has not before been noticed.

The names of the two strongholds built by the Israelites will now require our attention.

Pithom, פתם. We have elsewhere expressed our conviction that this was the city originally built by Sethos the father of Rameses on the easternmost branch of the Nile, which was named after it the Phathmetic, i. e. Pithometic branch; in the same way as all the other branches took the names of the principal cities on their banks. The hieroglyphic names of this city was 𓌞𓂆𓊪 *p-stmei*, " the lock or seal of Egypt;" written in the Coptic texts, it was *tamiati*, omitting the *p* at the beginning, which is the definite article. It retains the same name to this day, *Damietta*. It is several years since we published this our conviction : * our present inquiry entirely confirms it. The constructions of Israel at Damietta would doubtless consist of extensive fortifications, walls, and other military works.

Ramses, רעמסס. It was the custom of the kings of Egypt, at all times and from the first, to call by their own names the districts or lands reclaimed

* " Egypt, her testimony," &c.

and added to the actual surface of Egypt Proper, by the engineering operations carried on during their reigns, either by themselves or their subjects. In the tombs of the earliest epochs, when the first colonization was yet in progress, the princes of Egypt paraded long lists of fields and plots of ground, all named after the reigning Pharaoh in the inventory of their properties.* Other plots of ground registered in their tombs were named after more ancient kings. By this means the hieroglyphic names of Cechous and Reophis, both of the second dynasty, have been preserved. This consideration establishes the high probability, that the localities in Egypt called Ramses in the books of Moses, were so named after the monarch who had first added them to Egypt. Now we have found that the Delta had been accounted a strange land, and the cities acquired there recorded as foreign conquests, by the Theban Pharaohs, the predecessors of Ramses. So that the act of the 21st of Ramses, whereby the whole of it was annexed to and made a part of Egypt, was in effect analogous to the reclamation of a patch of the desert by means of channels from the Nile. It made an actual addition to the soil of Egypt, and therefore, by invariable prescription,

* History of Egypt, Vol. i.

the Pharaoh who had been the author of it, named the acquired district after himself. We have happily further monumental evidence which reduces this probability to a certainty. In the act of Pharaoh Ramses which adds the Delta to Egypt, he goes to Heliopolis, not under the name in his first ring, [hieroglyph] which was his name in Lower Egypt (*Sesostris*), but under the name in his second ring, [hieroglyph] i. e. *Meiamoun* (the beloved of Amoun), *Ramses*, (he is named in the lists Ramses Meiamun), which was his name in Upper Egypt. A haughty taunt is doubtless implied in this. The newly-acquired district shall be called, not by his name in Lower Egypt (of which nevertheless it forms a part), but by his name in Upper Egypt, thereby asserting the superiority of Thebes his capital over all the cities of Egypt, and of Amun his god over all the gods of Egypt. This was the reason why he named the Delta Ramses. The monumental evidence of the Delta itself is perfectly decisive of the question as to this identity. *There is not a single mound or ruin in any part of the Delta, on which the name of Pharaoh Ramses has not been engraved, and in nearly the whole of them his is the only king's name that occurs at all.* So clear is it that it was after him that the district wherein Israel sojourned was named Ramses. (See Gen. xlvii. 11.)

In the place now before us Ramses is also the name of a city of Egypt built by the Israelites. This was the new capital which Ramses built for Si-Ptha, his son-in-law, and Thouoris his daughter, and named after himself. The site of it bears to this day, and always has borne, the name of Ramses. A few sculptured stones, with the name of the founder, once marked the spot: but they have been destroyed by the barbarism of Mohammed Ali. It is situated on the extreme western border of the Delta, and about midway between the crown thereof and the sea. So that with Pithom by the sea on the opposite border, and Heliopolis at the southern angle (see map), it was well placed for holding the entire Delta in military subjection. The building of fortified camps was that upon which Ramses employed the forced labour of the Israelites, when he first placed them in bondage. These completed, and manned with a strong military force, and Pharaoh was in position to throw off the mask with which the power of the Israelites in the Xoite kingdom had compelled him to cover his first steps against them.

" And as they afflicted them, so they multiplied and grew, and they were grieved because of the children of Israel.

" And the Egyptians made the children of Israel to serve with rigour.

" And they made their lives bitter with hard

bondage, in mortar (asphalt), and in brick, and in all manner of service in the field. All the service wherewith they made them serve was with rigour." Exodus i. 12—14.

The children of Israel are now completely in the position of prisoners of war. They are made to work at the drudgery—the mere brute labour, both of the field and of the city, under task-masters from among themselves, appointed by the Egyptians, and beaten when their gangs fail in producing the required amount of labour. In this consisted the bondage in Egypt, and with certain mitigations, it continued until the time of the Exodus.

The reign of Pharaoh Ramses in Egypt was a very long one. According to the Greek lists, it lasted for sixty-eight years, and there is a tablet in the British Museum which is dated in his sixty-sixth year. As the decree to which we have so often alluded was made in his twenty-first year, it will follow that he held the children of Israel in bondage for forty-seven years.

The actual numbers of the children of Israel, at the time of this beginning of their captivity, are of course unknown. The expression "the land was filled with them," implies, however, that they must have been very many. At the Exodus, when the census of the fighting men was taken, there were upwards of 600,000 men in Israel between the ages of twenty and sixty; but assuredly in the captivity the Israelites would be compelled to begin to work long before the age of twenty, and to continue to labour long after that of sixty. If therefore we put down the number of prisoners of war or bond-slaves, which the policy of Ramses had placed at his disposal, at 500,000, we shall be sure to err considerably in defect. Yet is even this number incomparably out of proportion to any hieroglyphic record of captives that exist on the monuments of Egypt. The whole amount of prisoners taken alive in the wars of Amosis for the recovery of Memphis, scarcely exceeds 2400 (which is by far the greatest number extant). In the histories of other wars, the capture of 15, 10, or even 5 living prisoners, are deemed events worthy of commemoration on the walls of the temples they helped to build, so very generally did the combatants in ancient warfare prefer death on the battle-field to the horrors of captivity.

The works upon which the Israelites were compelled to labour would be in great part of a monumental character, for this was the prevailing taste in ancient Egypt at all epochs. And mechanical science in these times, not extending beyond the inclined plane, and possibly the lever, the quantity of work produced entirely depended upon the number of men whose forced services were at the command of the constructor. The Israelites would be marched in gangs to the quarries, and employed both in the hewing of blocks of stone and granite, and in the transport of them across the desert to Egypt, like the Canaanites in the reign of Solomon. They would also be employed in making bricks of Nile mud, wherewith to build the walls of the huge quadrangular precincts of the temples, and the cloisters for the priests, and the oval cells for the prisoners ◯ which they enclosed. Likewise, in the works actually in progress on the sites of temples, palaces, and other great constructions, very much more depended in these remote epochs upon the application of direct human force, and very much less upon mechanical contrivances, than in subsequent periods. We give a single example of this. The huge blocks and slabs of stone with which the walls were built, and the still more unwieldy masses that formed the architraves of the colonnades, were not raised from the ground by ropes, to workmen upon scaffolds, as in modern architecture. They were heaved and rolled with infinite toil and risk of life and limb, up the inclined surface of huge mounds of Nile mud, by the slaves who were attached to the building.* These labours were never

---

* So completely are many of the halls of the palace of Medinat Abou in Western Thebes, encumbered both within and without with these mounds, that I suspect they were never finished, and consequently the

performed by freedmen for hire in ancient Egypt. They were accounted penal and degrading, and were always wrung by the torture of the lash from slaves, prisoners of war, and malefactors. These circumstances in the customs of ancient Egypt suggest a conclusion of the very last importance for the monumental verification of "the king that knew not Joseph" of the Mosaic narrative. The number of commemorative remains of any Pharaoh being thus entirely dependent upon the amount of forced labour at his command, there must of necessity appear among the ruins of Egypt the name of one Pharaoh distinguished among all his predecessors and successors for the number of existing monuments of his reign, in an excess enormously disproportionate to the memorials of any other king of Egypt, if the Bible narrative be true. We shrink not at all from this alternative. If this be not the case, then is the Bible account of the bondage in Egypt either a fiction or an exaggeration, which we hold to be a sin of a still deeper die against the truthfulness which its own precepts inculcate. But there is a Pharaoh so distinguished among all his fellows on

---

scaffolding has not been removed. Herodotus relates that a man was killed, during the removal of a block of granite, at Sais; and that king Psametichus in consequence ordered it to be left where it was, and not put in its place in the temple. (lib. ii. c. 176.) But this was a modern refinement. The life of a workman was no such important matter in the days of Ramses.

the monuments of Egypt: and to an excess fully commensurate to the amount of human labour at his command, which the Bible assigns to "the king that knew not Joseph;" and this Pharaoh is Ramses, whom we have already identified as the oppressor of Israel from considerations altogether distinct from this, and independent of it.

The excess in the number of the existing monuments of Ramses over those of any other king of Egypt of any epoch, is so great, that the most sober statement of it sounds like exaggeration. The number of kings of Egypt of the Pharaonic period, that is from the foundation of the monarchy by Menes, to its conquest by Alexander the Great, amounts to about 150. The existing monuments of Ramses are more in number, and greater in magnitude and extent, than those of the whole of the rest of the Pharaohs put together. The same fact appears when we descend to the details. Of the nine Pharaonic obeliscs yet existing in the ruins of Rome, and brought thither by the emperors from Heliopolis and other cities in the Delta, six were either completed in the quarry of Ramses, having been begun there by his predecessors, or were executed by him altogether. Of the twenty-three other obeliscs of this epoch which yet exist in Egypt, and in the rest of the world, fifteen bear in like manner the name of Ramses, either alone or in connexion with some of his ancestry.* Of the eight temples which yet remain in the ruins of Thebes, there is but one which Ramses did not either complete or build from the first. His name has also been read on the fragments of other temples which once stood at Thebes, but are now razed to the ground. If we now turn to the localities in the rest of Egypt, in which the name of Ramses has been found, we are thrown into the same predicament as in our account of him in the Delta. There is scarcely a mound of ruins in the whole of Egypt and Nubia, on which the name of Ramses does not appear, either as the builder of a temple to the local divinity, or as the author of extensive additions to one already existing. So that to chronicle them would be pretty nearly to give a list of the whole of the localities where ruins have been found in Nubia, Egypt, and the Delta. Everywhere in the latter district, the name of Ramses stands all but alone. The greater monuments of ancient Egypt preserved in the museums of Europe, bear testimony to the same fact. The number of colossi, andriantes, statues, groups, sphinxes, and other memorials of the reign of Ramses that appears in them is out of all proportion greater than those of any other king of Egypt.

The traditionary account of Ramses preserved by the Greeks, is of an exactly corresponding character.

* Notes on Obeliscs, by J. Bonomi. Trans. Roy. Soc. Lit. vol. i. p. 158.

We have many particulars of his reign in the notices of Egypt, both of Herodotus and Diodorus Siculus. He is named by the first of these authors, Sesostris, and by the latter of them Sesoosis. Both are merely attempts to write the name in his first ring. ⟨hieroglyph⟩ *ra-merois-sothphre,* which in the narratives of the priests to the Greek travellers was abbreviated to *sesothphre.* This word Herodotus hellenized to Sesostris, and Diodorus to Sesoosis; for both authors were ignorant of hieroglyphics, and therefore merely wrote from the ear. He was called Sesostris at Heliopolis and Memphis, where they heard of him, because his name in Lower Egypt was in the first ring. In Upper Egypt, at Thebes, where Germanicus heard of him some time afterwards, he had the name of Ramses, which, being in the second ring, was his name in that division of the monarchy.* ⟨hieroglyph⟩

The testimony of all these ancient authorities regarding Sesostris Ramses is perfectly uniform. He was by far the greatest monarch that ever sate upon the throne of Egypt. He built in every city in Egypt a temple to the city god. (Diod. i. 56.) He made enormous additions to the temple of Ptha at Memphis. The propylon or porch which he built at the entrance, was supported by two andriantes

---

* See Tacitus, Ann. lib. ii. c. 60.

(pillar-like statues) of himself and his queen, each thirty cubits high. (Her. ii. 110. Diod. i. 57.) The statue of himself still remains prostrate, but almost uninjured, on the plain of Metrahenny. His constructions generally were remarkable for the enormous size of the blocks employed in building them. (Her. c. 108.)

Thus fully and clearly is the monumental fame of Ramses corroborated by the testimony of those who visited Egypt 2000 years ago.

We further learn, from these same authorities, many particulars regarding the great works of engineering, accomplished by Sesostris Ramses. He built a chain of fortifications along the entire northeastern frontier of his kingdom, to defend it from the attacks of the Syrians and the Arabs. These extended from Pelusium on the sea, across the desert, to Heliopolis; a distance of 1500 stadia—about 160 English miles. He likewise erected mounds to keep out the waters of the overflow from many cities which had suffered great inconvenience from this cause. His engineering works for the distribution of the waters of the Nile, were of the same colossal character. He intersected the entire district between Memphis and the sea with channels of irrigation so wide and so numerous that he altogether altered the character of that part of Egypt. It became from thenceforth impracticable either for cavalry or war-chariots; whereas before the times of Sesostris Ramses, it had been noted for equestrian warfare. (Diodorus, c. 57.) The older historian, Herodotus, confirms the whole of these particulars. He further states that Ramses measured out the land thus reclaimed in square blocks, and distributed it by lot among his Egyptian subjects (c. 109); clearly implying that the Delta was a new country, and that Ramses was the first to annex it to Egypt. We had already inferred the same fact from the existing monuments of the reign of this monarch.

Thus perfectly in harmony is the testimony of the Greek tradition with that of the cotemporary monuments regarding Sesostris Ramses. He had at his command a very far larger amount of forced human labour than any king of Egypt either before or after him.

The next question that arises in the order of our discussion is, What account do these same authorities give of the circumstances which placed at his command this vast body of slaves?

The priests of the temples carefully explained to Diodorus that no single native Egyptian had put his hand to any one of the great works of Sesostris. They were constructed altogether by the forced labours of his prisoners of war. (c. 56.) This we also might have anticipated; for it had been the

THE KING THAT KNEW NOT JOSEPH. 255

custom at all times. The memory of the builder of the great pyramid (Cheops or Suphis of the fourth dynasty) was infamous in Egypt, because he had employed upon it the forced labour of his own subjects. (Her. ii. 124.) Had Sesostris followed his example, doubtless his memory would have shared the same fate. It would have been execrated, and his monuments defaced.

The priesthood gave always the same account of the vast number of captives in Egypt in the days of Sesostris Ramses. They were the fruits of his victories. We have three versions of their story of his wars given at three different periods: That of Herodotus was related more than 450 B. C. Diodorus was in Egypt about the time of our Saviour; and Tacitus with Germanicus nearly a century afterwards. If we compare the three together we shall find that they are all agreed in the point that Sesostris Ramses spent many of the earlier years of his reign in foreign conquests: but, as we proceed, it is very amusing to discover that the extent of the geographical knowledge of the priestly narrators at each epoch, is the exact measure of the foreign conquests they assign to their hero. According to Herodotus, he embarked on the Red Sea, overran Asia as far as Scythia, and returned home through Europe. (c. 102, 103.) The hero of Diodorus throws all this into the shade. He subdues the whole south coast of Asia as far as India, a country scarcely known to Herodotus. He then marches inland and overruns Europe and Asia in a circuit which everywhere exactly overpasses the extreme limit of the conquests of Alexander the Great. He is made to subdue the nations immediately beyond this limit, whose very names had been before unknown either in Greece or Egypt. (Diod. lib. i. c. 55.) Had the names of any nations still more distant been familiar to them, doubtless their hero would have been sent thither also.

But what are even these to the deeds in arms of the hero of the Theban priesthood a century afterwards, when the Roman prince Germanicus stood before a temple at Thebes, and demanded an explanation of a huge battle-piece sculptured on one of the propyla ? He received for answer, that it was one of the exploits of the great [Sesostris] Ramses, who had left Egypt on foreign conquest at the head of 700,000 fighting men, and had subdued Lybia, Ethiopia, the Medes, the Persians, Bactria and Scythia; holding also in subjection Armenia and Cappadocia, and conquering Bythynia, on the one coast of Asia Minor, and Lycia on the other.* In a word, every tribe, nation, and country in East Africa and Asia which was at that moment contending for its independence with the arms of im-

* Taciti Annales, ii. c. 60.

THE KING THAT KNEW NOT JOSEPH. 257

perial Rome, had, by their account, been thousands of years before made by their hero the tributary of Egypt. These veracious narrators of history did not send their hero to Europe, it is true, and for precisely the same reason that their predecessors at Heliopolis forbore to make him conquer Tyre and Babylon to Herodotus. Germanicus had himself been there, and would therefore have been able to contradict them, from his personal knowledge.

The existing monuments of Egypt happily put us in a position to apply a perfectly conclusive test to these narratives, in which we have already detected such strong *primâ facie* evidence of falsehood. We have explained that of the war at the commencement of the reign of Ramses, no fewer than three different picture-narratives are still in existence, and that one of them (that at Abou Simbel) is all but perfect. In them therefore we have before us the one original, whence all these different versions of the story were read by the priests to their foreign visitors. It was a very inconsiderable and inglorious affair, ending in nothing but concession and pacification. Not a single stronghold was taken, not an ounce of tribute nor one living captive was brought to Egypt. Had such been the case, assuredly they would have been paraded in a triumph; but no such appears in any of the pictures of the campaign. It was apparently a mere march over the desert, a

s

battle and a retreat; never was ancient falsehood more easily detected than this!

The prisoners then, with whom Ramses built the vast constructions that distinguish his reign, were not taken in the wars at the commencement of it. We say so, inasmuch as the cotemporary records of those wars contradict it; which is only to say that they do not declare a thing in itself impossible.

These monumental remains however, enable us to carry the enquiry one step further. No subsequent war took place in the reign of Ramses, of any consequence; certainly none in which he could possibly have taken any great number of captives. The excavation of the speos or cavern-temple at Abou Simbel was not begun until his thirty-eighth year. Yet is its vestibule adorned with the details of this affair at the beginning of his reign. Had any great action of war befallen in this long interval, surely it would have been recorded, and not an old and then almost forgotten event. Some other wars of Sesostris Ramses are in fact mentioned on the monuments, but not one that approaches in importance to this of the fifth year from his accession, the first of his sole reign.

Yet all that the priests told the Greeks and Romans concerning the vast works of Sesostris Ramses in Egypt, was true. The temples whence they read them, stand to this day, and repeat unerringly the same story. Whence then had this man the enormous amount of human labour at his command which enabled him in one life to accomplish more than all the other kings of Egypt put together, who had preceded and followed him for more than 2000 years? The Scripture account of the subtle and deceitful policy whereby the children of Israel were made slaves about this time, presents, we submit, the only possible solution of this wonderful and otherwise perfectly unaccountable anomaly, to which there is no parallel in the monumental history of any other country!

" And the king of Egypt spake to the midwives of the Hebrews, of which the name of the one was Shiprah, and the name of the other Puah.

" And he said, When ye do the office of a midwife to the Hebrew women, and see that [the infant] is a son, then ye kill him; but if it be a daughter then she shall live. But the midwives feared God, and did not as the king of Egypt commanded them, but saved the men-children alive. And the king of Egypt called for the midwives and said to them, Why have ye done this thing, and saved the men-children alive? And the midwives said unto Pharaoh, Because the Hebrew women are not as the Egyptian women; for they are lively, and are delivered ere the midwives come in unto them. Therefore God dealt well with the midwives.

"And the people multiplied and waxed very numerous.

"And it came to pass, because the midwives feared God, that he made them houses." Exod. i. 15—21.

Every branch of the healing art was hereditary, and most strictly prescriptive in Egypt. It was, moreover, so absolutely identified with religion, that its practitioners were all priests. The two personages to whom Pharaoh gave this instruction were Egyptians, as their names import 𓏞𓏛 *Tshiphre* 𓏞𓏛 *Paith*. They were ladies of high rank, and at the head of the college, or guild of their profession throughout all Egypt. They were to issue to the entire body of their subordinates a secret order, for which they were to feign a revelation from the goddess, the patroness of their mystery, *Tun* 𓏞𓏛 * Their fear, however, of the invisible power whom they thus ignorantly worshipped, and their sense of the sacredness of their office, prevented them from obeying the mandate of Pharaoh. They thus subserved the divine purpose, Israel went on increasing, and therefore the divine blessing, giving abundant prosperity to the houses of their husbands, was their visible reward.

"And Pharaoh charged all his people, saying,

* She was the Lucina of the Egyptian Mythology. Her name was Tamar, she was the wife of Noah.

Every son that is born ye shall cast into the Nile, and every daughter ye shall save alive." Exod. i. 22.

Pharaoh now becomes himself religious. All sacrifice was in the first institution vicarious. The sin of the offerer was imputed to the victim. In Egypt this was especially the case, as the ceremonial for the sacrifice of beasts abundantly testifies. The victim was brought to the altar with fire upon it. Wine was poured upon its head. The priest then stabbed it, invoking at the same time the name of the god. He then cut off the head, pronounced curses over it, and threw it into the river. (Herod. ii. 39.) The victims at first had been young persons and children of either sex, but always virgins. They were thrown into the river. (Porphyr. de Abstin. 199 R.)* This was also the case with all the old idolatries. The grand and crowning rite of the entire round of service was a human sacrifice. The better feelings of men in Egypt, and other well-ordered countries, soon revolted against these murderous rites; and before

---

* He here mentions that human sacrifices were offered at Heliopolis up to the time of Amosis, who abolished them, and substituted figures of wax, which were thrown into the river instead of children.

Plutarch seems to have believed that human sacrifices were offered at Elythya (the god of which city was Sevek, the crocodile) even in his time. De Iside et Oscride, c. 73.

the time of Ramses, had substituted beasts or images for living boys or girls; though it is scarcely needful to remark that human sacrifices made a part of the ceremonial of the idolatries of Canaan, Babylon, and other heathen nations, up to their extinction. It would be a fact perfectly familiar to the subjects of Ramses, that it was a direction of the primitive ritual of Egypt, that, on stated occasions, children should be thrown into the Nile in sacrifice. He would therefore find no difficulty in persuading them, that when he commanded the male infants of Israel to be thus immolated, he spake the mind of the gods.

Ramses has now got the victims of his policy at considerable advantage. His strong military force keeps Israel in awe in the Delta. The flower of the manhood of all the tribes is dispersed over the whole of Egypt, and working under the whips of his taskmasters. He has now no more occasion to dissemble. He devotes the entire race to slavery and speedy extinction. The men will soon die out, under the hardships he meditates. The women will be the handmaids and drudges of the Egyptians. Such was his design, which doubtless, he would have accomplished, had not He that fought for Israel, been mightier than either Ramses or his gods.

We have already explained that the infanticidal

decree was probably issued in the interval between the births of Aaron and of Moses.

" And there went a man of the house of Levi, and took a daughter of Levi. And the woman conceived and bare a son ; and when she saw him, that he was a goodly child, she hid him three moons. And when she could no longer hide him, she took for him an ark (basket) of papyrus rushes, and daubed it with asphalt, and put the child therein ; and she laid it in the flags by the river's brink. And his (Amram's) sister stood afar off to see what would be done to him." Exodus ii. 1—4.

The tribe of Levi was at this time in very low estate. The causes of it we must now consider.

Levi was the third son of Leah the wife of Jacob, by a fraudulent trepanned marriage, the result of which wrong the inspired narrative has plainly recorded : Jacob hated Leah. Gen. xxix. 21—34. For the unhappy offspring of such a marriage, the chances of parental tenderness and careful training are but small in any state of society. Where polygamy prevails, they only who have been themselves the witnesses of the abominations of an eastern harem, can have the remotest idea of the incessant tempest of the fiercest and worst passions of our nature, in the midst of which the children of Leah were nurtured. Their mother's wrongs, and how they might be redressed and avenged, were the elements whence their entire characters were to be developed. There is not a single transaction recorded of the children of Leah, in which this fault of their early training does not appear. Hatred of the children of Rachel, contempt for their father, and that fierce, clannish, animal attachment to each other, which led them to hunt in couples, like wolves or hyænas, and to tear in pieces the perpetrators of dishonour upon their sept, by stratagems of which the wild beasts would have been ashamed, had their powers been equal to them, were its bitter fruits.

Even Reuben, though by nature mild, gentle, and amiable, had no more reverence for his father, than to perpetrate upon his house the unpardonable outrage which cost him the primogeniture. Gen. xlix. 3, 4. Judah, possessed of far more natural talent (see Gen. xliv. 14—34), and too shrewd, too sagacious, and too avaricious to compromise himself by overt acts of lust or violence, has left, nevertheless, the melancholy record of his utterly unbridled passions and ill-ruled household, in one of the most revolting passages in the entire volume of revelation. Of Levi and his next brother, their father himself shall speak, and in the spirit of prophecy.

" Simeon and Levi are brethren,
Their swords are weapons of violence.
O my soul, come thou not into their plot,

With their confederacy mine honour be not thou
    united,
For in their wrath they slew the men,
And in their wantonness they houghed the oxen.
Cursed be their anger, for it was fierce;
And their wrath, for it was cruel.
I will divide them in Jacob;
Yea, I will scatter them in Israel."
Gen. xlix. 5—7.

Of the doubtless innumerable instances in which the fierce passions that burnt in the bosoms of these men of blood had burst forth, two only are recorded. Their conspiracy to murder Joseph, we have already considered. The slaughter of the Hivites is even still more revolting. It maintains a bad eminence among the collected histories of the great atrocities that have been committed by man upon the earth. There is yet one aggravating circumstance in it which is not generally understood. They murdered Dinah their sister, as well as her paramour, and the whole of his kindred. There can be no doubt of this. It was this deed amid those of the rest of their lives of rapine, that drew down their father's most emphatic curse upon their guilty heads. This was an occurrence too disgraceful to his own ancestry for Moses to record. No perceptible good purpose moreover would have been answered by the disclosure, and therefore it was graciously permitted him to spread the veil of oblivion over it: but there is every reason to believe that it took place: for Dinah is never mentioned afterwards.

Here then was the sin which brought upon its perpetrators this fearful denunciation of the Divine vengeance; and, moreover, he who spake by the lips of the dying and agonized father when he uttered it, "is not a man that he should lie, neither the son of man that he should repent! Hath he said, and shall he not do it? or hath he spoken, and shall he not make it good?" Its fulfilment however, is no where directly recorded: for the arrangement in the Holy Land whereby Levi had Jehovah and His service for his patrimony was preeminently a blessing; the direct reversal of a curse; as it is invariably styled in the language of Scripture. (See Num. xviii. 20. Deut. x. 8, 9, &c.) It is well known also, no such fate befel Simeon, who was equally included in the malediction.

The prophecy therefore must have received its fulfilment during the sojourn in Egypt; and in the well-known gap in the genealogy of Levi and in the census afterwards, we point to the silent but highly significant evidences of it. The ruffian propensities of these men would soon fulfil their curse without any miraculous interposition, when the death of their father had in some measure freed them from the restraint which his authority had imposed upon them. In order rightly to apprehend this, the state of society which prevailed among the children of Israel in Egypt after his death must be considered.

There is but one passage in the whole Bible in which any event that befel Israel in Egypt after the death of Jacob, and before the rise of the king that knew not Joseph, is recorded. It occurs in the genealogy of Ephraim. 1 Chron. vii. 20—23. The history narrated in it amounts to this: The Ephraimites crossed the desert on a predatory expedition into Philistia, for the purpose of driving off cattle. They were defeated with great slaughter by the men of Gath. Eliad in the direct line from the first-born of Ephraim was among the slain.

This circumstance tells of a state of society in the Delta, on the death of Joseph and the first immigrants, perfectly analogous to that which our knowledge of the elements of which it was composed would have led us to anticipate. It consisted of

I. The Lower Egyptians. The professors of the man-worship of the Pyramids.

II. The Egypto-Canaanites, or Shepherds, their co-religionists and the close imitators of all their customs.

III. The Canaanite rangers of the Desert, the inhabitants of Canaan Proper, and professing its local idolatry.

IV. The children of Israel, now rapidly increasing in numbers.

The transition from barbarism to civilization commenced by the regulations of Joseph at the famine, (above p. 134.) was also in progress at this time, and upon all these classes, for we shall presently find that long afterwards the change was still far from complete. Quarrels, feuds, broils, and deeds of violence would inevitably attend such a state of things, and in the midst of these, the wild fierce propensities of Simeon and Levi would drive them with uncontrollable vehemence. Their sons would also follow them : and close at their heels. Had the government of Egypt been a weak one instead of a strong one, Simeon and Levi might have stood in its annals for great conquerors. But law in Egypt was always very powerful, and society therefore wonderfully peaceable and well-ordered; so that Simeon and Levi would only figure among their cotemporaries as violent, quarrelsome, turbulent men, and their tribe as bad subjects, and troublesome, dangerous neighbours. Retribution would speedily follow. The entire population of every class would rise against them. They would be overpowered, and the laws both of social order and of war would take their course upon them. It was as bond-slaves and prisoners-of-war among the cities and tents of their brethren of the other tribes that Simeon and Levi were divided in Jacob, and scattered in Israel. As we have already explained, the misfortunes of Simeon and Levi during this interval are not recorded, but the fact that they underwent them is very significantly indicated by their places in the census of Israel in the Desert. In the first census, Simeon brings forward 59,300 fighting men, Numb. i. 23., shewing that the increase in his tribe had been at least as rapid as in that of those of his brethren. But the Levites were left out of this census by express command, the reason for which is not given, (verses 47—50.) It appears however, and very clearly, in the following census. The whole of the living males of Levi of all ages, was then only 23,000; considerably less than half the average number of the fighting men (i. e. the men between 20 and 60) of each of the other tribes. Levi therefore had been omitted from the former census, because his numbers were so insignificant, that to have recorded them would have been to set him forth as a reproach in Israel. Simeon also partook in the curse of his progenitor, as this second census shows unmistakably. His 59,300 has dwindled down to 23,000 only,—scarcely the half of the numbers of any one of the rest of his brethren, in the same enumeration. The men of the former census therefore had been far advanced in life, and past the age of prolificness. They fell in the wilderness and left few representatives behind them; for the young men of the tribe had already perished in Egypt.

Amram, the head of the tribe of Levi and his family, are now household slaves attached to one of the palaces of Si Phtha the viceroy of the Delta at Heliopolis. He himself is probably far away from his family, as head of his tribe, and task-master over them in their forced labours in some distant quarry. His wife and sister, with his child, were housed in a wretched hovel in the court of the palace, and worked under the baton of the master of the house.

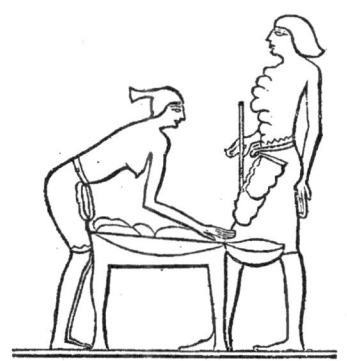

FROM NAHRAI AT BENIHASSAN.

The birth of Moses would not be an event in which their oppressors took any interest. Had they detected the concealment, they would merely have thrown the infant into the river, and beaten the mother:—occurrences too frequent in the house of bondage everywhere to have attracted notice.

Baskets of the papyrus-rush were in common use in Egypt. The word translated *ark* is not Hebrew but Egyptian. תבה. It is the name of the cage in which birds and small animals taken in the chase were kept alive for the purpose of domesticating them, according to the universal practice in these ancient times. It is written ▭ *tb*.

"And the daughter of Pharaoh came down to bathe at the river, and her maidens walked in train or file [after her] along the bank of the Nile. And she saw the basket among the flags, and she sent her hand-maid to fetch it. And when she had opened it she saw the child; and behold the babe wept. And she had compassion on him and said, This is one of the Hebrews' children." verses 5, 6.

This was *Thouoris* ⟨hieroglyphs⟩ the daughter of Pharaoh Ramses, and the wife of Si-Phtha the last of the Xoite kings of the Delta. At this time she was united with her husband in the vice-regency of this division of Egypt. On the death of her father and younger brother, she became queen-regent over all Egypt. The clear monumental indications of this identity will appear in the progress of our enquiry. Thouoris was the priestess of the goddess Hathor,* the wife of Athom (Adam) the tutelary of

---

* Hathor ⟨hieroglyph⟩ was the Egyptian Venus. She was a deification of Eve.

Heliopolis. This is recorded in her tomb. It was, moreover, the universal custom in Egypt. All the princesses of the earliest epochs were also ministers to the worship of the goddesses. The occasion on which she went down in state to the water was, a religious solemnity, the commencement of which was an act of ablution in the sacred waters of the river. It was the festival of the new moon. Jochebed, the mother of Moses, was, as we have seen, one of the household slaves of the palace. She was therefore cognizant of all the movements of the princess. She put the basket with her infant in the place where the procession would approach the bank of the river, and set her husband's sister, and her fellow-slave to watch it afar off. The stage or quay by which the princess would descend to the water's edge would no doubt have an enclosure fenced off from the rest of the river, to keep out the crocodiles which at that time swarmed in the Nile everywhere. Within this enclosure the poor outcast was in comparative safety. All the river was sacred: but it was especially so in those portions of it which ran by the temples and were enclosed off for the many ceremonies of ablution which formed so important and large a portion of the entire ritual of the worship of Ancient Egypt. When the princess first perceived the cage, she probably supposed it might have been left there by some profane person who had dared to commit the act of impiety of "netting the water-fowl of the gods." *   The burst of natural feeling which gushed from her heart when she saw, and heard the cries of, the wretched forsaken infant whom the cruel edict of her father directed her to cast at once out of the enclosure, to be torn in pieces almost before it touched the water by the hungry monsters, who probably enough lay basking and wallowing by dozens together on the sand-banks adjacent, and excited by his cries, already gnashed their teeth for their prey, suggests a very important conclusion. The milk of human kindness had stirred in the breasts of other women in Egypt, besides the princess Thouoris, at the sight of these unoffending and helpless sufferers. The expedient adopted by the mother of Moses was a common one,—and thereby many of the sons of Israel had been rescued from the fate to which the law of Ramses had consigned them. That no great number of infants had perished by this barbarous persecution, the census at the Exodus makes abundantly apparent. The whole tenor also of the subsequent notices of the Egyptians in the books of Moses goes to prove, that the bondage with its attendant cruelties was the work of Pharaoh, and his councillors, not of his subjects. The inspired history

---

* This was one of the forty-two mortal sins of the moral code of Ancient Egypt.

combines moreover with the monuments to acquit Si-Phtha and his illustrious spouse from any very active share in the sorrows of Israel.

"Then said his sister to Pharaoh's daughter, Shall I go and call to thee a nurse of the Hebrew women, that she may nurse the child for thee? And Pharaoh's daughter said to her, Go, and the maid went and called the child's mother. And Pharaoh's daughter said unto her, Take this child and nurse it for me, and I will give thee thy wages. And the woman took the child and nursed it." Verses 7—9.

The name Thouoris in the Greek lists, and the dynasty to which she belonged (the 19th, that of Ramses her father) are all that profane tradition has handed down regarding her.* The history of this illustrious lady is, with these exceptions, altogether monumental. Nevertheless, the few notices they embody, very remarkably confirm the inspired

---

* She is made the third successor of her father Ramses. She was in fact his second successor. She is also said to be a man, but the motive of this change of sex is very obvious. According to the chronological computations of the Greek compilers of these lists, the siege of Troy took place during her reign; and as Homer says, that Polybus was the king of Egypt at that time, of course this is king Polybus; and the account of him which appears in Homer's verses they have appended as an historical notice to the name of Thouoris in the lists. This fact is very instructive. It discloses the notions of writing history that prevailed among the compilers of the Greek tradition regarding Egypt. The name Thouoris is plainly that of a woman, if it be an Egyptian name.

narrative. She had no family, and her husband survived her for nearly forty years. She was queen of all Egypt for a short period on the death of her younger brother Amenephthis. These monumental facts suggest the certainty that she was the eldest daughter of Ramses, and that at the time of her marriage she was of somewhat advanced age, and had been for many years attached to the service of religion as one of the vestals or *pallaces*,* which was the usual fate of the princess royal of Egypt. Her husband, on the other hand, was not a child merely; he was an infant at the time of their marriage. No unusual disparity in these matches of policy and convenience. Probably enough, it had been the troubles consequent upon an infant succession that had furnished the pretext for the interference of Ramses in the affairs of the Xoite kingdom which had issued in this marriage. These circumstances seem to be all implied in the inspired narrative of the transaction before us, which we assume to have taken place in the tenth year of the captivity, and of the marriage of Siphtha and Thouoris. Pharaoh's daughter was evidently a sovereign queen. The edict of her father was nothing to her. She disregarded it openly, deliberately, and in the face of her whole court. Thouoris was at this time sole administratrix of the

* An order of priestesses, generally the daughters of Pharaoh.

monarchy of her husband, who was still a mere child, under tutors and governors. The operation of the law therefore, and its suspension in the Delta, were altogether in her own breast. In regard to the succession, moreover, Thouoris was most painfully situated. In all probability it was by the laws of nature impossible that a child of hers should sit on the throne of her husband, and she had for this reason been selected from among the many daughters of Ramses for the wife of Siphtha. In these circumstances, her public adoption of the outcast infant of a tribe whom the same policy whereby she had been condemned to childlessness, had also doomed to a cruel death, was noble and most womanly.

The circumstances of Amram, the father of Moses, and head of the tribe of Levi, would be materially altered by this event. As nurse of a son of the house of Pharaoh, Jochebed his wife would take rank in Egypt next to the princesses of the blood.

The census of the tribe afterwards, when it entered the holy land, renders it far from improbable that the mitigations which would follow upon this change in the circumstances of its head, had saved it from extinction.

" And the child grew; and she [his mother] brought him unto Pharaoh's daughter, and he became her son. And she called his name Moses;

and she said, Because I drew him out of the water." Verse 10.

The name is an Egyptian one. It was written thus 〔hieroglyphs〕 litt. *nu-mu-shf*, " received, [taken] from Nu (Noah) of the waters." This name, like Sesostris, was abbreviated in common parlance to *mu-she*, as the Hebrews wrote it.*

" And it came to pass in the days when Moses was grown up." Verse 11.

" And Moses was learned in all the wisdom of the Egyptians, and was mighty in words and deeds. And it came to pass when he was full forty years old." Acts vii. 22, 23.

The collation of these two inspired passages elicits the fact, that an interval of forty years elapsed after the last event recorded, during which nothing has been written regarding the history of Israel. It is incumbent upon us to supply this interval from the monumental history of Egypt.

The commencement of the captivity falling upon the 21st of Ramses, the birth of Moses took place in his 31st, or thereabout, by our calculation. As

---

* In Manetho's account of the Exodus, preserved by Josephus, (Cont. Apion. I. 25.) his name is said to be *Osarsiph*, or Moses. The former name is 〔hieroglyphs〕 *oshir-shf* " taken from Osiris; " and its use by Manetho, shows him to have been the votary of a philosophic modification of the ancient superstition which was first invented in his days. It made Osiris to represent every thing *wet*, and Seth or Typhon, every thing *dry*.

the whole reign of Ramses lasted for 66 or 68 years, it follows that 35 or 37 years of this unrecorded interval were occupied by the termination of it. The particular of this reign, directly pertinent to the history of Israel, namely, his identification with "the king that knew not Joseph," has been already sufficiently discussed. The following tabular arrangement of all the dated monuments of it that are known to exist, is instructive as to its general history :

Year of the reign of Ramses.

1st tablet at the quarry of Gebel Silsili commemorating the hewing of stone for a temple 4
1st war (with Sheth) . . . 5
  the first of his sole reign.
2nd war with Asiatics (papyrus at Turin) 8
3rd war (with Sheth) Karnak . . 9
4th war with Asiatics (Sallici papyrus) 14
Pacification with Sheth . . . 21
  Commencement of captivity.
2nd tablet at Gebel Silsili . . 30
3rd tablet at Gebel Silsili on the occasion of hewing stone for a temple . . 34
The speos at Abou Simbel in Nubia commenced 35
4th tablet at Gebel Silsili . 37
  Hewing stone for a building.

THE KING THAT KNEW NOT JOSEPH. 279

	Year of the reign of Ramses.
Speos of Abou Simbel completed	38
5th tablet at Gebel Silsili	40
6th ditto ditto	44
Funeral tablet at Florence, one of the officers of Ramses who died in the year of his reign	62
Tablet at the British Museum	66

Some historical deductions of considerable interest arise from this synopsis of the dated cotemporary monuments of the reign of Ramses.

I. All the wars of Ramses took place in the first twenty years of his reign.

This is conformable with the Greek tradition.

II. The treaty with Sheth was of the definite and important character which its hieroglyphic record states it to have been. It was a permanent pacification. No war occurred afterwards during the reign of Ramses.

Here again the Greek tradition is literally correct. There was peace in Egypt with all the world throughout the latter years of the reign of Sesostris. So many were his captives, that all the drudgery of Egypt was performed by them, and never did the country enjoy such a measure of temporal prosperity as at this period.

III. It was the 30th year of his reign that he

began to hew blocks of red sand-stone from Gibel Silsili for the construction of temples at Thebes. This is, according to our computation, within a year of the birth of Moses. We have assumed that the building of the fortifications of Pithom and Ramses, and the vast engineering works wherewith he intersected the Delta, would occupy about this period ; and at this time it is very supposeable that Ramses would permanently reside either at Heliopolis or Xois. Here, in the midst of the Israelites he would have abundant opportunities of observing their rapid increase, notwithstanding his grievous oppression of them, and notwithstanding the murderous instructions he secretly gave to Shiphrah and Puah. We have already ascertained that his infanticidal decree must have been issued in the interval between the birth of Aaron and that of Moses. We now find that the year before the latter event, Ramses was in all probability in Upper Egypt superintending the building of the temples of Thebes. Nothing is more probable than that soon after passing this revolting law he should have fled from the odium which it evidently excited in his subjects of all ranks in that part of his dominions where it came into operation, leaving the execution of it to his officers under the viceregency of his daughter.

The entire independency of the edict which Tho-

THE KING THAT KNEW NOT JOSEPH. 281

uoris displayed in the adoption of Moses, is also well accounted for by this date. Ramses, her father, had at this time finally left the Delta to her sole government, probably only returning thither afterwards on rare occasions: for we find that the great constructions of the following years of his reign were all in Upper Egypt and Nubia.

IV. The war of the 5th of Ramses (the first of his sole reign) was assuredly the great military exploit of his life: inasmuch as he has left three repetitions of it on three of his greatest constructions; the first of which he did not begin to build until more than thirty years afterwards.

V. The same monumental facts reduce to a simple impossibility the statement of the Greek traditions, that they were prisoners of war who built the constructions of Ramses.

The condition of Israel in Egypt must necessarily have undergone considerable mitigation after the adoption of Moses by Pharaoh's daughter. The silence of the inspired historian implies this fact, which appears still more clearly in the constant murmurings of the entire body of the people while in the wilderness after the Exodus, and the frequent conspiracies among them to displace Moses and return to Egypt under the leadership of the heads of the tribes. Had the cruelties and horrors which marked the commencement and termination of the captivity, been in no way mitigated in the interval of the century for which it lasted, surely the remnant of so unparalleled a persecution would never have conspired against their liberator, to return to the lash of the taskmaster and the house of bondage!

The fact thus strongly implied in the history of Israel, we now find to be rendered probable by the monumental history of Egypt. The government of the Delta seems at this time to have been a viceroyalty, administered from the throne of the kings who had known Joseph, and by a princess who had shown by her adoption of Moses, her sympathy with the sentiments of her predecessors. The immediate author of the captivity had left the Delta to her sole regency. So that, not only did the infanticidal edict fall into utter disuse, (we never hear of it again in the inspired narrative) but the circumstances of the Israelites would be similar to their condition under the Xoite kings, with the exception that they were now strangers in Egypt, and that their forced services were in constant requisition at the quarries, the temples, and other public works which were in progress in every city throughout the land of Egypt.

The date of the death of Ramses is the only particular concerning it, preserved in the history of Egypt, traditive or monumental. His successor was named Amenemnes, or Amenephthis, in the lists. The monuments declare him to have been his thirteenth son. He wrote his name as king of Egypt thus.

The monumental history of this monarch is very scanty. His traditive history is confined to a single fact. He reigned in Egypt for five years only. There is no evidence that the death of Ramses exercised any particular influence on the Delta, or that Amenephthis interfered at all with the viceroyalty of his sister. At his death, however, many changes took place, which brought the period now under review to its termination in the forty-second year of the age of Moses, which corresponds with the " full forty years old " of the inspired narrative.

CHAPTER VI.

MOSES IN MIDIAN.

"And it came to pass in those days when Moses was grown, that he went out unto his brethren and looked on their burdens." Exod. ii. 11.

"And when [Moses] was cast out, Pharaoh's daughter took him up and nourished him for her own son. And Moses was learned in all the wisdom of the Egyptians, and was mighty in words and in deeds. And when he was full forty years old it came into his heart to visit his brethren the children of Israel." Acts vii. 21—23.

"By faith Moses when he was come to years refused to be called the son of Pharaoh's daughter; chusing rather to suffer affliction with the people of God, than to enjoy the pleasures of sin for a season. Esteeming reproach for Christ greater riches than the treasures of Egypt, for he had respect unto the recompence of reward." Heb. xi. 24—26.

This is the whole of the direct inspired history, and of the traditions which have had the subsequent sanction of inspiration regarding the life of Moses, at the epoch at which we have now arrived. These inspired writers throw, at the least, as much light on the cotemporary monumental history of Egypt, as they receive illustration from it. We do not hesitate to give it as a marvellous coincidence, that the death of Amenephthis took place when Moses was forty-two years old; and that on this event the aged and childless princess, his foster-mother, became Queen of all Egypt. So that the history of Egypt at this epoch—faintly traced upon its cotemporary monuments—renders not only possible, but highly probable, that which the Bible states to have been the fact. When Thouoris became queen of all Egypt, she proposed to inaugurate Moses her foster-son as her successor and co-regent with her husband on her demise. But Moses refused to "be called the son of Pharaoh's daughter," and thereby to be afterwards Pharaoh himself. We now understand at what a sacrifice of all the noblest and most exalting ties and ambitions of human nature, Moses chose the "reproach of Christ;" and perceive the extent to which his refusal illustrates the power of the faith, which was his motive in doing so.

And he [Moses] spied an Egyptian smiting an

Hebrew, one of his brethren. And he looked this way and that way, and when he saw no man, he slew the Egyptian, and hid him in the sand. And when he went out the second day, behold two men of the Hebrews strove together; and he said to him that did the wrong, Why smitest thou thy fellow? And he said, Who made thee a prince and a judge over us? Intendest thou to kill me as thou killedst the Egyptian? And Moses feared and said, Surely this thing is known. Now when Pharaoh heard this thing he sought to slay Moses. But Moses fled from the face of Pharaoh." Exodus ii. 11—15.

The events in the history of Egypt which have taken place since we last considered it, are required to harmonize this narrative with that which precedes it. It is, as we have explained, only by the aid of the facts contained in the inspired narrative that the history of Egypt at this time can be written.

Thouoris seems from the first to have married the infant heir to the throne of the Xoites, on the condition that on his father's death she should succeed to the throne of all Egypt. As, however, was too often the case, she, together with a host of her brothers and sisters, were passed by, by her father in his extreme old age, and his thirteenth son Amenephthis, a very young man, was named his successor. On the death of this young king, after a short and monumentally inglorious reign of five years, Thouoris was called to the throne ; probably by the states of Egypt, to redress the wrong which her father's appointment had done her. It would seem from the coincidence of dates, that her first act on her accession was prompted by her affection for her foster-son. His refusal to be named her successor, would not fail to be a deep mortification and grief to her, however fully she might enter into and appreciate the purity of his motives. She seems from the monuments to have left to her husband, now Pharaoh Siphtha, the administration of the affairs of Lower Egypt, and to have retired to Thebes; when she not only appointed for her successor the infant son of Amenephthes, but directed that the government should be carried on in his name; constituting Siphtha, her husband, his tutor, and co-regent during life. Queen Thouoris seems thenceforward to have led a religious life at Thebes; interfering but little with affairs of state, and occupying herself in the decoration of the tomb for herself and her husband, which is more tastefully and elaborately furnished than any other in the valley of the kings, and in other works of a devotional character: such being the nature of all the existing memorials of her reign.

After the departure of his foster-mother, Moses still resided at the court of Pharaoh Siphtha, as a prince of Egypt. At this time the metropolis and ordinary residence of Siphtha seems to have been the city of Ramses in the Western Delta.

It would be in some official capacity that Moses went down to the opposite border of Egypt to inspect the forced labours of the Israelites. The description of these labours in the passage before us, shews that we have correctly estimated the position of Israel in Egypt at this time. All the men of Israel were at all times liable to be called out to serve in the gangs of workmen, but there were no circumstances of aggravation and insult added to this coercion by the government. So that they were not in a worse position than the Canaanites in the Holy Land in Solomon's reign. Their sufferings arose from acts of individual oppression and cruelty from the Egyptian officers and the taskmasters of their own brethren that were over them. They were not systematically enacted as before and afterwards.

The scene which took place when Moses "looked upon the burdens of his brethren," affords clear evidence that he had hitherto been a stranger to the actual sight of their sufferings. It is, moreover, one that would hardly fail to have taken place on the first visit of a high-minded, kindly-natured man, hitherto only accustomed to command, to the house of bondage. This circumstance which excited Moses, is one of daily, hourly occurrence at all times, and in all places, where man is slave to man. Upon any pretext, or no pretext, a slave is laid down, and cruelly, mercilessly beaten by his tyrant. It is a hard matter! (we speak from personal experience in the land of Egypt and elsewhere) for a man to restrain himself from acts of violent retribution, to whom the spectacle is yet a strange one; even when the tyrant is of his own race, and the slave a stranger. We can therefore readily understand that the indignation which would fire the soul of Moses at the sight of one of his own brethren thus maltreated by an Egyptian, should burst forth uncontrollably, and that, seizing the opportunity when none but Israelites were present, he should cut down the oppressor with his scymitar and bury him in the sand. The act was a perfectly natural one:—a consideration which strongly corroborates the truth of the narrative, though (as we scarcely need observe,) this consideration by no means justifies the act itself.

The transaction of the following day disclosed the extent of the error into which the impetuosity of Moses had betrayed him. The narrative is again wonderfully truthful. A Hebrew task-master, in sedulous imitation of his superiors, is avenging upon the person of one of his unoffending brethren under him, the stripes which still smart on his own. How exactly this is true wherever slavery prevails, they who are most conversant with it will be best able to declare. Even to this day, in every slave-plantation in the west, in every slave-bazaar and compound in the east, the cruellest task-masters are the slaves themselves over their fellow-slaves. The expostulation of Moses with the oppressor, shews him the position in which his rash act has placed him. The Hebrew task-masters will confederate with the Egyptian officers, and be the first to impeach him as a violator of the laws of Egypt. If Moses had seen much of slavery, he might have been well assured of this, though the threat of the Hebrew task-master had never been uttered. It is the one circumstance that perpetuates slavery all over the world. The slaves in authority are in league with the masters against their fellow-slaves.

In the eye of the law in ancient Egypt, as in every well-ordered country, human life was very precious. It awarded the punishment of death not to the shedder of blood merely, but to the bystander also, who, seeing the outrage, forbore to defend the sufferer to the peril of his own life.* The impeachment of Moses therefore which immediately followed, left no choice to Pharaoh Siphtha but the issue of the order for his arrest and trial. Moses, however, had notice of this in time to escape into the desert, and leave the bounds of Egypt, according

* Diod. Sic. i. § 77.

to the invariable practice of accused parties in that country at the present day.

"And Moses fled from the face of Pharaoh, and dwelt [sate down, rested] in the land of Midian, and he sate by a well." Exod. ii. 15.

Midian crossed the peninsula of Sinai, and extended along the eastern coast of the gulf of Akaba. It was probably at some mine or quarry in the desert that Moses had killed the Egyptian officer. The Midianites were descendants from Abraham (Gen. xxv. 2); they were therefore akin to Israel, which was doubtless the reason why Moses sought refuge in their country.

"Now the priest-prince * of Midian had seven daughters: and they came and drew water, and filled the troughs to water their father's flock. And the shepherds came and drave them away, but Moses stood up and helped them, and watered their flock. And when they came to the seer [prophet] their father, he said, How is it that ye are come so soon to-day? And they said, An Egyptian delivered us out of the hand of the shepherds: and also drew water enough for us, and watered the flock. And he said unto his daughters, And where is he? Why is it that ye have left the man? Call him that he may eat bread. And Moses was content to dwell

* See Genesis xiv. 18.

with the man, and he gave Moses Zipporah his daughter.

"And she bare him a son, and he called his name Gershom; for he said, I am a stranger in a strange land." Exod. ii. 16—22.

These transactions took place out of Egypt: they are merely quoted here to continue the narrative.

"And it came to pass after many days, that the king of Egypt died. And the children of Israel sighed by reason of their bondage." ver. 23.

Another long period has now elapsed, during which no single event is recorded in the history either of Israel or Egypt. Its termination is marked by the death of the Pharaoh who had sought the life of Moses. In consequence of this event the sufferings of Israel in Egypt were fearfully aggravated, so that "they sighed by reason of their bondage." The phraseology of the passage leaves no doubt on this head. After the death of the king, Israel sighed by reason of his bondage, as he had not sighed while Pharaoh lived. The circumstances in the history of Egypt which occasioned this change, we have now to consider.

The period we find, Acts vii. 30, to be forty years proximately, or in round numbers. This is assuredly the sense in which the epochs in the life of Moses are to be interpreted. For, as has been very justly remarked,* to assume an exact tripartite division of his life into three equal periods, is also to assume a miraculous interference on a very trivial occasion, and for no conceivable purpose; inasmuch as without it the events of human life never do, in this manner, conform to the rules of arithmetic.

The Pharaoh who had died, we have ascertained to be Siphtha, the last of the line of the Aphophean kings. This his place in the annals of Egypt (for which it is incumbent upon us to explain that we are ourselves alone responsible) solves entirely the many anomalies that otherwise beset his monumental history. He is not named in the lists, yet assuredly he was a king in all Egypt, and for a very long period. He was evidently cotemporary with Ramses, and one of his near successors on the throne. He was also of the family of Ramses, for in a tablet at Gournou he worships Ramses and his progenitors as his ancestry. Nevertheless, he is the only one of this entire line of Pharaohs who has rejected the name of Amun from both the rings of his royal titles, styling himself in the first of them the worshipper of Ra at Heliopolis, and in the second, of Ptha at Memphis. Thus utterly ignoring the existence of Thebes, the third capital of Egypt, and, in the days of the illustrious line of kings to which he claims affinity, the greatest of all, and the only royal

* Bunsen's Egypt's Place, vol. i.

residence, ["light of the sun, proved by the sun,"] ["one with Phtha, Siphtha *the son of Ptha*"] and identifies himself altogether with the northern portions of the monarchy. These circumstances are all explained by the assumption that he was the infant son of the last of the Xoite kings, and that Ramses took advantage of the death of his father to annex his dominions to the crown of Egypt, by espousing Siphtha to his daughter Thouoris, to whom he confided the viceroyalty of the Delta in the name of her infant husband.

We have already explained that, on the refusal of the crown of Egypt by Moses, Thouoris, his foster-mother, went to Thebes, when she appointed the infant son of Amenephthis his successor in the monarchy, administered the government in his name, and employed herself in works of piety. Her husband probably remained in the Delta.

The character of Siphtha appears, from the few monuments of his reign that are known to exist, to have been precisely that which the inspired narrative leaves to be inferred regarding him. He was an unambitious, mild, humane monarch, very likely to have acquiesced in the arrangement whereby his queen adopted for her son the Hebrew boy who probably had been his playmate in their childhood, inasmuch as after the death of Thouoris, and up to the period of his own death, we find him always religiously conforming to the still more humiliating arrangement of which she also was the author, and which imposed upon him the cares and toils of sovereignty, but conferred all its honours upon her infant nephew.

Thouoris survived for seven years only the refusal of Moses to be her son and heir.* She seems to have from the first associated the infant her nephew, whom she made her successor, with her in the sovereignty; and also to have administered the kingdom in his name. So that his reign dates its commencement from his own birth two years before the death of his father, while she and her husband appear merely as his co-regents.

Except their tomb, the extent and elaborate beauty of which we have often mentioned, the memorials of the reign of Siphtha and Thouoris are but very few, and they altogether of a religious character, commemorating acts of worship to their ancestry in the temples of Thebes. They seem to have employed the Israelites in the completion of the many temples and other constructions begun by their father, and which they were contented to complete in his name, omitting their own altogether. The abundance of the monuments of Ramses requires some such circumstance, notwithstanding the

* Lists of Manetho, Dynasty XIX.

number of workmen at his command, and the length of his reign. They may also have proceeded with works of utility, which leave no monumental trace behind them, but nevertheless, there cannot be a doubt that the sufferings of the captivity were considerably mitigated when Siphtha and Thouoris had the sole rule in the Delta.

We find from the passage before us, that the death of Siphtha took place in the 39th year of the reign of his nephew and co-regent, which was likewise 37 years after the death of Amenephthis, and 30 years after that of Queen Thouoris.

The name of this Pharaoh was written in hieroglyphics, (*rois kru ra mn-amun*) (watcher of the transmigrations of the sun, *one* with Amun); (*stei mn-pth*) (*Sethos* one with Phtha.) It appears from the comparison of the lists with the Scripture narrative, that Sethos was born when his father Amenephthis had been for three years king of Egypt; and that on his father's death, two years afterwards, he was adopted by Queen Thouoris, his aunt, who not only made him king of Egypt from his birth, but carried on the affairs of government in his sole name, constituting herself and her husband Siphtha his guardians and co-regents during life. In the ninth year of his age and reign, his foster-mother died. The circumstance that both Moses and Pharaoh Sethos II. had been the adopted sons of this queen of Egypt, we shall find hereafter to be one well worthy of note.

The temple-records of Egypt, which were quoted by the historian Josephus,* make Sethos II. to have been a great warrior, who left his own dominions at the commencement of his reign to conquer foreign countries, and committed the affairs of the monarchy altogether to his relatives and councillors. We have already read the same story from the same records of the grandfather of this king, and detected its utter falsehood. The monuments are equally explicit in the present instance. They give not even a shadow of support to the tradition. So that this fable of the warrior was the screen wherewith the lying priests of the Egyptian idolatry covered over equivocal and disgraceful transactions in the reigns of their ancient kings. Sethos II. was an irreligious, vicious, idle profligate. His tomb, in the valley of the kings, is the instinctive chronicle of his infamy. The excavation and decoration of the tomb of a king of Egypt began on the day of his accession, and ended on the day of his death. The superintendance and direction of it were duties so sacred, that even Pharaoh could not perform them by proxy. His own presence, his own directing mind must be there, or the work stood still. At the instant of his death, it ceased altogether. In what-

* Contra Apion. i. 15.

ever state of imperfection it might be, no stroke of
the chisel, no trace of the pen, passed over it again.
The mummy of Pharaoh was laid in the vault—
finished or unfinished—and the tomb was closed.
So that there is much history to be read in the wild
and desolate valley of the kings, in the desert of
Western Thebes. The long reign of a pious monarch is marked by a suite of corridors and halls
excavated in the mountain, to an extent which
threatens the stability of the superincumbent mass,
and gorgeously and elaborately decorated with hieroglyphics and reliefs, like the vault of Sethos I.*
A reign, suddenly terminated by untimely death,
appears in the abrupt cessation of works in progress, promising great excellence and beauty when
complete, like the tomb of Amenephthis.† It is
thus that the tomb of Sethos II.‡ writes his history.
In grandeur of design his tomb is equal to the
largest in the valley, and an immense range of corridors and halls is excavated : so that this Pharaoh
had at his command a supply of labour equal to the
greatest of his peers. The parts of it also that are
finished are of exquisite execution ; so that he had
no lack of skilled artists. Nevertheless this vault
is distinguished from all the other tombs in the
valley by a very remarkable peculiarity. No single

* No. 17, of Sir G. Wilkinson's enumeration.
† Ibid. No. 8.   ‡ Ibid. No. 15.

corridor or hall throughout it was ever finished, though they were all begun. I was not able to discover even a wall which had been completed, except perhaps the roof of the inclined corridor, which forms the entrance. Yet in every part there are bits which have been finished with the utmost care; the rest of the picture of which they formed a part, being merely traced with minium or charcoal on the stucco. The opposite wall of the apartment has not been stuccoed or even dressed preparatory to it. It has been merely roughed out with the chissel, and the chips and fragments encumber the floor of the hall to this day. This is the case with the entire tomb, from its entrance to the last or *golden hall*, ⌸ in which stood the sarcophagus. It is not so, we repeat it, with any of the other tombs in the valley. Up to the furthest point they are all finished with the utmost care. It is only there that the work of decoration ceases suddenly: making it evident that the commencement of each of the halls in the tomb of Pharaoh, took place on the recurrence of some stated festival; and that it was his duty to see that in the interval, the works both of excavation and decoration, were complete, and that all was ready to proceed with the new work. In this his duty, which was esteemed of the most sacred and awful obligation in ancient Egypt, Sethos II. failed altogether. The work in his tomb was merely continued during the actual celebration of the festival: that ended, and all the workmen were withdrawn, save a few unskilled drudges to carry on the excavation, that the treasure which the states of Egypt had assigned to him for this purpose might be lavished in sensual indulgences. The skilled workmen at his disposal would be hired out to his princes and nobles, and their wages would be speedily absorbed in the same insatiable vortex. There is no other mode of accounting for these appearances in the tomb of Sethos II.

At the period now under review, Sethos II. had been for thirty-seven years actual king of Egypt. That his reign was a long one, appears from his sarcophagus as well as his tomb. This receptacle was most elaborately and exquisitely finished. With the means of working the hard red granite at the disposal of ancient Egypt, it must have employed any number of workmen that could be engaged upon it at the same time, for many years. The fragments lie scattered to this day on the floor of the last hall in his tomb, together with the chips that have fallen there from the chisels of the excavators, the rude marks of which still remain on the unsightly walls of this mere hole in the rock. The name of Sethos II. is not unfrequently written on the great remains of Thebes and other cities throughout Egypt, but everywhere they are upon trifling additions to the constructions of his ancestors.

The death of Siphtha, which is recorded in the inspired narrative, would render it needful that Sethos II. his co-regent, and now sole king of Egypt, should visit the Delta. Probably enough it would be the first time that he had been in that part of his dominions, where his guardians had been supreme for so many years.

Assuming this very probable circumstance, the first thing that would attract the attention of Sethos on his arrival in the Delta, would be the utter failure of his grandfather's design for the extermination of the strangers that sojourned therein. Notwithstanding nearly a century of oppression, the thousands of Israel swarmed every where, and the land was filled with them.

He would also not fail to observe the great falling off in the products of their forced labours which had marked the reign of his uncle and co-regent, as compared with the works wrung from the Israelites by the tyrannies of Ramses his grandfather. The crowd of courtiers, flatterers, and needy adventurers that always surround a sovereign, would help on this impression. They would remind him of the leaning of Siphtha towards the liberal policy of the Aphophean Pharaohs his ancestors, and of the mild gentle character of his queen. The weak humanities towards Israel, which had characterised their reigns, would furnish a constant theme for their banter, and jibe, and ridicule, and the defect in the work of Israel, of their indignation. Under the pressure of these circumstances the character of Sethos II. underwent a very common change. The reckless careless profligate, suddenly started forth the morose inexorable tyrant. The most stringent and cruel orders were issued to the officers over the forced labours of the strangers. No mitigation of their toils was to be allowed for a moment. Let them die under their burdens,—no matter. The lash of the taskmaster resounded every where, and there was a great cry throughout the land of Egypt.

" And the children of Israel sighed by reason of their bondage, and they cried,

" And their cry came up unto God by reason of their bondage. And God heard their groaning, and God remembered his covenant with Abraham, with Isaac, and with Jacob. And God looked upon the children of Israel, and God had respect unto them." Exod. ii. 23—25.

" Now Moses kept the flock of Jethro his father-in-law, the priest of Midian: and he led the flock to the back-side of the desert, and came to the mountain of God, even to Horeb.

" And the angel of the Lord appeared unto him in a flame of fire out of the midst of a bush: and he looked, and, behold, the bush burned with fire, and the bush was not consumed. And Moses said,

I will now turn aside, and see this great sight, why the bush is not burnt. And when the Lord saw that he turned aside to see, God called unto him out of the midst of the bush, and said, Moses, Moses. And he said, Here am I. And he said, Draw not nigh hither: put off thy shoes from off thy feet, for the place whereon thou standest is holy ground. Moreover he said, I am the God of thy father, the God of Abraham, the God of Isaac, and the God of Jacob. And Moses hid his face; for he was afraid to look upon God.

" And the Lord said, I have surely seen the affliction of my people which are in Egypt, and have heard their cry by reason of their taskmasters; for I know their sorrows; and I am come down to deliver them out of the hand of the Egyptians, and to bring them up out of that land unto a good land and a large, unto a land flowing with milk and honey; unto the place of the Canaanites, and the Hittites, and the Amorites, and the Perizzites, and the Hivites, and the Jebusites. Now, therefore, behold, the cry of the children of Israel is come unto me: and I have also seen the oppression wherewith the Egyptians oppress them. Come now therefore, and I will send thee unto Pharaoh, that thou mayest bring forth my people the children of Israel out of Egypt.

" And Moses said unto God, Who am I, that I

should go unto Pharaoh, and that I should bring forth the children of Israel out of Egypt? And he said, Certainly I will be with thee; and this shall be a token unto thee, that I have sent thee: When thou hast brought forth the people out of Egypt, ye shall serve God upon this mountain. And Moses said unto God, Behold, when I come unto the children of Israel, and shall say unto them, The God of your fathers hath sent me unto you; and they shall say to me, What is his name? what shall I say unto them? And God said unto Moses, I AM THAT I AM: and he said, Thus shalt thou say unto the children of Israel, I AM hath sent me unto you. And God said moreover unto Moses, Thus shalt thou say unto the children of Israel, Jehovah the God of your fathers, the God of Abraham, the God of Isaac, and the God of Jacob, hath sent me unto you: this is my name for ever, and this is my memorial unto all generations. Go, and gather the elders of Israel together, and say unto them, Jehovah the God of your fathers, the God of Abraham, of Isaac, and of Jacob, appeared unto me, saying, I have surely visited you, and seen that which is done to you in Egypt: and I have said, I will bring you up out of the affliction of Egypt unto the land of the Canaanites, and the Hittites, and the Amorites, and the Perizzites, and the Hivites, and the Jebusites, unto a land flowing with milk and honey.

And they shall hearken to thy voice: and thou shalt come, thou and the elders of Israel, unto the king of Egypt, and ye shall say unto him, The Lord God of the Hebrews hath met with us: and now let us go, we beseech thee, three days' journey into the wilderness, that we may sacrifice to the Lord our God.

" And I am sure that the king of Egypt will not let you go, no, not by a mighty hand. And I will stretch out my hand, and smite Egypt with all my wonders which I will do in the midst thereof; and after that he will let you go. And I will give this people favour in the sight of the Egyptians: and it shall come to pass, that, when ye go, ye shall not go empty: but every woman shall borrow of her neighbour, and of her that sojourneth in her house, jewels of silver, and jewels of gold, and raiment: and ye shall put them upon your sons, and upon your daughters; and ye shall spoil the Egyptians." Exod. iii.

" And Moses answered and said, But, behold, they will not believe me, nor hearken unto my voice: for they will say, The Lord hath not appeared unto thee. And the Lord said unto him, What is that in thine hand? And he said, A rod. And he said, Cast it on the ground. And he cast it on the ground, and it became a serpent; and Moses fled from before it. And the Lord said unto Moses, Put

x

forth thine hand, and take it by the tail. And he put forth his hand, and caught it, and it became a rod in his hand: That they may believe that the Lord God of their fathers, the God of Abraham, the God of Isaac, and the God of Jacob, hath appeared unto thee.

"And the Lord said furthermore unto him, Put now thine hand into thy bosom. And he put his hand into his bosom: and when he took it out, behold, his hand was leprous as snow. And he said, Put thy hand into thy bosom again. And he put his hand into his bosom again; and plucked it out of his bosom, and, behold, it was turned again as his other flesh. And it shall come to pass, if they will not believe thee, neither hearken to the voice of the first sign, that they will believe the voice of the latter sign. And it shall come to pass, if they will not believe also these two signs, neither hearken to thy voice, that thou shalt take of the water of the river, and pour it upon the dry land: and the water which thou takest out of the river shall become blood upon the dry land.

"And Moses said unto the Lord, O my Lord, I am not eloquent, neither heretofore, nor since thou hast spoken unto thy servant: but I am slow of speech, and of a slow tongue. And the Lord said unto him, Who hath made man's mouth? or who maketh the dumb, or deaf, or the seeing, or the

MOSES IN MIDIAN.

blind? have not I the Lord? Now therefore go, and I will be with thy mouth, and teach thee what thou shalt say. And he said, O my Lord, send, I pray thee, by the hand of him whom thou wilt send. And the anger of the Lord was kindled against Moses, and he said, Is not Aaron the Levite thy brother? I know that he can speak well. And also, behold, he cometh forth to meet thee: and when he seeth thee, he will be glad in his heart. And thou shalt speak unto him, and put words in his mouth: and I will be with thy mouth, and with his mouth, and will teach you what ye shall do. And he shall be thy spokesman unto the people: and he shall be, even he shall be to thee instead of a mouth, and thou shalt be to him instead of God. And thou shalt take this rod in thine hand, wherewith thou shalt do signs.

"And Moses went and returned to Jethro his father-in-law, and said unto him, Let me go, I pray thee, and return unto my brethren which are in Egypt, and see whether they be yet alive. And Jethro said to Moses, Go in peace. And the Lord said unto Moses in Midian, Go, return into Egypt: for all the men are dead which sought thy life. And Moses took his wife and his sons, and set them upon an ass, and he returned to the land of Egypt: and Moses took the rod of God in his hand. And the Lord said unto Moses, When thou goest to return into Egypt, see that thou do all those wonders before Pharaoh, which I have put in thine hand: but I will harden his heart, that he shall not let the people go. And thou shalt say unto Pharaoh, Thus saith the Lord, Israel is my son, even my firstborn. And I say unto thee, Let my son go, that he may serve me: and if thou refuse to let him go, behold, I will slay thy son, even thy firstborn." Exod. iv. 1—23.

The time for the deliverance has come at length. The leader is prepared by long discipline for his arduous office, and the people that are to follow him now cry unto God. Forty years before, they had denounced Moses unto Pharaoh when he smote one of their oppressors. In Egypt also, all who in the remotest degree had favoured Israel are dead, and a heartless profligate and cruel tyrant wields the thong of the taskmaster. All was ready. Then, and not till then, God will work. Our impatient struggles and cries avail nothing with him while our sorrows are working for our benefit: that once accomplished, and the fiercest efforts of our enemies cannot for a single moment delay our deliverance.

CHAPTER VII.

THE PLAGUES OF EGYPT.

" AND the Lord said unto Aaron, Go into the wilderness to meet Moses. And he went, and met him in the mount of God, and kissed him.

" And Moses told Aaron all the words of the Lord who had sent him, and all the signs which he had commanded him." Exod. iv. 27, 28.

The tribe of Levi is now no longer in the low estate in which the narrative of the birth of Moses displayed it. His adoption by queen Thouoris, and the appointment of his mother to nurse him as one of the sons of Pharaoh, were distinctions which would not fail to be accompanied with large accessions both of influence and wealth. This would give to Amram and the rest of the elders of Levi the means of protecting the small remnant of their tribe from the tyranny of the Egyptian officers, so as to restore them in some measure to their place among their brethren. Aaron the head and first-born of Levi, is now a prince in Egypt. He leaves the boundaries of the kingdom, he goes into the presence of Pharaoh at his pleasure. He could have done neither had he not been of high rank.

The brothers met in Mount Sinai. They will meet there hereafter. They returned to Egypt together; each as a prince in his own right; for the death of Pharaoh Siphtha took off his proscription of Moses if it had ever been issued. Such was the law of Egypt.*

It had been in humble guise that Moses set out from Midian. (See verse 20.) But he went forth at God's command, and he bore God's commission: and " them that honour Him, He will honour."

" And Moses and Aaron went and gathered together all the elders of the children of Israel. And Aaron spake all the words which the Lord had spoken unto Moses, and did the signs in the sight of the people. And the people believed: and when they heard that the Lord had visited the children of Israel, and that he had looked upon their afflictions, then they bowed their heads and worshipped." Exodus iv. 29—31.

Thirty-seven years before, Moses " supposed that his brethren would have understood how that God by his hand would deliver them, but they under-

* Rosetta Inscription, Greek lines 12—14.

stood not." Acts vii. 25. Both Moses and his brethren have suffered much during this interval. Both have learnt much also.

"And afterward Moses and Aaron went in and told Pharaoh, Thus saith Jehovah the God of Israel, Let my people go that they may hold a feast unto me in the wilderness. And Pharaoh said, Who is Jehovah that I should obey his voice to let Israel go? I know not Jehovah, neither will I let Israel go?" Exod. v. 1, 2.

This was Sethos II.; and we have here another event in his monumental history to relate. It was an act of gross and mad impiety to which the monuments of Egypt have recorded no parallel, in the history of any other individual that ever lived there. It appears that when the tidings of the death of Siphtha reached Thebes, it became the duty of Sethos as his co-regent and successor, to visit the valley of the kings, for the purpose doubtless of being present at certain ceremonies preparatory to the sepulture. Here the exquisite beauty of the resting-place of his kind and most indulgent relatives Siphtha and Thouoris, and the disgraceful contrast to it, presented by his own slovenly, unfinished, and neglected vault, would be strongly impressed upon him. The course he adopted would send a thrill of horror and disgust through the entire of his subjects, of which we can form but a feeble conception. He ordered the names and portraits of his aunt, to whom he owed it that he was king of Egypt, and of his uncle, who had carried on the affairs of the nation for him, and built temples whereon he had inscribed the titles of Sethos to the exclusion of himself, to be covered with stucco, and wrote over them his own recreant name. It would not have been possible to have framed any other act of daring wickedness, whereby the higher and better feelings of ancient Egypt would have been so grossly outraged.

The next act of Sethos II. is recorded in the present passage, and is worthy that which went before it. The answer of the infatuated king to the message from the God of Israel is exactly that which we might have anticipated from the violator of the tomb of his benefactors. The tyrant knew not his country's gods, for he had despised and neglected the elementary precept of their religion regarding his own tomb. He knew not the natural feelings of affection and respect towards his deceased relatives, nor even the still commoner obligation of gratitude to the memories of liberal and disinterested benefactors. Upon these, the very elements of all right and reverential feeling in man, he had trampled ruthlessly and with mockery. How should such a man know the God of Israel, or care to obey him?

THE PLAGUES OF EGYPT. 313

" And they said, The God of the Hebrews hath met with us : let us go, we pray thee, three days journey into the desert, and sacrifice unto Jehovah our God, lest he fall upon us with pestilence or the sword. And the king of Egypt said unto them, Wherefore do ye, Moses and Aaron, let the people from their works ? Get you unto your burdens. And Pharaoh said [to his courtiers], Behold the people of the land are many, and ye make them rest from their burdens." Exod. v. 3— 5.

The moral identification of the monumental Sethos with the Pharaoh of the Exodus, yields in perfectness of coincidence to no other in the entire history. A reckless, hardened profligate, and impudent contemner of the commonest conventionalities of outward decency, ignorant through the wanton neglect of abundant opportunities of learning wisdom, and heady, headstrong, boisterous, and uncontrollable in the exact measure of his ignorance, the same individual must have sat for both portraits. The man who could perpetrate the grossest of all outrages upon the memory of his foster-parents before their funeral ceremonies were commenced, at the same time petrifying with horror the whole kingdom by the blasphemous impiety of the act, and this merely to gratify a whim of vanity and self-opinion,—this is the king of Egypt we should have chosen from the entire list of them for the opponent of Moses, even if there had been no chronological data to guide us in the selection!

The tyrant's address to the Egyptians around him, further illustrates the view of the real oppressors of Israel, of which other passages had also afforded us the shadow and outline. The kings of Egypt, and not the people of Egypt, were the enemies of Israel. It was to the authorities and great officers of the city of Ramses that the sordid and brutalized tyrant addressed the last of these objurgations. We could not have had a more convincing proof of the correctness of our previous assumptions regarding this matter, than the passage before us.

"And Pharaoh commanded the same day, the taskmasters of the people [Egyptians] and their officers [Israelites] saying,"—ver. 6.

This also was addressed to the whole body of the executive of the officers over the forced labours of Israel, whom he had peremptorily summoned into his presence. The Egyptians and the Israelites both stand before Pharaoh, and listen to the commands of the tyrant.

"Ye shall no more give the people straw to make brick as heretofore: let them go and gather straw for themselves. And the tale of the bricks which they did make heretofore ye shall lay upon them: ye shall not diminish ought thereof; for they be idle, therefore they cry, saying, Let us go and sacrifice to our God. Let there more work be laid upon them, that they may labour therein, and let them not regard vain words."

"And the taskmasters of the people [Egyptians] went out, and their officers, [Israelites] and they spake to the people saying, Thus saith Pharaoh, I will not give you straw. Go ye, get you straw where you can find it: yet not ought of your work shall be diminished.

"So the people were scattered abroad throughout all the land of Egypt, to gather stubble instead of straw.

"And the taskmasters were urgent, saying, Fulfil your works, even your daily works, as when there was straw.

"And the officers of the children of Israel, which Pharaoh's taskmasters had set over them, were beaten, saying, Wherefore have ye not fulfilled your daily task both yesterday and to-day, as heretofore? Then came the officers of the children of Israel and cried unto Pharaoh, saying, Wherefore dealest thou thus with thy servants? There is no straw given unto thy servants, and they say unto us, Make brick, and behold thy servants are beaten; but the fault is in thine own people. But he said, Ye are idle, ye are idle: therefore ye say, Let us go and do sacrifice to Jehovah. Go therefore now and work;

for there shall no straw be given you, yet shall ye deliver the tale of bricks." Exod. v. 6—18.

It was on the third day after the delivery of God's message that the disgusting scene took place which is described at the conclusion of this passage. To comment upon, or to amplify it, would be only to weaken its effect.

That bricks made of Nile mud, held together with chopped straw, have at all times, from the beginning until now, been used for building in Egypt is well known. It is not equally well known, that in the ancient kingdom, bricks made by the king's slaves for public works, were all stamped with the name of the reigning Pharaoh. Bricks made in eighty different reigns were collected in Egypt by the Prussian commission. (1843.)

Another circumstance connected with the brick-work of Ancient Egypt is also well worthy of note. The temples and palaces of Ramses at Thebes are distinguished from those of all the other kings of Egypt, by the enormous size of the quadrangular precincts that surround them, and by the vast series of ruined halls, corridors, and oval cells with which they are crowded. All these, together with the wall that encloses the precinct, were built of bricks of Nile mud, all of them stamped with the name of Ramses. Not dwelling upon the strong presumptive evidence afforded hereby, that he was the king that knew not Joseph, (the proof of that being sufficiently clear without it), we find from hence also, that the captive Israelites had been from the first principally employed upon the unskilled and very debasing drudgery of making bricks. There is no violation of probability in the supposition, that the works now especially in hand, would be such precincts and outer buildings for the numerous temples erected by the grandfather of Sethos in the Delta; and that by this display of excessive zeal for his own gods, and of contempt for the God of the oppressed people, whom his grandfather's subtle treachery had made the public slaves, he should endeavour to atone to the priesthood for the act of abominable impiety he had just committed in the valley of the kings, and to appease the justly offended prejudices of his Egyptian subjects generally.

The picture representing Israelite malefactors (Levites?) at work making bricks in the tomb of Rekshare, one of the architects of Thothmosis, is moreover highly illustrative of the passage before us. We find from it, that the Egyptian as well as the Israelite task-masters, were beaten when the work failed, and also that they were in that case themselves set to work by the superior officers of the king.

The season of the year at which these transactions took place, appears from the inspired narrative of them. It was shortly after the wheat-harvest, and the plains of the Delta were yet covered with the long stubble left by the reapers, who in Ancient, as in Modern Egypt, cut off the corn close to the ear. Instead of being any more supplied with straw from the threshing-floors, which was short enough to be at once available for mixture with the clay, without cutting, the tyrant will compel them to go forth and collect the stubble, and cut it, and yet not all diminish the tale of the bricks. The wheat-harvest is over in Egypt about the end of April; at the time when the Nile is at the lowest, and the hot sand-wind from the Sahara blows incessantly across the valley of the Nile for fifty days, rendering it as barren in appearance, and in temperature as intolerable as the surrounding deserts. It was into this burning atmosphere that the Israelites were driven forth to waste their strength and lives upon their impossible tasks.

"And the officers of the children of Israel did see that they were in evil case, after it was said, Ye shall not minish ought from your bricks, of your daily task.

"And they met Moses and Aaron who stood in the way as they came forth from Pharaoh. And they said unto them, Jehovah shall see you, and shall judge how ye have made our savour to stink in the sight (perception) of Pharaoh, and in the sight of his servants, even to the putting of a sword into their hands to slay us.

"And Moses returned unto Jehovah, and said, Lord, why is it that thou hast sent me? wherefore hast thou so evil entreated this people? For since I came to Pharaoh to speak in thy name, he hath done evil to this people, neither hast thou delivered thy people at all.

"Then said Jehovah unto Moses, Now shalt thou see what I will do to Pharaoh: for with a strong hand shall he let them go, and with a strong hand shall he drive them out of his land." Exodus v. 19—23; vi. 1.

The third day has scarcely yet declined in Egypt since the first interview of Moses and Aaron with Pharaoh. Yet the faith of Moses, and of all Israel, has broken down, because they are not already delivered from their oppressors. Their faith must be increased. This is a condition of spiritual gifts, inseparable from the religion of Jehovah under all its dispensations.

"And God spake unto Moses, and said unto him, I am Jehovah. I appeared unto Abraham, and unto Isaac, and unto Jacob, under [the name of] Elshaddai, but in my name Jehovah, did I not make myself known unto them. Yet did I establish my covenant with them, to give them the land of Canaan, the land of their pilgrimage, wherein they were strangers. Now also I have heard the groaning of the children of Israel, whom the Egyptians keep in bondage, and I have remembered my covenant. Wherefore say unto the children of Israel;

"I Jehovah will surely bring you out from under the burdens of Egypt.

" Yea, and I will deliver you from their service.

" And I will redeem you with a stretched-out arm, and with great judgments.

" And I will take you to me for a people.

" And I will be to you for a God.

" And ye shall know that I am Jehovah your God,

" Who bringeth you forth from under the burdens of Egypt.

" And I will bring you into the land,

" Which I lifted up my hand to give it,

" To Abraham, to Isaac, and to Jacob.

" Now will I give it to you for a possession. Even I, Jehovah.

" And Moses spake unto the children of Israel; but they hearkened not unto Moses, for anguish of spirit, and for cruel bondage." Exodus vi. 1—9.

This is a very remarkable passage. The Israelites are groaning, bleeding, and dying by hundreds under the merciless inflictions of the task-masters of Pharaoh. Moses, whose message from God had been the sole cause, however unintentional, of this fearful increase of their sufferings, expostulates with

THE PLAGUES OF EGYPT. 321

God upon the present distressing effect of his message, so different from that which he, as well as Israel, had anticipated. God's answer is addressed to the wants, and not to the wishes; to the faith, and not to the sufferings, either of Moses or Israel. For the confirmation thereof, he vouchsafes to them a two-fold revelation of his own thoughts.

He assumes to himself a new name. By the name *Elshaddai*, he was known to the whole earth. Egypt knew it familiarly, and habitually profaned it by applying it to the whole host of her men and women gods, dead and alive!* Jehovah is his new name, whereby he will reveal himself to Israel only, and to his sons, whether of the flesh or of the faith.

In His second revelation of himself to Moses, God was pleased to repeat and solemnly ratify the Abrahamic blessing and covenant in a prophetic hymn or ode.

God's message of peace was faithfully delivered, but the faith of his people was as yet too weak to receive it. The spirit of Israel was not attuned to the song of Moses. It was " as vinegar upon nitre," to his " heavy heart." Prov. xxv. 20.

* אֵל־שַׁדַּי Gr. παντοκρατωρ " God almighty. The hieroglyphic transcription of this name of God ⬚ *iri* or *el-chet* " the doer of all things " is a constant epithet in the texts both of the gods and kings of Ancient Egypt. It is applied to Ramses the oppressor of Israel on hundreds of monuments yet in existence.

" And Jehovah spake unto Moses saying, Go in and [command unto] Pharaoh the king of Egypt that he send the children of Israel out of his land.

" And Moses spake before Jehovah saying, Behold the children of Israel have not hearkened unto me. How then shall Pharaoh hear me, who am of uncircumcised lips?

" And Jehovah spake unto Moses and unto Aaron, and gave them a charge unto the children of Israel, and unto Pharaoh king of Egypt, to bring the children of Israel out of the land of Egypt." Verses 10 —13, 28—30.

The faith of Moses and Aaron must now undergo a yet severer test. With no other defence than the promise of God,—with no other weapon than the message of God,—they are again to go into the presence of the rabid tyrant, and deliver to him the words of God as the mandate of a king! It is not easy to conceive of a commission involving more imminent personal peril. It was ever thus: they whom God designs to do eminent service to his cause, must be prepared for it by searching trials of their confidence in him. " Without faith it is impossible to please God." Heb. xi. 6.

" And Jehovah said unto Moses, Behold I will make thee as God unto Pharaoh, and Aaron thy brother will I make thy prophet. Thou shalt speak all that I command thee: yea, Aaron thy brother shall command Pharaoh to send the children of Israel out of his land.

"But I will harden Pharaoh's heart and multiply my signs and my wonders in the land of Egypt. Yea Pharaoh shall not hearken unto you, that I may lay my hand upon Egypt and bring forth mine host, even the people of the children of Israel, out of the land of Egypt by great judgments. And all Egypt shall know that I am Jehovah, when I stretch forth my hand over Egypt, and bring forth the children of Israel from the midst of you [O inhabitants thereof!]

"And Moses and Aaron did as Jehovah commanded them; so did they." Exod. vii. 1—6.

To encourage his servants in the arduous and perilous mission on which he sent them forth, God was pleased to raise yet higher the veil that hid the glorious future from their gaze. Now is faith triumphant! They go forth in the name of Jehovah and doubt no longer.

"And Jehovah spake unto Moses [by the way] saying, When Pharaoh shall speak unto you, saying, Give ye forth a sign, then thou shalt say unto Aaron, Take thy staff and cast it before Pharaoh; it shall become a serpent.

"And Moses and Aaron went in unto Pharaoh, and they did so as Jehovah had commanded; and

Aaron cast down his staff before Pharaoh and before his servants, and it became a serpent.

"Then Pharaoh also called for the wise men and the sorcerers, and the magicians of Egypt. They also did in like manner with their enchantments. For they cast down every man his staff, and they became serpents: but Aaron's staff swallowed up their staves. Yet Pharaoh's heart was strong [obstinate] that he hearkened not unto them, as Jehovah had said." Exod. vii. 8—13.

The issue of this their second interview with Pharaoh had been foretold. The supernatural powers of the false gods of Egypt are called forth to assist the delusion of the infatuated monarch. It is now happily no longer needful to show the reality of the powers possessed by the ministers of the Egyptian idolatry, or to combat the ignorant illogical assumption that they practised tricks of jugglery on this and other similar occasions. Had they done so, the miracles of Moses and Aaron were the most powerful means of helping forward their delusion that could possibly have been devised, and the God in whose name they performed them, ministered to the sin of the idolatrous priests of Egypt!

The epithets and titles of the various orders of the Egyptian priesthood are not yet well ascertained. There are but few students of a vast subject, so that the progress of Egyptian archæology is

THE PLAGUES OF EGYPT. 325

now necessarily but slow. More than to state that they are all Egyptian words written with Hebrew characters, we do not, for this reason, enter upon their derivation.

"And Jehovah said unto Moses, Pharaoh's heart is hardened; he refuseth to let the people go. Get thee unto Pharaoh in the morning; lo, he goeth out unto the water; and thou shalt stand by the river's brink against he come; and the staff that was turned to a serpent shalt thou take in thy hand. And thou shalt say unto him, Jehovah the God of the Hebrews hath sent me unto thee to say, Let my people go, that they may serve me in the wilderness: and behold, hitherto thou wouldst not hear. Thus saith Jehovah, In this shalt thou know that I Jehovah [am God]. Behold I [Aaron] will smite with the staff in my hand upon the waters in the Nile, and they shall be turned to blood. And the fish that is in the river shall die, and the Nile shall stink, and the Egyptians shall lothe to drink of the water of the Nile.

"And Jehovah spake unto Moses, Say unto Aaron, Take thy staff, and stretch out thy hand upon the waters of Egypt, upon the canals, נהרות, upon the branches of the Nile, יאורות, and upon their pools, אגם, and upon all their tanks of water, מקוה, that they may become blood, and that there may be blood throughout all the land of Egypt, both in the channels of wood and in the channels of stone.

" And Moses and Aaron did so as Jehovah commanded, and Aaron lifted up the staff and smote the waters that were in the Nile, in the sight of Pharaoh, and in the sight of his servants; and all the waters that were in the Nile were turned to blood. And the fish that was in the Nile died, and the Nile stank, and the Egyptians could not drink of the water of the Nile. And there was blood throughout all the land of Egypt.

" And the magicians of Egypt did so with their enchantments, and Pharaoh's heart was hardened; neither did he hearken unto them, as Jehovah had said. Yea, Pharaoh turned and went to his house, setting not at all his heart upon the matter.

" And all Egypt digged on the banks of the Nile for water to drink; for they could not drink the water of the Nile." Exodus vii. 14—24.

The entire agreement of this passage, with all the circumstances and accessories under which we have assumed from the analogy of other passages, that the event must have occurred, is well worthy of note, and very extraordinary.

Pharaoh Sethos was residing at Ramses, in the western Delta. The site of this city is about six miles further west than the Bolbatine, or westernmost mouth of the Nile. (See Map.) This circumstance is clearly intimated in the narrative. Pharaoh would " go out unto the water " on the morning following the last interview. Moses and Aaron were to stand by the brink of the Nile against he came

The occasion on which Sethos went in procession to the edge of the Nile, surrounded by the civil and ecclesiastical authorities of Egypt, must have been a stated and a solemn one. The period of the year at which the transaction occurred, makes it apparent that such would actually be the case. The yearly overflow had just begun. The river had risen considerably. The first change in the appearance of the waters had already taken place. This is called, from the colour they assume, "the Green Nile." It is occasioned by the stagnant pools on the plains of Ethiopia, the contents of which are propelled into the bed of the river by the rise of the flood. The Nile water is then unfit to drink for three or four days, and the Egyptians prepare against it by storing the water in tanks and pools before its commencement. It is just at the time of this phenomenon (about the middle of June) that the stubble is collected into heaps in the wheat-fields, in order to burn it. It was the sight of the stubble yet abroad that had doubtless suggested to Sethos the cruel expedient of withholding straw from the Israelite workmen. He designed thereby to save this labour to the Egyptians.

In this state of the river it was the duty of

Pharaoh in person, and attended by the pomp of a religious procession, to inspect the waters, in order to decide upon the ceremonies of worship which were requisite, and upon the sluices of irrigation which were then to be opened. Every thing connected with the Nile was religion in Ancient Egypt. Over every different phase of the overflow a separate god presided : and to open the sluice which diverted its sacred waters one day before the prescription, or to keep it open one day after, were both mortal sins in the code of her mythology. On such an occasion, and for such a purpose, Sethos went down in state to the brink of the Nile, to direct the observances which were prescribed by religion on the appearance of the next phenomenon in the course of the overflow. In this second condition of the Nile, the waters are deeply tinged with the ferruginous clay of the lower hills and plains over which they flow at the commencement of their devious course. This change is called from its colour, the Red Nile, and on its first appearance the broad turbid tide certainly has a startling resemblance to a river of blood : we can testify to this fact, having seen it. Of this natural occurrence the God of Israel was pleased miraculously to avail himself in order to rebuke the obduracy of Sethos. The appearance became reality when Aaron lifted his staff. The red waters of the overflow were changed into that which they seemed to be ; clotted blood, reeking and rotting in the burning sun of Egypt. The plague extended throughout all the branches of the Nile, and the canals and channels of irrigation, whether of wood or stone. In the reedy pools formed by the waste waters on the edge of the desert, in the tanks and reservoirs which supplied the garden and the city with this indispensable requisite for life in Egypt, all was blood. The fish died, the river stank, and the Egyptians loathed to drink of its water, just at the time when this most delicious and refreshing of draughts is in its highest perfection.

If any doubt had before existed that the scene of this terrific display of the power of God was the Delta, the phraseology of the present passage must have removed it. Nowhere else in Egypt could the expressions whereby the several receptacles of the waters of the Nile are signified, have been used with any propriety. One only of them will require special notice. The word we render "Nile," is Egyptian. Heb. יאר. Coptic *iaro*. Hieroglyphic 𓇋𓂋𓈗 This word is never used but of the Nile and its natural branches ; so that the expression "Niles," decides the question of the locality definitively. There is but one Nile anywhere in Egypt, save in the Delta only.

The haughty tyrant is once more encouraged in

his obduracy by the display of the same miraculous power in the priesthood of his own idolatry. He makes light of God's message, disdains any reply to His messengers, and returns in state to his palace at Ramses.

This terrible judgment was confined to the Delta, the principal scene of the oppression and sufferings of Israel. The fact appears in the circumstance that sweet water was still to be obtained by digging in the sand at the banks of the river. This was the water of the inundation of the higher parts of the valley that filtered through.

"And seven days were fulfilled after that the Lord had smitten the Nile." Verse 25.

This is just about the time that would be required for the inundation to pass from the head of the Delta to the sea. In the course of it, the loathsome putrescence rolled onward before the waters of the rising flood which restored the Nile to its ordinary condition. " In the midst of wrath, God remembers mercy."

"And Jehovah spake unto Moses, Go unto Pharaoh, and speak unto him, Thus saith Jehovah, Let my people go, that they may serve me. Else if thou refuse to let them go, behold I will smite all thy borders with frogs. And the Nile shall bring forth frogs abundantly, which shall go up and come into thine house, and into thy bed-chamber, and upon thy bed, and into the house of thy servants, and upon thy people, and into their ovens, and into thy kneading-troughs, and the frogs shall come up both upon thee and upon thy people, and upon all thy servants.

" And Jehovah spake unto Moses, Say unto Aaron, Stretch forth thy hand with thy staff over the canals, and over the Niles, and over the pools, that the frogs may come up over the land of Egypt. And Aaron stretched forth his hand over the waters of Egypt; and the frogs came up and covered the land of Egypt. And the magicians did so with their enchantments, and brought up frogs upon the land of Egypt.

" Then Pharaoh called for Moses and Aaron, and said, Intreat Jehovah that he may take away the frogs from me and from my people, and I will let the people go, that they may do sacrifice to Jehovah. And Moses said unto Pharaoh, Declare to me when I shall intreat for thee and for thy people, to destroy the frogs from thee and from thy houses, that they may remain in the Nile only. And he said, To-morrow. And he said, Be it according to thy word, that thou mayest know that there is none like unto Jehovah our God. For the frogs shall depart from thee, and from thy houses, and from thy servants, and from thy people. They shall remain in the Nile only.

"And Moses and Aaron went out from Pharaoh, and Moses cried unto Jehovah because of the frogs that he had brought against Pharaoh. And Jehovah did according to the word of Moses; and the frogs died out of the houses, out of the cities, and out of the fields. And they gathered them together upon heaps, and the land stank.

"But when Pharaoh saw that there was respite, he hardened his heart, and hearkened not unto them, as Jehovah had said." Exod. viii. 1—15.

This is again the natural appearance next in the order of occurrence to the Red Nile, and of it also the God of nature availed himself to vindicate his power before Pharaoh, and before Egypt. The Nile, its branches and the great canals of irrigation are all bank-full, and the exuberant moisture has aroused from their summer torpor into life and activity the frogs of the Nile, in numbers inconceivable to those who have not been in hot countries. Even in ordinary years the annoyance of these loathsome creatures night and day, gives some idea of what this plague must have been, and renders abundantly reasonable the creation of a goddess, *Ranipula*,* at the very commencement of the mythology of ancient Egypt. In the whole of this fearful succes-

---

* "Driver away of frogs." Her name was Heki: *Birch* ap. Bunsen. She was the *Buto* of the Greek authors.

sion of judgments, there is not one more personally revolting than the plague of frogs.

" And the magicians did so with their enchantments, and brought up frogs upon the land of Egypt." Probably out of the tanks or *impluvia* in the centre of the open courts round which their temples were built. But were there not frogs enough upon the land of Egypt already? Why bring up more? A more useful display of their supernatural attainments would have consisted in calling forth the frog-expelling energies of the goddess to whom they had entrusted this needful office. That would have affected the whole question between Jehovah and the gods of Egypt. The power of Moses and the priests both flowed from the same source. The ministers of the idols can somewhat divert its course, so as to encourage the reprobate king in his wickedness, but they can no more turn it back upon Him who sent it forth, than the loiterer on the sea-beach can roll back the rising tide with his staff.

The frogs are in Pharaoh's palace, in the halls and rooms of state, in the offices and secret chambers, on his table and on his bed. The food of himself and his family is polluted by them. The palace rings incessantly with their hideous croakings, when undisturbed; and with their yet more discordant shrieks and yells when attacked and in danger. He could laugh at the river running blood, for Ramses was on the extreme border of Egypt, and water might be had for the supply of the palace from the springs in the desert. But now he suffers personally. There is no rest night or day. His family expostulates, and Pharaoh relents. Jehovah hears the prayer of his servant. The frogs die, or leave the land for the river. With them the relentings of Pharaoh depart also, as Jehovah had said.

" Then Jehovah said unto Moses, Say unto Aaron, Stretch forth thy staff and smite the dust of the land, and it shall become gnats [musquitoes] in all the land of Egypt. And he did so, and Aaron lifted up his staff, and smote the dust of the land, and it became gnats upon man and upon beast, all the dust of the land became gnats throughout all the land of Egypt.

" And the magicians did so with their enchantments to bring forth gnats, but they could not. Yet there were gnats upon man and upon beast. Then the magicians said unto Pharaoh, This is the finger of a god. But Pharaoh's heart was hardened, and he hearkened not unto them, as Jehovah had said." Exod. viii. 16—19.

The overflow has risen above the level of the canals and channels, and is rapidly flowing over the entire surface. The fine dust or powder, into which the Nile mud of last year's overflow is triturated, and with which the fields are entirely covered, now presents a very extraordinary phenomenon. Immediately on its being moistened with the waters, gnats and flies innumerable burst from their pupæ, and spring into perfect existence. The eggs that produce them were laid in the retiring waters of the former flood. They have matured in the interval, and they vivify instantaneously that the dust has absorbed moisture enough to discolour it. As the flood advances slowly onwards, a black line of living insects on its extreme verge moves with it. The sight of them, and of the birds and fishes that prey upon them, is a curious and a wonderful one. Once more the God of all the earth avails himself of the natural event actually occurring in the course of the year in Egypt. Aaron lifts his staff over the teeming dust, and the swollen germs of insect life that are mingled with it break forth into mosquitoes, a fearful pest in Egypt, but principally confined to the coast in the present day.

The priests once more go forth and sing their incantations and mutter their charms over the dust, but the permissive power of the spirits that obeyed them is withdrawn, and no musquitoes appear at their bidding. The conviction was forced upon them which they declared to Pharaoh. The finger of the God of Israel was more powerful than all the gods of Egypt. However, by the aid of curtains and attendants, the apartments of the palace would be kept tolerably free from the buzzing swarms that were tormenting his subjects outside. Sethos suffered but little personal inconvenience, and therefore the expostulations of his own priests were as little regarded as those of Moses and Aaron. He hardened his heart, and hearkened to neither of them, " as Jehovah had said."

" Then Jehovah said unto Moses, Rise up early in the morning, and stand before Pharaoh ; lo, he cometh forth to the water ; and say unto him, Thus saith Jehovah, Let my people go, that they may serve me. Else if thou wilt not let my people go, behold I will send swarms upon thee, and upon thy people, and upon thy houses ; and the houses of the Egyptians shall be full of swarms, and also the land around them.

" And I will sever in that day the land of Goshen in which the people dwell, that no swarms shall be there ; to the end that thou mayest know that I am Jehovah in the midst of the land [of Egypt] ; therefore will I put a division between my people and thy people. To-morrow shall this sign be.

" And Jehovah did so, and there came a grievous swarm into the house of Pharaoh, and into his servants' houses, and into all the land of Egypt; and the land was corrupted by reason of the swarm." Exod. viii. 20—24.

The overflow being nearly at its height, it seems to have been the custom of Egypt, in all ages, for the supreme ruler to go forth in solemn procession to the brink of the Nile, and there with much ceremony to direct the opening of the sluices at the mouths of the great canals; the occasion being further marked by feasts and rejoicings which last for many days.

Here again also the messenger of Jehovah met Pharaoh Sethos. The threatened plague on this occasion also, we believe to have been the natural phenomenon next in order of occurrence. At this period of the overflow, when so much of the country is under water, the common flies infest the cities of Egypt to a fearful extent. The attempt to read the word, rightly translated "swarms," (ערב) of some blood-fly, is altogether supererogatory, to those who have actually experienced the torment of the common fly in Egypt, during the overflow, at the present day. The plague of flies will take its place as a round in the entire climax of the plagues, without the aid of any such interpretation.

Goshen, "the land of flowers," was at first the name of a district in the east of the Delta. It was there that Israel and his tribe were first located. It was also, like Ramses, a name for the whole Delta. The Egyptians in the Delta were principally settlers brought thither by the Pharaoh of that name. We infer from this passage that they were for the most part located in the western portion of it, around the city of Ramses. The Israelites still clung to the settlements of their forefathers, and inhabited Goshen and its eastern portions.

"And Pharaoh called for Moses and for Aaron, and said, Go ye, sacrifice to your God in the land.

"And Moses said, It is not meet so to do: for we shall sacrifice the dread [or reverence] of Egypt to Jehovah our God: see now, may we sacrifice the dread of the Egyptians before their eyes, and will they not stone us? We must go three days' journey into the wilderness, to sacrifice to Jehovah our God as he shall command us.

"And Pharaoh said, I will send you forth, and ye shall sacrifice to Jehovah your God in the wilderness, only go not very far away [but] intreat for me.

"And Moses said, Behold, I go out from thee, and I will intreat Jehovah that the swarms may depart from Pharaoh, from his servants, and from his people to-morrow: but let not Pharaoh act deceitfully any more in not sending forth the people to sacrifice to Jehovah.

"And Moses went out from Pharaoh and intreated Jehovah. And Jehovah did according to the word of Moses, and removed the swarms from Pharaoh, from his servants, and from his people. There remained not one.

THE PLAGUES OF EGYPT. 339

" And Pharaoh hardened his heart at this time also ; neither would he let the people go." Exodus viii. 25—32.

No curtains, no precautions, no assiduity on the part of attendants can keep out the flies of Egypt. They creep in at every crevice, however minute, through which the air circulates. It will only be by a detail of actual and personal suffering from this pest in an ordinary year, that the amount of torment they are capable of inflicting will appear to those who have not been to Egypt ; and these details are too revolting. It may suffice to remark, that the suffering from the nausea that ensued when a fly was accidentally swallowed, and from the countless swarms of them that settled on every morsel of food, the moment it was exposed to them, had nearly in one instance issued in loss of life during the inundation of 1848. The cause of these fearful swarms was, on that occasion, rendered perfectly apparent. Not only has a far greater number been hatched (as we have already explained), but so large a proportion of the whole land being under water, their supply of food is greatly diminished by the circumstance ; so that they are literally mad with hunger, and throw themselves headlong upon whatever offers to satiate it. They rush into an apartment in which food is set forth like a snow-storm, and in spite of all the attendants can do, every drinking-vessel is filled with them, and they are heaped in huge black masses alive and dead upon every dish. Nothing escapes their voracity. Bread and fruit are polluted by them just as eagerly as animal food. We have described that which we saw under the ordinary circumstances of the overflow. What the plague must have been when Jehovah " hissed to the fly " from the entire Delta, and settled their noisome swarms upon the narrow strip of country around the city of Ramses, we must confess our own utter inability to imagine. From the inspired narrative before us, we may form some judgment of their numbers. They died of hunger in such quantities, that their bodies rotted on the mud, and corrupted the land. The amount of torment they inflicted we also learn from thence. The suffering bowed the stiff-neck and smote the stout heart of Pharaoh Sethos.

Oxen, sheep, and goats were all worshipped as gods in Egypt. To have offered them in sacrifice would have been to have slain the gods of Egypt before the eyes of their worshippers. Such would evidently have been the impression which such an act would have produced. These animals were slaughtered in Egypt for food, not for worship.

Of course Sethos disregarded and laughed at his promise, the moment the plague was removed. Doubtless he still laid the flattering unction to his soul, that Jehovah was after all like his own idols, only a little more powerful. The enchanters are already beaten. Moses will yield after this or another trial, and then Sethos will be master of the field.

"Then said Jehovah unto Moses, Go in unto Pharaoh, and say unto him, Thus saith Jehovah the god of the Hebrews, Send forth my people, that they may serve me; for if thou refuse to send them forth, and holdest them still, Behold the hand of Jehovah is upon thy cattle which is in the field, upon the horses, upon the asses, upon the camels, upon the oxen and upon the sheep, even a very grievous murrain. And Jehovah shall sever between the cattle of Israel and the cattle of Egypt. There shall nothing die of all that is the children's of Israel.

"And Jehovah appointed a set time, saying, Tomorrow shall Jehovah do this thing in the land. And Jehovah did that thing on the morrow, for all the cattle of Egypt died; but of the cattle of the children of Israel died not one. And Pharaoh sent, and behold, there had died not one of the cattle of Israel.

"Yet the heart of Pharaoh was hardened, and he would not send the people forth." Exodus ix. 1—7.

From those marvellous treasure-houses of ancient knowledge, the tombs of Egypt, we have the perfect illustration of this plague, and of the natural causes of which, in the unity of this his dispensation, the God of nature was again pleased to avail himself. The inundation had advanced considerably, and the pastures of the Delta were now under water. This was an anxious time for the herdsmen of Egypt. The cattle were penned for the night in mounds above the level of the water. In the day-time they were driven forth before the herdsmen into the higher parts of the fields, where the water permitted them to browse upon the young shoots of the lentils that were sprouting abundantly in the fertile mud below. The herdsmen, some in papyrus rafts, others wading or swimming, were in constant and anxious attendance upon them, to keep them out of the deep water, and to protect them from the crocodiles.

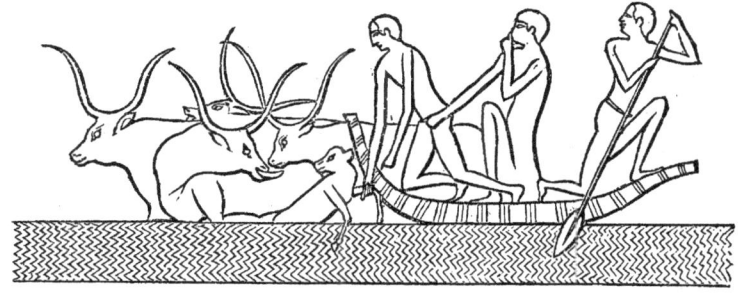

The cattle of Egypt were also at this season in requisition for an agricultural purpose of great importance in the tillage of the land. The seeds of many species of lentils, vetches, and other similar

THE PLAGUES OF EGYPT. 343

plants, were scattered upon the surface of the water at the beginning of the inundation, and trodden in by the cattle, great and small, so as to secure them in the mud, that they might not be washed away by the retreating waters. This was accomplished by incessantly driving them through the plashy mud, backwards and forwards, by men armed with heavy whips.

The cattle suffered greatly from these operations, so contrary to their ordinary habits. This circumstance is most significantly represented in these ancient reliefs. In the same plane, with cattle in the water, are also diseased cattle, tended by skilled herdsmen who are administering medicine to them.

This picture we believe to be thus associated with cattle in the water in every tomb in which it is repeated.

These were, so to speak, the suggestive circumstances of the present plague. In the administration of it, however, a character more decidedly miraculous and discriminative was imparted to it than to any of the former plagues. The murrain seizes the camels and horses of Pharaoh and his princes in the desert, as well as their cattle in Egypt. Yet the cattle of Israel, intermixed with the cattle of Egypt, breathing the same air, browzing the same marshes, are miraculously free from the ordinary unhealthiness of the season. All the cattle of Egypt died of the murrain; but of the cattle of Israel there died not one. Sethos sent and ascertained this wonderful fact. Yet he went on still in his wickedness: he refused to let the people go. The cattle of Egypt were all dead. He will seize upon the cattle of Israel. This was, doubtless, the suggestion that Satan put into his heart.

"Then Jehovah said unto Moses and unto Aaron, Take to you handfuls of ashes of the burning,* and let Moses sprinkle it towards heaven in the sight of Pharaoh. And it shall become small dust in all

---

* כִּבְשָׁן "conflagration," "tract of country on fire." See Genesis xix. 28; Exodus xix. 18, which are the only other places in the Bible where this word occurs.

the land of Egypt, and shall be a boil breaking forth with blains upon man and upon beast, throughout all the land of Egypt. And they took ashes of the burning and stood before Pharaoh; and Moses sprinkled it up toward heaven; and it became a boil breaking forth with blains upon man, and upon beast.

" And the magicians could not stand before Moses because of the boils; for the boil was upon the magicians, and upon all Egypt.

" And Jehovah hardened the heart of Pharaoh, and he hearkened not unto them, as the Lord had spoken unto Moses." Exodus ix. 8—12.

Again in strict analogy to the actual succession of the phenomena of the yearly overflow in Egypt, Jehovah selects the next occurrence in the course of it for the instrument of his vengeance upon Pharaoh. The inundation has touched its highest point, aud the last great work of the husbandman is now being performed. The stubble and the weeds of the low lands have all been carefully gathered off and collected upon the highest mounds, which at the present time are out of the reach of the overflow, and to be watered with the *shadoof* or balance-bucket. Here they are set on fire and burnt to ashes. The custom seems to be universal in Egypt at the present day. The cotemporary monuments are our unerring authority for stating in addition that it prevailed also in Ancient Egypt. Every occupation in agriculture being associated with religion, it was celebrated there in a high and solemn festival, lasting probably for some days, the first day of the feast being named 𓂋𓐍𓏛 *rkh*-na-hb*—" the feast of the greater burning;" and the last day, 𓂋𓐍𓏛 *rkh-tsb-hb*—" the feast of the lesser burning." These names are of very frequent occurrence. They seem to indicate that the heaps were frequently fired in order to insure their entire destruction. There is the same superstitious notion in Egypt at the present day. The peasants are very particular in burning up the whole.

The highest land in Egypt now is that on the brink of the river, and it is there that the burning takes place. It is a strange but beautiful sight in the thick darkness of an Egyptian night, to see the river as far as both horizons rolling along between two broad belts of fire. It is a yet stranger sight in the day-time, when the smoke and ashes of these conflagrations drive in whirls and eddies over the land before the rude blasts of the Elesian wind. It was gazing at this sight, and seeing the clothes of all present covered with the light and feathery particles of the ashes, that it first occurred to us, that this was the agent of God's vengeance in the plague of boils; though we did not then understand that

* Coptic, "to burn."

all the preceding plagues had in like manner been produced through the agencies of the successive phenomena of the overflow. It seemed to us then, and it still seems to us, to solve entirely a great difficulty connected with this miracle, according to the common interpretation of the passage. Fuel is scarce in Egypt, and in consequence fire for all purposes is used in the smallest possible quantity, and for the shortest possible time. This peculiarity in the present customs of Egypt we find from the paintings on the tombs to have always prevailed there. The fires used both for cooking and the arts were very inconsiderable. Under these circumstances it is hard to understand how a handful or two of ashes thrown up from one furnace could be diffused over an entire district to " become boils breaking forth with blains upon man and beast." But the difficulty vanishes altogether when we find that it was the season for consuming the weeds and field-refuse of all Egypt, and that the white ashes of their burning was drifting in clouds before the north wind, which at this time blows very fiercely.

Sethos appears to have been engaged in some public pomp, prescribed for the observance of this festival of the burnings, when Moses and Aaron denounced and inflicted upon Egypt the plague of boils. The magicians, or priests, suffered severely from it, so much so that the ceremonial was probably interrupted thereby; but the inspired narrative leaves us to infer that Pharaoh was not personally inconvenienced by it. The fans of his attendants at the time, and the cares of the guardian of the king's apartments in the palace would accomplish this without difficulty. The whole process of the burning lasts but for a few days. The plague passed away with that which Jehovah had miraculously constituted the cause of it, and Pharaoh once more despised the chastening of the Almighty.

"Then Jehovah said unto Moses, Rise up early in the morning, and stand before Pharaoh, and say unto him, Thus saith Jehovah the God of Abraham, Send forth my people, that they may serve me. For yet once again I send forth all my strokes [blows] upon thy heart, [self] and upon thy servants, and upon thy people; that thou mayest know that there is none like me in all the earth. For now again I stretch forth my hand to smite thee and thy people with plague; then thou shalt be cut off from the earth." Exod. ix. 13—16.

The terms of this passage seems to imply the lapse of some time after the occurrence of the events narrated in that which precedes it. Such we shall find by the passage that next follows to have been actually the case. The condition of Israel during this interval, we gather from the same kind of occasional notices of it. The direct pressure of the

THE PLAGUES OF EGYPT. 349

bondage had certainly ceased. It is never mentioned after the first plague. The overflow alone would render the cessation of all great public works of construction in Egypt a measure of necessity. The gangs of forced labourers would on this occasion return home to Goshen from the distant scenes of their sufferings; and the six fearful miracles of judgment which God had displayed on their behalf before the eyes of all Egypt, would present a perfectly effectual bar to the attempt on the part of any one to reimpose their burdens upon them. Even had Pharaoh been capable of such audacious wickedness (of which there is no evidence) his subjects would not have dared to have executed his decrees. The question between Moses and Sethos was now simply that of the departure out of Egypt. The sufferings of the captivity were at an end.

Another equally important consideration is suggested by this passage. Jehovah does not condescend to Pharaoh. He hath a controversy with the gods of Egypt. The king of Egypt he leaves to Moses his servant. This was a style of international communication well known in Egypt in those days. To the treaty of the 21st of Ramses, which had enslaved Israel, the high contracting parties were Amun and Ptha, and Ra, (or the sun) for Egypt; and Ashtar and Ashtoreth for Moab. It is in the conflict with this confederacy that Jehovah now brandishes his glittering sword. Who is Pharaoh? "Even a man that is a worm, and the son of man that is a worm!"

"And thou (Pharaoh) shalt be cut off from the earth. For in very deed for this have I raised thee up, to show in thee my power, and that my name may be declared in all the earth." Ver. 15, 16.

"What shall we say then? Is there unrighteousness with God? God forbid. For he saith to Moses, I will have mercy on whom I will have mercy, and I will have compassion on whom I will have compassion. So then it is not of him that willeth, or of him that runneth, but of God that showeth mercy. For the scripture saith unto Pharaoh, Even for this same purpose have I raised thee up, that I might show my power in thee, and that my name might be declared throughout all the earth. Therefore he hath mercy on whom he will, and whom he will he hardeneth." Rom. ix. 14—18.

We give this text with its inspired commentary without at all entering upon the mysterious question which the Divine author of both addresses to the faith, and not to the understanding of man. The only remark upon the passage that is incumbent upon us, we make with regret. For the sake of chronological convenience it has been assumed by some writers, that after all, Pharaoh did not perish in this conflict with Jehovah, but survived for many years the departure of Israel, and the destruction of his army. If this really is the case, the history before us is a fable, and the inspired comment we have just quoted a mistake. Such defences are mere subterfuges, deeply injurious to the cause they are intended to serve.

" As yet exaltest thou (Pharaoh) thyself against my people, that thou wilt not send them forth? Behold, to-morrow about this time, I will cause it to rain a very grievous hail, such as there hath not been in Egypt from the foundation thereof even until now. Send therefore now, gather thy cattle and all that thou hast in the field. Every man and beast which shall be found in the field and not brought home, the hail shall come down upon them and they shall die. He that feared the word of Jehovah among the servants of Pharaoh made his servants and his cattle flee into the houses. And he that regarded not the word of Jehovah left his servants and his cattle in the fields.

" Then Jehovah said unto Moses, Stretch forth thine hand toward heaven, that there may be hail in all the land of Egypt, upon man and upon beast, and upon every herb of the field throughout the land of Egypt. And Moses stretched forth his staff toward heaven: and Jehovah sent thunder and hail, and the fire ran along upon the ground, and Jehovah rained hail upon the land of Egypt. So there was hail, and fire mingled with the hail, very grievous, such as there had been none like it in all the land of Egypt since it became a nation.

" And the hail smote throughout all the land of Egypt, all that was in the field, both man and beast; and the hail smote every herb of the field, and brake every tree of the field. Only in the land of Goshen, where the children of Israel were, was there no hail." Ver. 17—26.

It is here again our painful duty to have to notice another of the mistakes into which the Christian commentators upon this history have fallen. Between the months of November and February, rain and hail are not uncommon in the Delta and Middle Egypt. They are most frequently accompanied by thunder and lightning; and the storms are very violent, though not of long continuance. Here again then, God created no new thing in the earth, as has been assumed in ignorance of the facts. He merely displayed his mastery over the occurring phenomena of the season.

The preface to the narrative of this plague implies, as we have explained, a longer interval of time between it and the plague that preceded it, than had been interposed between the previous plagues: so that the entire visitation seems here to separate into two sections.

An interval, then, has evidently elapsed. We

THE PLAGUES OF EGYPT. 353

will endeavour very shortly to estimate this interval more precisely. The overflow had attained its height and gradually subsided, leaving throughout Egypt successive flats of intense fertility, ready for the labours of the husbandman. In the earlier days of this interval, the prevalence of the waters would prevent the progress of all great works of construction in Egypt. Afterwards, all Egypt would be abroad in the field and at work; so that there would be neither time nor men for building temples, and the forced labours of Israel would at this season cease of necessity in good measure.

Sethos appears to have left the Delta for some other part of his dominions at this time. Israel, in his absence, had collected in Goshen around the princes of the several tribes, and withdrawn themselves from their previous intermixture with the Egyptians. This appears in the progress of the narrative. Doubtless these movements took place at the command of Jehovah, and under the direction of Moses and Aaron.

The labours of the field being now ended, Sethos has returned to the Delta. Probably enough, in doing so, it had been in his heart and purpose, if not in his counsels, to reimpose the burdens upon Israel.

"And Pharaoh sent and called for Moses and Aaron, and said unto them, I have sinned this time. Jehovah is righteous, and I and my people are wicked. It is enough. Intreat Jehovah that there be no more voices of the $_{gods}$ (thunder) and hail: and I will send you forth, and ye shall stay no longer.

" And Moses said unto him, As soon as I am gone out of the city, I will spread abroad my hands unto Jehovah, and the thunder shall cease, neither shall there be any more hail: that thou mayest know that the land [of Egypt] is Jehovah's. But as for thee and thy servants, I know that ye will not yet fear the Lord Jehovah.

" And the flax and the barley was smitten: for the barley was in the ear, and the flax was bolled; but the wheat and the spelt* were not smitten, for they were not grown up.

" And Moses went out of the city (Ramses) from Pharaoh, and spread abroad his hands unto Jehovah: and the thunders and the hail ceased, and the rain was not poured upon the earth.

" And when Pharaoh saw that the rain and the hail and the thunders ceased, he sinned yet more and hardened his heart, he and his servants. Yea the heart of Pharaoh was hardened, neither would he let the children of Israel go, as Jehovah had spoken by Moses." Exod. ix. 27—35.

It is quite clear from this passage that Pharaoh

* כסמת " short awmed or beardless wheat."

and his councillors had from the first well understood the strictly religious nature of the conflict in which they were engaged, and betaken themselves to the gods of Egypt for aid against the God of Israel. They had deemed (according to the doctrine of local gods which prevailed universally in the ancient world) that it was a war between the divine protectors of the two races; that the powers of the combatants were at the least evenly balanced, and that they had only to persevere, and the victory might yet be with the gods of Egypt. It was to expose the utter futility of these vain imaginations that Jehovah was pleased to effect his own purpose through the agencies of the several phenomena of the Egyptian year in the cycle of their ordinary occurrence, converting each in succession into a fearful plague. For these were the divine attributes with which the fables of their mythology had invested the dead men and women whom they worshipped as gods. In the instance now before us the ritual of the gods of fire (the Eumenides, or avenging gods) had been exhausted. Earnest prayers, gorgeous processions, and costly sacrifices had been offered in vain. The voice of a greater than the idols still pealed through the heavens. The lightnings of a mightier than they still flashed in the eyes of their votaries, and ran along the ground diffusing blight and ruin, and the hail and rain continued hour after hour, yea, for successive days, breaking the trees, beating down the growing herbs into the mud, and destroying the hopes of the gardens and the fields of Egypt. "Only in Goshen where were the children of Israel was there no hail." The God of Israel then is contending with the gods of Egypt, and the latter are utterly impotent before him to help either themselves or their votaries. No fabling of the priests, no enchantments of the magicians can veil the truth from the eyes of all Egypt. It was in this dilemma that Pharaoh sent for Moses and Aaron, and enacted a brief scene of penitence before them. Most vain mockery! Moses was prescient of Pharaoh's hypocrisy, but he was the minister of the God that delighteth in mercy. For the sake, not of Pharaoh, but of his subjects, the plague passes away and the scene changes. Pharaoh and his councillors once more defy the God of Israel.

The barley is in the ear, and the flax bolled in Egypt at the present day, about the end of December and the beginning of January. This makes the interval between the plague of boils and the plague of hail about five months. Such a period would seem to be implied by the tenor of the narrative. All the varieties of wheat now cultivated in Egypt are sown after the barley, when the land is much drier, and are not carried until late in April.

Whereas the barley-harvest is in February and March. This was also the case in Ancient Egypt, for at the time of the plague of hail the wheat was not grown up.

" Then said Jehovah unto Moses, Go ye unto Pharaoh, for I have hardened his heart, and the heart of his servants, that I might shew these my signs before him:

" Yea, that thou mayest tell in the ears of thy son, and of thy son's son, what things I have wrought in Egypt, and my signs which I have done among them; that ye may know how that I am Jehovah." Exod. x. 1, 2.

After so fearful a display of the omnipotence of Jehovah as the plague of hail, it is not in the nature of man that Sethos and his councillors should immediately on its cessation determine to disobey the command, to enforce which it had been so expressly sent. Some weeks would doubtless first be spent in parley, and equivocating with Moses and Aaron. The fear of a return of the plague must be removed to a safe distance, before the decision which was in their hearts would be uttered by their lips. The children of Israel in this interval would complete the assembling of themselves in Goshen, and be busily occupied with preparations for departure. It was on the day that Pharaoh pronounced his decision, and before Moses went to the king's palace to hear it, that he received the message from God in the text before us. The patience with which the thousands of Israel had waited hither to the time of their Divine deliverer, instead of bursting their bonds at once with a strong arm, as was fully in their power, now drew from the heart of God this most gracious revelation of his purpose in the delay.

In this interval a scene of exquisite beauty has developed itself in the Delta. The rain and the hail which had somewhat interfered with its first disclosure are over and gone. The voice of the turtle-dove is heard in every bush and tree, amid fresh springing leaves and sweet blossoms. At times the north wind awakes, cool and refreshing; at other times the south wind blows, soft and balmy. Before both, the beans, the pease, the lupins, the vetches, the lentils, the endless variety of plants of this order that cover the plains of the Delta, all in full blossom, and all sweet scented, roll in green undulations, interchanged with more gorgeous tints, and shake forth their spicy odours, copious as the blue and sparkling river that slowly meanders in the sunshine, and grateful to the senses as the draughts of its delicious waters to him who first reaches its brink from the thirsty desert. There is not in nature any thing more charming! There is not on the wide world a spot that can advance a stronger claim to its ancient epithet; GOSHEN, "the land of flowers."

"And Moses and Aaron came in unto Pharaoh and said unto him, Thus saith Jehovah the God of the Hebrews, How long wilt thou refuse to humble thyself before me? Send forth my people, that they may serve me. Else, if thou refuse to send forth my people, behold to-morrow will I bring the locusts within thy borders. And they shall cover the face of the land, so that one cannot be able to see the land: and they shall eat the residue of that which is escaped, which remaineth to you from the hail, and shall eat every tree which groweth for you out of the field. And they shall fill thy palaces, and the palaces of thy [servants, attendants,] princes, yea the habitations of all Egypt, such as neither thy fathers have seen nor thy fathers' fathers, since the day that they were upon the earth unto this day. Then he [Moses] turned away and went forth from Pharaoh.

"Then said Pharaoh's princes unto him. How long shall this man be a snare unto us? Send the men forth to serve Jehovah their God! Knowest thou not that already Egypt is destroyed?

"Then Moses and Aaron were ordered to return unto Pharaoh, 'and he said to them, Go serve Jehovah your God. Who are they that will go? And Moses said, We will go with our young and with our old, with our sons and with our daughters : yea, we will go with our flocks and with our herds; for we must hold the feast of Jehovah.

" And he [Pharaoh] said unto them, Will Jehovah be thus with you (as hitherto) when I shall have sent you forth and your little ones. Take heed lest evil be before you. It will not be so; [therefore] ye that are men go forth and serve Jehovah; for that ye have asked of me. Then they were dismissed from the presence of Pharaoh." Exodus x. 3—11.

The stout hearts of Pharaoh and his princes melt within them at the mention of the locusts. They will no longer contend with the mighty arm that is stretched out against them. Moses and Aaron are recalled to the council-chamber, and the conditions of the departure of Israel are demanded. Moses answers in the spirit of prophecy. The royal rejoinder is highly characteristic, and places the mind and heart of Sethos in an aspect at least as revolting as any that the monumental and historical notices of it in our possession had set before us. Now that his power is gone, the tyrant turns hypocrite. He takes an affectionate interest in the women and children of the tribe he has enslaved and oppressed. They will never be equal to the fatigues and dangers of the desert. The men may go, but these must remain behind, lest they perish in the wilderness.

THE PLAGUES OF EGYPT. 361

This is Pharaoh's decision. He does not wait for any rejoinder, but at once closes the interview. As if the God of Israel could be mocked with this stale device! As if " the eyes of Jehovah, that run to and fro throughout the whole earth," (2 Chron. xvi. 9,) could not see through the flimsy veil of this pretext!

"Then said Jehovah unto Moses, Stretch out thine hand over the land of Egypt for the locusts, that they may come up upon the land of Egypt, and eat every herb of the land, even all that the hail hath left. And Moses stretched forth his staff over the land of Egypt, and Jehovah brought an east wind over the land all that day and all that night. When it was morning the east wind brought the locusts. And the locusts went up over all the land of Egypt, and rested in all the borders of Egypt in exceeding multitudes. Before them were there no such swarms (of locusts) as they, neither after them shall be such. For they covered the face of the whole earth, so that the land was darkened; and they did eat every herb of the land, and all the trees which the hail had left: and there remained not any green thing on the trees or on the herbs of the field, through all the land of Egypt." Exodus x. 12—15.

There is but one brief season of the Egyptian year during which a descent of locusts there would be possible, and that is the few weeks next following the cold (and in the Delta rainy) month, which corresponds to the winter of less-favoured climates. At all other times of the year, a flight of locusts would only alight in Egypt to die of hunger or be drowned. They would find the land covered with the straws of ripe corn and herbs, which are not the food of the locust, or as barren as the desert, or under water, But for this short spring-tide, the entire surface is covered with luxuriant vegetation. It is a striking coincidence that the view of the plagues which has been forced upon us by the consideration of the preceding ones, requires the plague of locusts to occur in exactly this place in the Egyptian calendar.

To one who has seen the locust at work, and also past through the green beauties of the Delta at this season, the idea of this plague is most appalling. The pen of inspiration alone can describe the ravages of this awful pest:

" A day of darkness and gloominess,*

A day of clouds and thick darkness.

As the morning light on the tops of the mountains

Comes a great people and a strong.

There hath not ever been the like,

Neither shall there be any more after it

To the years of many generations.

* The locusts darken the day in their flight.

A fire devoureth before them,
Behind them a flame burneth.
As the garden of Eden is the land before them,
And behind them as the desolate wilderness,
For truly nothing can escape them.
The appearance of them was the appearance of horses.*
As trained horses, so do they bound†
As the noise of chariots over the [rugged] tops of mountains, they take wing,‡
Yea, as the roar of fire that devoureth stubble,
As [clash the arms of] warriors in battle array.
At the sight of them the people are in anguish;
All faces gather blackness.
They rush forward like mighty men,
They climb the wall like men of war,
They march every one on his way,
They break not their ranks,
Neither does one thrust another,
They go on every one on his path,§
And where the weapon alights it wounds them not.‖

* The head of the locust bears considerable resemblance to that of a horse.

† The locust leaps like the grasshopper. It moves by a succession of bounds, strongly resembling the gallop of a fleet horse.

‡ This description of the deafening buzz and clatter with which a flight of locusts takes wing is wonderfully true to nature.

§ These peculiarities of a descent of locusts is well known.

‖ The locust is so extremely agile that it is very difficult to kill it.

They run to and fro in the city,
They mount upon the wall;
They climb up upon the houses,
They steal in at the windows like a thief."

Joel ii. 2—9.*

To comment upon this sublime and most faithful description of a flight of locusts would be to weaken its effect.

"Then Pharaoh called for Moses and Aaron in haste: and he said, I have sinned against Jehovah your God, and against you: now therefore, forgive, I pray thee, my sin only this once, and entreat Jehovah your God, that he may take away from me this death only.

"And he went forth and entreated Jehovah. And Jehovah turned a mighty strong west wind, which took away the locusts, and cast them into the Red Sea: there remained not one locust in all the borders of Egypt." Exodus x. 16—19.

This act of penitence had been performed before, but not under circumstances of equal urgency. The Delta is a dreary plain of black Nile mud, as barren as the desert, and the locusts having consumed every green thing, are commencing their ravages upon the

---

* The flight of locusts in this passage is used metaphorically for the Assyrian invasion of Palestine. The figure was suggested by the actual occurrence of the pest at the time of the delivery of the prophecy. (See c. i. v. 4.)

bark of the fruit-trees. The humiliation of Sethos is as abject as the occasion is urgent. He rolls in the dust. He confesses his sin against Moses and Aaron, as well as against Jehovah; he humbly begs pardon of both. He asks for the intercession of Moses with God in terms of distressing meanness.

For his people's sake the hypocritical prayers of Sethos were heard once more. The west wind arose; the parched wind of the desert. The locusts were driven like the sand before its rude fitful gusts, to perish in the Red Sea. Their work was done. They had come to Egypt on the east wind from Syria and Palestine. It was the ordinary course and season of their migration. They were on their way to the parts about Cyrene, to lay waste the gardens of Carthage, to ravage the vineyards and olive-yards of Mauritania as far as the pillars of Hercules, when the call of their Creator arrested their flight, and his finger pointed to the land of Egypt.

Once more a few weeks elapsed, during which the Israelites proceeded with their preparations to depart, no man hindering them; while Pharaoh parleyed and equivocated with Moses and Aaron. At length all fear of the return of the locusts was at an end. The clover and other leguminous herbs, that had been eaten down, would begin to spring again. Something might even then be done to save Egypt, but it must be by means of irrigation and the labour of man. Never before had the Israelite slaves been wanted in Egypt as at that moment. In a mind constituted like that of Sethos, motives as selfish and as sordid as these would doubtless preponderate in his final decision.

" But Jehovah hardened Pharaoh's heart, so that he would not send forth the children of Israel." ver. 20.

The divine judgments marched majestically onwards, utterly regardless of Sethos, his paroxysms of rage, or his collapses of meanness. But one being remains, and then Jehovah will have contended with and conquered every thing that is called God, or that is worshiped in Egypt. Over the river and the land, with all that inhabit them, over " the air, the flood, the flame," he has already asserted his absolute unbounded sovereignty. They have bowed to his behests, and done his commandments in the eyes of all Egypt. But the sun, the father-god of the whole mythology, the dread protector of the oldest and most venerated of the cities of Egypt, still shines serene in heaven, untouched by the wonders which the God of Israel has wrought. Is not he then also a god as well as Jehovah? The question soon receives an answer.

" Then Jehovah said unto Moses, Stretch out thine hand toward heaven, that there may be darkness over the land of Egypt, even darkness that may be felt. And Moses stretched forth his hand towards heaven, and there was a thick darkness in all the land of Egypt three days. They saw not one another, neither rose any from his place for three days.

" Yet had all the children of Israel light in their dwellings." ver. 21—23.

The sun then is the minister of Jehovah as absolutely as the rest of the elements of nature. He listens as implicitly to the voice of His word, and gives or withholds his light at His bidding as obediently as they.

Once more the agent of this fearful judgment is the occurring event of the season. No one who has been in Egypt to experience it, will doubt for a moment the agency whereby Jehovah wrought. The plague of darkness was a sand-storm. It is impossible for words to describe this fearful visitation more accurately, than the passage before us.

In ordinary years the wheat would have ripened and the harvest have been gathered in the warm sunny month that had elapsed, since the last display of the power of God. In this disastrous year there was no harvest to gather. About the middle of April a west wind sets in strongly, and continues to blow from that quarter for about fifty days. It is named by the Arabs in Egypt *hamseen,** from

---

* " Fifty." Arabic.

this circumstance. During the whole season of the prevalence of this wind, the atmosphere is excessively dry, and loaded with the fine particles of the sand of the Sahara,—to the great discomfort of the inhabitants of Egypt. But occasionally the west wind suddenly freshens to a perfect hurricane, and sweeping before it the light sands of the desert, precipitates them in columns and drifts upon the valley of the Nile. The sufferings of man and beast during these dreadful storms, in ordinary years, baffle description. No man leaves his dwelling, for to face a violent gust would be certain death by suffocation. They who are overtaken by them, wrap their faces in their mantles, and lie prostrate on the ground. It is their only chance of life. The light of noon-day is but a red angry twilight. At intervals, though brief ones, it is obscured, and the darkness is total while the heavy drifts pass the sun's disc. We testify that we have seen, on this point. It is impossible by any expedient to keep the sand out of the houses. So saturated is the air with the sand, that it seems to lose its transparency, so that artificial light is of little service. The sand also gets into the eyes, producing ophthalmia; so that men " see not one another."

We have described the sand-storm of an ordinary year, which seldom lasts more than a few hours. When the storm raged incessantly for three days, the amount of suffering, of disease and death among the aged, the weak, and the young of the subjects of Pharaoh, we are unable in any way to estimate. We speak from personal endurance, when we say, that for intense and universal misery the plague of darkness would far surpass all that went before it, and that as it was the last, so was it also the most fearful, of the plagues which Jehovah inflicted on Egypt through the agency of the powers of nature.

The locusts had eaten every green thing throughout all Egypt. The children of Israel did not need the rising crops that they destroyed, but they were protected by the power of their God from the horrors of the sand-storm. The west wind threw down its heavy burden of sand over Ramses. The children of Israel, in Goshen to the eastward, had light in their dwellings, and suffered comparatively but little inconvenience otherwise. Such partial exemptions sometimes occur in sand-storms at the present day.

" Then Pharaoh called for Moses, and said, Go ye, serve Jehovah, only let your flocks and herds remain; your little ones also shall go with you.

" But Moses said, Thou shalt also give up into our hands sacrifices and burnt-offerings, that we may do sacrifice unto Jehovah our God. Our cattle also shall go with us, there shall not a hoof be left behind; for thereof must we take to serve Jehovah our God; yet know we not with what we must serve Jehovah until we come thither.

"Then Jehovah hardened Pharaoh's heart, that he would not send them forth." Exodus x. 24—29.

The sordid meanness of motive, whereby this wretched monarch had been actuated throughout, is at length stripped of its last covering, and comes forth in its naked deformity.

The cycle of the year in Egypt is now complete. It is just twelve months since Moses first stood before Pharaoh. In the course of it the God of Moses has wielded the nine prominent occurrences in its several seasons to scourge therewith the contumacy of Pharaoh and his princes.

"But Jehovah had said unto Moses, Pharaoh shall not hearken unto you, that my wonders may be multiplied in the land of Egypt. So Moses and Aaron did all these wonders before Pharaoh; but Jehovah hardened Pharaoh's heart, so that he would not send the children of Israel forth from the land." Exod. xi. 9, 10.

Some displacements and omissions have occurred in the Hebrew of the text that continues the narrative. The sense of the passage readily adjusts the displacements. The Samaritan transcription of the Pentateuch supplies the omissions.

"Then Jehovah said unto Moses, Yet will I bring one plague upon Pharaoh and upon Egypt; then will he send you forth from hence altogether, yea, he will thrust you forth with violence. Speak now in the ears of the people, that every man ask of his neighbour, and every woman ask of her neighbour, vessels [objects] of silver and vessels of gold. For I Jehovah do give the people favour in the sight of the Egyptians, so that they shall give them what they ask.

" For about midnight I will go forth into the midst of the land of Egypt, and every firstborn in the land of Egypt shall die, from the firstborn of Pharaoh that sitteth upon his throne even unto the firstborn of the maid-servant that is behind the mill, and all the firstborn of beasts. And there shall be a great cry throughout all the land of Egypt, such as there has been none like it, nor shall be like it any more. But against any of the children of Israel there shall not a dog move his tongue, against man or beast ; that thou mayest know that Jehovah doth put a difference between Egypt and Israel. Thou also shalt be very great in the eyes of Pharaoh's princes and in the eyes of his people.

" Then Moses [went in unto] Pharaoh, and said unto him. Thus saith Jehovah,

" Israel is my son, even my firstborn ;

" And I said unto thee, Send my son forth that he may serve me.

" But thou hast refused to send him forth : therefore, behold, Jehovah slayeth thy son, even thy firstborn.

"Therefore thus saith Jehovah, About midnight I will go forth into the midst of Egypt, and all the firstborn of the land of Egypt shall die, from the firstborn of Pharaoh that sitteth on the throne even unto the firstborn of the maid-servant that is behind the mill, and all the firstborn of beasts.

"And there shall be a great cry throughout all the land of Egypt, such as there was none like it nor shall be like it any more; that ye [Pharaoh and his princes] may know how that Jehovah doth put a difference between Egypt and Israel. And all these thy princes shall come down unto me, and bow themselves unto me, and say, Go forth, and all thy people that is at thy feet. Then will I go forth." Exodus xi. *Sam.*

There is no space for repentance now. Moses, as the prophet of God, denounces the wrath of God upon Pharaoh and his guilty councillors. The majestic bearing of the messenger and the tone of his message rouse the haughty despot to a transport of uncontroulable fury, in which he altogether forgets the fearful purport of it.

"Then Pharaoh said unto him (Moses), Get thee from me; take heed to thyself, see my face no more: for in the day thou seest my face thou shalt die.

"And Moses said, Thou hast spoken well, I will see thy face again no more. So he went out from Pharaoh [who was] in the heat of wrath." Exod. x. 28, 29 ; xi. 8.

Now is the long-suffering of God exhausted. Pharaoh is given over to desperate folly. He defies the God who had desolated his land, and decimated his people already. He drives from his presence with execrations and insults, the prophet who had nine times denounced the divine judgments upon him, and whose threats in every instance had been strictly verified.

For twelve months the children of Israel have been occupied in assembling themselves in the eastern Delta, and in preparations for their departure. Now all is ready. In that very day when their last act of faith in the word of Jehovah was accomplished, came forth the command to their first act of obedience.

"And the Lord spake unto Moses and Aaron in the land of Egypt, saying, This month shall be unto you the beginning of months : it shall be the first month of the year to you.

"Speak ye unto all the congregation of Israel, saying, In the tenth day of this month they shall take to them every man a lamb, according to the house of their fathers, a lamb for an house : and if the household be too little for the lamb, let him and his neighbour next unto his house take it according to the number of the souls; every man according to his eating shall make your count for the lamb. Your lamb shall be without blemish, a male of the first year; ye shall take it out from the sheep, or from the goats: and ye shall keep it up until the fourteenth day of the same month: and the whole assembly of the congregation of Israel shall kill it in the evening. And they shall take of the blood, and strike it on the two side-posts and on the upper door-post of the houses, wherein they shall eat it. And they shall eat the flesh in that night, roast with fire, and unleavened bread; and with bitter herbs they shall eat it. Eat not of it raw, nor sodden at all with water, but roast with fire; his head with his legs, and with the purtenance thereof. And ye shall let nothing of it remain until the morning; and that which remaineth of it until the morning, ye shall burn with fire.

"And thus shall ye eat it; with your loins girded, your shoes on your feet, and your staff in your hand; and ye shall eat it in haste: it is the Lord's passover. For I will pass through the land of Egypt this night, and will smite all the firstborn in the land of Egypt, both man and beast; and against all the gods of Egypt I will execute judgment: I am the Lord. And the blood shall be to you for a token upon the houses where ye are· and when I see the blood, I will pass over you, and the plague shall not be upon you to destroy you, when I smite the land of Egypt. And this day shall be unto you for a memorial, and ye shall keep it a feast to the Lord throughout your generations; ye shall keep it a feast by an ordinance for ever. Seven days shall ye eat unleavened bread; even the first day ye shall put away leaven out of your houses: for whosoever eateth leavened bread from the first day until the seventh day, that soul shall be cut off from Israel. And in the first day there shall be an holy convocation, and in the seventh day there shall be an holy convocation to you; no manner of work shall be done in them, save that which every man must eat, that only may be done of you. And ye shall observe the feast of unleavened bread; for in this selfsame day have I brought your armies out of the land of Egypt: therefore shall ye observe this day in your generations by an ordinance for ever.

" In the first month, on the fourteenth day of the month at even, ye shall eat unleavened bread, until the one-and-twentieth day of the month at even. Seven days shall there be no leaven found in your houses: for whosoever eateth that which is leavened, even that soul shall be cut off from the congregation of Israel, whether he be a stranger, or born in the land. Ye shall eat nothing leavened; in all your habitations shall ye eat unleavened bread.

"Then Moses called for all the elders of Israel, and said unto them, Draw out and take you a lamb according to your families, and kill the passover. And ye shall take a bunch of hyssop, and dip it in the blood that is in the basin, and strike the lintel and the two side-posts with the blood that is in the basin; and none of you shall go out at the door of his house until the morning. For the Lord will pass through to smite the Egyptians; and when he seeth the blood upon the lintel, and on the two side-posts, the Lord will pass over the door, and will not suffer the destroyer to come in unto your houses to smite you. And ye shall observe this thing for an ordinance to thee and to thy sons for ever. And it shall come to pass, when ye be come to the land which the Lord will give you, according as he hath promised, that ye shall keep this service. And it shall come to pass, when your children shall say unto you, What mean ye by this service? that ye shall say, It is the sacrifice of the Lord's passover, who passed over the houses of the children of Israel in Egypt, when he smote the Egyptians, and delivered our houses. And the people bowed the head and worshipped. And the children of Israel went away, and did as the Lord had commanded Moses and Aaron, so did they." Exod. xii. 1—28.

It was on the tenth day of the month that Moses, going forth from his final interview with Pharaoh, assembled all the elders and princes of the people, and instituted the passover. The institution itself, the types thereof and their deep significance, need, thank God, no amplification of ours to the English reader.

In this his last great work in the land of Egypt, God will wield the common elements of the material world no longer. The angel of his presence is coming forth to do his pleasure. This judgment shall surpass all that have gone before it, as in severity, so also in close and strict discrimination. Every stroke shall be guided by intelligence; every victim shall be a selected one. God's dealings with Israel on this occasion undergo a change as strongly marked as the occasion itself. The strength of his faith is to be tested by the observance of a new prescription. An act of domestic worship, suited in all its details to their present position, as sojourners in a land that was not theirs, is instituted for a yearly feast, to serve for a memorial of that which Jehovah is about to do, throughout all future generations. The paschal lamb was to be selected, as on this day, by every family in Israel, and to be fed apart from the flock until the day of the judgment; when its slaughter, and the sprinkling of its blood on the door-posts, would not only commemorate the deliverance from Egypt, but be for a sign to the destroying angel to pass over the habitations of Israel, and also for a sign unto Israel of a truth elementary to all God's dealings with sin in man ;—" without shedding of blood there is no remission."

That the twelve months which had elapsed since Moses first appeared in Egypt with the divine command to Israel to depart, had been diligently employed by them in making all needful preparations for so great an event, there cannot be a doubt. It is equally certain that the divine wisdom would be with Moses and the princes of Israel in all the detailed arrangements for the harmonious and orderly march of the host of Jehovah. What these details were, we are not informed; and the narrative of the following events affords but little insight into them. It seems, however, certain, that the Israelites had now altogether left the cities of the Delta, and lived in tents, depasturing their flocks on its fertile plains. We may with probability suppose the general arrangement to have been, that the heads of each tribe were encamped in the vicinity of different cities in the Delta, and that the individual members of each pitched their tents around them. These cities appear to have lain on, or very near, the line of their march, and to have extended across the entire Delta. The princes of all the tribes, with Moses and Aaron, were at Ramses, on the western bank of the Bolbatine branch of the Nile, in attendance upon Pharaoh. The thousands of Israel lay encamped in a broad belt extending from thence to the eastern desert, a distance of more than seventy miles.

The sun of the last day of the sojourn of Israel in Egypt had set. It was the fourth day after the interview with Moses. Pharaoh, his princes, and the priests of his idols would doubtless take courage from this unwonted delay. Jehovah and his minister are beaten at length, for now the gods of Egypt prevail against them. The triumph would be celebrated in pomps and sacrifices, in feasts and dances. Nothing is more likely than that the banquet-halls of Pharaoh at Ramses were blazing with lamps, and that he and his princes were pouring forth libations of wine to their gods, and concerting schemes amid their revelry, for the perpetuation of the thraldom of Israel.

The paschal lamb was slain that night in all the tents of Israel. The sprinkled blood was yet moist on the door-posts of every habitation. Their flocks and herds were ruminating in the pens, their little ones were sleeping in the tents, and the men of Israel, having partaken of the mystical feast, stood awe-struck and silent, listening for the footsteps of the coming God.

" And it came to pass that at midnight Jehovah smote all the first-born in the land of Egypt, from the first-born of Pharaoh that sat on the throne, unto the first-born of the captive that was in the dungeon, and all the first-born of cattle. Then Pharaoh rose up in the night, he and all his princes, and all Egypt. And there was a great cry in Egypt, for there was not a house where there was not one dead." Exod. xii. 29, 30.

Pharaoh Sethos started from his couch that night, yelling in fierce and bitter agony, and gnawing at the sharp arrow that was rankling in his vitals, like a wounded lion. His son, his first-born, his only son, just arrived at man's estate, just crowned king of Egypt, and associated with his father in the cares of sovereignty, writhed before him in mortal throes, and died. His transports of grief were re-echoed, and with no feigned voice, by the princes, the councillors, and the priests that partook of his revelry. Each one rends his garments and clasps to his bosom the quivering corpse of his first-born son. On that fearful night "there was a great cry throughout all the land of Egypt," but if we have rightly read its history, the loudest, wildest wail of remorseful anguish would arise from Pharaoh's banquet hall!

The name and brief history of the first-born of Sethos are recorded in the valley of the tombs of the kings. The tomb numbered 11 by Sir G. Wilkinson, was commenced by him on a scale of great magnificence, and his name was inscribed over the entrance, and once on each wall of the inclined corridor. But the work ended when it had scarcely advanced beyond the external surface of the cliff. Probably the absence of Sethos from the Delta in the interval between the sixth and seventh plagues had been occasioned by the coronation of this ill-fated youth, whose memory, like that of his father, was afterwards made infamous in Egypt. His name on the tomb was covered over by his successor long afterwards, who completed the excavation, making it one of the largest and most magnificent vaults in the entire valley.*

"Then he (Pharaoh) cried (sent) to Moses and Aaron by night, saying, Arise! go forth from the midst of my people, both ye and the children of Israel, and go serve Jehovah as ye have said. Also take your flocks, and your herds, as ye have said, and be gone, and bless me also. Egypt also was urgent upon the people, and hasted to send them forth, for they (the Egyptians) said, We be all dead men." Ver. 31—33.

Thus was the Exodus of Israel accomplished. It was extorted from the haughty despot of a proud, prosperous, and most superstitious nation, in the fulness of his power and surrounded by the splendours of his court. For twelve months together he

* It is the well known Harpers' tomb of Bruce.

had resisted the command of Jehovah, and called forth to the conflict the gods of Egypt. He and they were foiled in every rencontre, and his obstinacy did but fulfil the purpose of his omnipotent enemy. It was now impossible to conceal from the Egyptians that Jehovah was God in Egypt as well as the God of Israel, and that their gods were no gods, but wood and stone, the work of men's hands, lying fables, the devices of men's hearts ; for the very deified elements of nature they ignorantly worshipped, Jehovah had wielded as the scourges wherewith to chastise their contumacy and folly.

CHAPTER VIII.

THE EXODUS.

" Now the sojourning of the children of Israel, wherein they dwelt in Egypt, was four hundred and thirty years. For it came to pass at the end of the four hundred and thirty years, even the self-same day it came to pass, that all the hosts of Jehovah set out from the land of Egypt. This is a night of observances for the children of Israel throughout their generations." Exod. xii. 40—42.

We follow here again the rule we have already prescribed to ourselves, in forbearing all discussion as to the duration of the sojourn.

In the passage that next follows we also restore the natural arrangement of the sentences.

" And the people took their dough before it was leavened, the remnant being bound up in their cloaks on their shoulders. And they baked unleavened cakes with the dough which they brought out of Egypt, for it was not leavened, because they were thrust out of Egypt and could not tarry, no not even to bake themselves bread." Exod. xii. 34, 39.

The fact here recorded was perpetually commemorated in the observances of the Passover. It conveys in the East the strongest possible impression of the haste with which Israel went forth from Egypt. Even under the most cruel tyranny of Mohammed Ali, the boatmen on the Nile can demand of those that engage them, a time at stated intervals to bake their bread. For journeys in the desert it is important to have the bread baked as near as possible to the commencement of the journey.

Such is the custom to this day in Egypt. It was this preparative only for their journey through the wilderness which Israel had not time to make. All other things were ready. Our authorized version, which was made when oriental customs were little known in Europe, conveys a somewhat erroneous impression on this point.

" And the children of Israel did according to the word of Moses, and they demanded of the Egyptians objects of silver, and objects of gold, and raiment. And Jehovah gave the people favour in the eyes of the Egyptians, so that they yielded to their demands. Thus they spoiled Egypt." Ver. 35, 36.

The ancient versions have misled our English translators in this passage. To borrow with no intention of repayment is to steal; but such was not the command of Jehovah to Israel. The original word has no such meaning. The children of Israel had been for nearly a century bond-slaves to the princes and nobles of Egypt. At the command of Jehovah they now *demanded the hire*, שאל, of these their services, and through his favour they obtained it, on the condition of their instant departure. Our modern neologian commentators are at no pains to correct palpable mistakes like these: while on the other hand, they are never weary of finding out and inventing readings which give absurd or grotesque imports to the sacred text.

Thus the hosts of Jehovah went forth from Egypt as conquerors, bearing the spoil thereof.

" And all the children of Israel did so: as Jehovah had commanded Moses and Aaron, so did they: and it came to pass on that very day that Jehovah led forth the children of Israel out of the land of Egypt by their hosts." Ver. 50, 51.

The expression " by their hosts," [or " armies," צבאות] is a remarkable one, which brings out clearly the view we had already taken of the assembling of the Israelites in the Delta before their final departure. They collected in twelve divisions, each of which was stationed round the city in which the prince of the tribe dwelt, and " had his possessions." Gen. xlvii. 27. The sale of these possessions would entitle the Israelites to a very large amount of the wealth with which they went out from Egypt.

"Then the children of Israel journeyed from Ramses to Succoth, about six hundred thousand on foot that were men, besides children." Ver. 37.

There are few passages in the Bible upon which more has been written than this. It is melancholy to have to add that there are still fewer regarding which, notwithstanding, less is really known. The two cities mentioned in it remain in Egypt to this day, and still retain their ancient names. Succoth moreover lies due east from Ramses, which is exactly the direction in which the Israelites must have journeyed on their way from thence to the desert of Sinai. Ramses, as we have already explained, was the city built by the Israelites at the command of Pharaoh of that name, and was situated on the extreme western border of the Delta where the settlements of the Egyptians were. The modern name of *Succoth* סֻכּוֹת is in Arabic *Sakha*, in Coptic *Schoou*. Its ancient name was written in hieroglyphics sichos,* which the Greeks transcribed Ξωις, Xois. That facts so palpable as these, and at the same time of such paramount importance to the illustration of the sacred text before us, should nevertheless have entirely escaped the notice

---

* *s* for *th*. The German Jews pronounce the letter ת *th*, *s*, at the present day.

of all commentators ancient and modern, is a circumstance concerning which we cannot refrain from the expression of our unfeigned astonishment. Xois, as we have seen, became the capital of the shepherd-kings after they had lost Memphis. The first grand preparatory movement therefore of the Exodus, was the departure of Moses and Aaron, with the rest of the princes of Israel, from the court of Pharaoh at Ramses, to Xois, the old capital of the Delta.

The name of the city of Xois, or Succoth, which is Hebrew, and signifies " tents," shows it to have been built by the Israelite or Canaanite settlers in the Delta. In all probability it had been the residence of one of the princes of the tribes ; so that here the comparatively small company that had left Ramses, consisting only of the little tribe of Levi, acting as guards or attendants upon the princes, were joined by one of the great sections of the host of Israel. Among the conquests of Sethos I. recorded at Karnak is a city of the Delta named *Manasseh*, which doubtless had been built by the prince of this tribe of Israel. It appears from hence that Israel had voluntarily built cities in Egypt before the captivity.

The number of the children of Israel at the time of the Exodus is another of those vexed questions, with which, in the order of our design, it is now incumbent on us to deal fully and faithfully.

The vague reckoning of about 600,000 footmen or infantry of the text, appears by the two exact censuses taken in the first and thirty-ninth years that followed the Exodus, to have been justly calculated. The census of the first year makes the fighting men of Israel to amount to 603,550 (Numbers i. 1—44.) The same class in the enumeration at the end of the wanderings in the Desert, amounts to 601,730 (Numbers xxvi. 51.) The individuals enrolled in this class were men only, and between the ages of twenty and sixty. All below this limit were accounted *lads* (ילד) and infants. All the men beyond it took their places among the elders of Israel, and were no longer liable to military service in the field. The censuses being in fact those of the armies of Israel,—the whole of the women, as well as the old men and children, are left out of them : so that the number of which the host of Israel consisted at the Exodus is a question in statistics. An easy reckoning gives us 4,000,000 as the lowest possible approximation to the sum of the entire host that left Egypt at the Exodus. The probability is that it was much greater. We make this statement with the full consciousness of the smile of sarcastic pity with which it will be received by the modern philosophical writers who have condescended to this our subject. If in our calculations of the rate of the increase of Israel in Egypt, we followed their example in working with factors derived from the tables of the latest census of London, or Paris, or Berlin, it is indeed " difficult to imagine how 70 or 75 persons can have become 4,000,000 and upwards in this period," to adopt their considerate phraseology; but we humbly submit that these their factors have nothing whatever to do with the question; inasmuch as the circumstances of society which govern the census were entirely different at the two epochs. The age of puberty was the same then as now, but the expectation of life was greater by at least 40 years. This would of course swell the ancient census. Polygamy and concubinage also prevailed among the Israelites, not as moral offences, but as sanctioned and established practices of society: the offspring of such connexions taking their assigned places in the father's household, and being enrolled in the family records as his lawful descendants. Whether their prevalence had, or had not, in the times when they had the divine sanction, the tendency to multiply the species, we have no means of knowing. They now only exist on the earth as disgraceful crimes. Of this, however, there can be no doubt. They would inevitably tend to the rapid increase of a thriving prosperous race of people among whom they prevailed, and at the expense of all the less prosperous races with which they were in contact. These were exactly the circumstances under which Israel had sojourned in Egypt. The men of Israel grew rich in possessions. According to the universal practice of the ancient world, they would, on this account, seek to increase and extend also their influence and the number of their descendants. They took to them wives abundantly, both from among the Egyptians and Canaanites. In consequence, the men of these races must of necessity intermarry with the Israelitish women, when there seems to have been no impediment to their admission into the tribes of Israel in the right of their wives. The inevitable effect of this process would be that Israel would increase far beyond the natural order of reproduction, while Egypt and Canaan would correspondingly decrease. The prevalence of this custom among the Israelites in Egypt is demonstrated by the divine prohibition and regulation of it shortly after the Exodus. Deut. vii. 2, 3, xvii. 10, seq., &c. Had the custom not existed, the law regarding it would never have been enacted. The consequence we have forestalled is expressly said to have taken place by Pharaoh Ramses, in his counsel with the princes of Egypt for the enslaving of Israel. " See! the people of the children of Israel are more and mightier than we." Exodus i. 9. Israel in Egypt outnumbered the Egyptians themselves.

THE EXODUS.

As this question is to be dealt with in a pre-eminently wide and extended sense, in order to meet the dignified spirit of high philosophy which now assails the Scripture account of it, we state further upon this point, that such is the inevitable consequence at all times, of this close contiguity with intermarriage between any two races of mankind. The one absorbs the other. No half-caste or mulatto race is perpetuated; but the peculiarities of the weaker race gradually disappear, merging in those of the stronger. This is the case even with the European and the African negro, the two opposite poles of the varieties of man. It is pre-eminently so with all the intermediate races. One familiar instance will illustrate this.

Less than 400 years ago, the Portuguese settled in great numbers in the south-western portions of the island of Ceylon. They have exercised considerable influence here. A *patois* of their language is still spoken through the entire district, and the names of nine-tenths of the inhabitants are Portuguese. Yet the race is extinct. There is not a trace of the European form or feature left in the purest and loftiest of the families of their descendants. The Dutch followed them about 200 years afterwards, when many settlers from Holland occupied the same district. They likewise are just on the verge of extinction. The personal appearance of the descendants of both is in nothing distinguishable from that of the Cingalese.

In the case of Israel in Egypt the assimilation would be far more rapid and decided than in this; owing partly, to the greater resemblance between the two amalgamating races, and still more, to the prevalence of polygamy among the Israelites. The circumstance that Joseph was a ruler and a prince, would give very great advantages to the first immigrants, which were certainly continued during the seventy years that he survived that event: nor is there any evidence that they were afterwards withdrawn before the times of Ramses. The events that we know to have befallen the shepherd kingdom during this its final epoch, would on the other hand, be highly favorable to the increase of Israel. The losses it sustained on its southern and western frontiers, which were mainly inhabited by Egyptians, would render the Israelites still more preponderant in the state, and increase their opportunities of aggrandizement. We found on the monuments, evidence of the power of Israel in the Delta at the time of its annexation to the Theban kingdom, so strong as to suggest, that jealousy of it, and apprehension of its consequences, might have induced the guardians of the infant Siphtha to call in the assistance of Ramses. His counsel on the occasion, which is recorded in Scripture, (Exod. i.

9,) plainly hints at such a motive. The design of the policy recommended by him and adopted, though not successfully, was the repression of the numbers of Israel.

These considerations, we submit, combine with the analogy of the similar instances we have cited, to remove all improbability from the Mosaic account of the numbers of Israel at the Exodus, even if, in obedience to the canon of modern philosophy, we choose to forget God in the matter, and to view it as altogether the result of natural causes. That the great increase of the Israelites was the effect of God's blessing, is nevertheless very distinctly stated in this account, which has now stood unflinchingly the test of so long and close an examination, that we do not hesitate to express our conviction of its truth, notwithstanding the derision which our avowal is sure to elicit from its philosophic assailants.

Through God's blessing, then, upon the universal laws of human increase, the seventy or seventy-five persons composing the clan of Jacob who had immigrated into Egypt, were represented by more than 600,000 fighting men, and at least four millions of souls, all lineally descended from them, when Israel had been in Egypt four hundred and thirty years.

" Also a great mixture [of people] went out with them: and flocks and herds, even very much cattle." Exod. xii. 38.

The word in the original of this place is the name common to all the nomade tribes of the desert of Sinai. The distinctions of race which were so strictly observed among the men of these very remote times, seem to have been neglected by them, probably through the necessities of their manner of life, in the rugged and barren district over which they wandered as merchants, with the products of the adjacent countries. For this reason they were very early named ערב *Arab*, "the mixed people;" and they retain the name to this day. These were the hired servants and bond-slaves of the Israelites. They were of both sexes. They were Egyptians, Canaanites, and Cushites,—some, prisoners of war, others malefactors, but all purchased in Egypt, and accompanying their masters as part of their property. It is in vain to attempt any conjecture as to their number. The passage, as well as the nature of the case, leave us to infer that it must have been considerable.

It is evident from hence that the number in the preceding sentence must be taken with its accompanying limitation in the strictest possible sense. The 600,000 fighting men were all the lineal descendants of Israel. Their servants and camp-followers are not included in it, as some commentators are disposed to imagine.

The Exodus was the last of the great movements

THE EXODUS. 395

among the primitive families of man to which the first impulse had been given on the plains of Shinar, more than 1500 years before. It admits of no comparison with the subsequent emigrations of mankind, by whatsoever motive they may have been influenced. It is with those earlier and vaster movements, when, impelled by the judgments of God, and guided by the hand of God, men went forth from one common centre by nations together, to people the districts which the divine sovereignty had assigned to them, that the comparison must be instituted, if the parallel is to be either just or relevant.

Pharaoh Ramses made no mistake in his calculation of the increase of Israel. They far out-numbered his own people. The population of all Egypt at no time exceeded eight millions. In this stupendous display of the sovereignty of Jehovah over the destinies of mankind, more than five millions left its borders in one host, never to return !

" It is a night of observances unto Jehovah who brought them forth out of the land of Egypt. Yea this is the night of Jehovah to be observed of the children of Israel throughout many generations." Exodus xii. 42.

" Then Moses said unto the people, Remember this day in which ye came out from Egypt, out of the house of bondage : for by strength of arm doth

Jehovah bring you out from hence. There shall be no leavened bread eaten this day when ye came out in the month Abib." Exod. xiii. 3, 4.

We had before been informed that the Exodus took place on the 14th day of the month, or moon. The name of the month is here specified for the first time. It is the eleventh month of the Egyptian calendar, which is written in the Coptic texts, *Ephip*. The Arabic transcription of the name used in Egypt at this day is identical with the Hebrew of the place before us, אביב. The Israelites in Egypt used of course the Egyptian calendar, which only differed from that of Noah and the patriarchs in giving names to the months, instead of merely enumerating them. The month was thirty days, and the year twelve months, in both. This division of time corresponds with the actual phenomena, neither of the moon nor of the sun. The moon revolves round the earth twelve times in 354 days. The earth moves once round the sun in $365\frac{1}{4}$ days. A year of 360 days agrees with neither. The consequence would be that the year in both countries was vague. It did not agree with the seasons. The Nile would very rarely overflow in the month in the Egyptian calendar marked for that event. The moon and the almanack would in like manner be constantly at variance. The mode of restoring the agreement seems to us to have been at the time now before us the same in both countries. A whole moon was occasionally added at the end of the year —the Veadar ואדר of the later Hebrews. We have already stated that, according to the Greek chronologers, a much more exact and systematic mode of effecting this was invented by the Shepherd kings. If such were really the case, it was too intricate for general practice, for there is not a particle of monumental evidence for its application at this epoch. We do not make the statement unadvisedly, or without having given the best attention in our power to all that has been advanced in support of the opposite opinion, especially by Dr. Lepsius.*

---

* Einleitung, pp. 123—245.—A wonderful display of learning, but a very forced and inconclusive argument. If we rightly understand the author's reasoning, it proceeds upon a mistake. According to the Greek authorities which he follows, the year in Egypt began on the day that the dog-star rose heliacally, that is, exactly at sun rise. But if the hieroglyphic calendar is to be regarded as authority, the year began on the first day after the entire subsidence of the river, that is, about the end of November.; and at this time the dogstar rises cosmically in Egypt, that is, exactly at sun set. It is however very doubtful to us, that the dogstar had anything to do with the matter. The Sothic cycles and other periods of the Alexandrian astronomers of the second and third centuries after Christ, are all evidently back-reckonings. If Sothis (or the dogstar), had any connection with the beginning of the Egyptian year, it was regulated by his cosmical rising, which is by much the easier to observe; but if this was the case, at the time of the Alexandrian astronomers, the calendar had gone so long unadjusted by the epact, that the first day of the year had receded to his heliacal rising, or thereabouts; and without any regard to the hieroglyphic names of the months, the philosophers have assumed this to have been the original observation. Strange as this

Abib was made the beginning of months, throwing hereby the Hebrew year two months in advance of the Egyptian year, by express command. (see above) The other names of the Egyptian months were not adopted by the Israelites, nor indeed was the name Abib, except in connexion with the passover;— the reason for its adoption is perfectly obvious. The passover was the feast of celebration of the deliverance from Egypt. Equally obvious is the reason why the Israelites rejected it in any other association, together with the rest of the Egyptian names of the months, after the Exodus. They were the names of idols whom their superstition made to preside over the twelve months. (Lepsius, u.s.) To this superstition Israel was sufficiently prone, without the aid of such a sanction as the adoption of the whole calendar would have afforded to it.

Israel, at the Exodus, used the patriarchal calendar at the command of Jehovah. The months were each lunations actually observed and named by the numbers one to twelve. They appear still to have retained for civil purposes the ancient computation in which the Abib of the Exodus fell on the seventh month.

may sound in the ears of modern philosophers, mistakes at least as ridiculous have nevertheless been made by their predecessors of the Alexandrian school.

"Then it came to pass when Pharaoh had sent forth the people, that God led them not the way of the land of the Philistines, although that was near: for God said, Lest peradventure the people repent when they see war, and they return to Egypt." Exodus xiii. 17.

The Philistines had attained a conspicuous place among the confederated nations of Canaan, apparently but a short time before the Exodus. Some time afterwards they took advantage of the disasters of the Exodus, and at the head of a vast alliance of Canaanites invaded Egypt and held large possessions in it for many years. The Israelites had not been trained to military service in Egypt after the commencement of the captivity; they would therefore have been unequal to the arduous service of cutting their way through a warlike and powerful clan, inhabiting a rough country abounding with strongholds.

"But God led the people about, the way of the wilderness of the Red Sea. So the children of Israel went up harnessed out of the land of Egypt." v. 18.

The people went forth to prepare for the execution of the decree of God in the extirpation of the Canaanite idolaters. Not then inured sufficiently to the toils of war, it was the design of Jehovah to train them in the wilderness for the service he would afterwards demand of them. How could they go forth on such a mission without arms? It is truly distressing to find modern commentators betrayed into the unspeakable absurdity of an interpretation of this passage, which deprives all the fighting men of Israel of weapons, and for a reason which the context expressly stultifies. "It is very improbable," say they, "that Pharaoh would have allowed them the use of arms:" But how was Pharaoh to enforce the prohibition? He and his people were too happy to be rid of Israel on any terms! Such is the Scripture account of the Exodus. The utter folly of the reading is so palpable that it is marvellous to see it proposed and advocated by otherwise deservedly high authorities in Scripture interpretation.

"And they [the children of Israel] took their journey from Succoth and encamped in Etham in the edge of the wilderness.

"And Jehovah went before them by day in a pillar of a cloud, to lead them by the way; and by night in a pillar of fire, to give them light; travelling day and night: he took not away the pillar of cloud by day, nor the pillar of fire by night, before the people." Ver. 20—22.

Having now no longer to imagine the sites of Ramses and Succoth, the rest of the journey to the Red Sea becomes divested of many of the difficulties which had hitherto seemed to beset it. Etham אתם

THE EXODUS. 401

on the edge of the wilderness, is the city called Patumos by the Greeks. Its site is named Thoum by the Arabs at this day. It stood just on the border of the arable land, a little to the north-east of Heliopolis. (See Map.) Etham lay in the direct line from Succoth to the Red Sea.

The order of march up to this point appears to have been as follows. Succoth was the appointed rendezvous for the tribes that dwelt in the western portions of the Delta, and Etham for the great bulk of the people, who had been living around the first settlements in Goshen proper, which was the eastern division of the Delta. At Etham, the whole host united, and marched forward day and night under the guidance of the token of the Divine presence to the Red Sea.

Israel from this point entered upon a new dispensation, of direct supernatural interference, of a far more marked character than ever before. The ordinary laws of universal nature were reversed in their behalf. To discuss this awful subject is no part of our present design. We merely repeat the caution which has been already so often suggested to us. If we have succeeded at all in establishing the truth of the Mosaic history, the miracles are a perfectly inseparable element in that history. If this history be true, the miracles cannot be poetry, or seeming, or jugglery. They are that which they are declared to be, and nothing else.

The route by which Israel moved on in mystic pomp from Egypt to the Red Sea has never been forgotten. It is called to this day *Wady-el-Tih,* " the Valley of the Wanderings," and *Wady-Mousa,* " the Valley of Moses." It commences in Egypt on the southern side of the Gebel Mokattam, a hill in the immediate vicinity of the modern city of Cairo, at a desert-station now called Bassatin, about twelve miles to the south of the mounds of Thoum, the Etham of the Bible. The direct course of Israel would have been due eastward, but the inspired narrative expressly mentions that, on account of the Philistines, by which term we are doubtless to understand the desert-rangers generally, their way was made circuitous. The Wady-el-Tih is the northernmost route that could with any propriety be styled " the way of the wilderness of the Red Sea," as it is the first that imposes upon the traveller the necessity, either of crossing the Red Sea, or of making a long detour round the head of the Gulf of Suez in order to reach the Peninsula of Sinai (see Map). The several routes to the modern city of Suez could only have been so named by an uncouth prolepsis: for they do not lead the traveller journeying to Sinai to the Red Sea at all: but point to the Isthmus as his direct route. Such has nevertheless been the assumption of certain writers, in order to support an infidel theory regarding the passage of the Red Sea. The assumption has also been taken up by Christian commentators, as we think, somewhat too hastily.

"Then Jehovah spake unto Moses, saying, Command the children of Israel to turn and encamp before Pihahiroth, between Migdol and the Red Sea, over against Baal-zephon: before it shall ye encamp by the sea." Exodus xiv. 1, 2.

This was the first encampment of Israel. It would occupy some considerable period in forming. Moses and Aaron with the princes of the people went first, marching day and night. Having reached the shore of the Red Sea, they, by the command of Jehovah, marked out the boundary of the camp. The rest of the people, the women, the little ones, the flocks, the herds, the provisions, the inconceivably numerous troop of beasts of burden, laden with the baggage of this vast host, would follow at leisure. The Wady-el-Tih, though very desolate, is by no means absolutely desert, like the Sahara. Green spots, and even groups of tamarisk-bushes, may be seen here and there. There are also wells of water there. The gazelles likewise bound over its rocks and plains in vast numbers; so that there must be pasturings in it, with which the Israelites would be acquainted. Through such a district the migration of the host of Israel would be accomplished without difficulty; and, with their supplies from Egypt yet undiminished, without distress to man or beast.

The termination of the Wady-el-Tih at the Red Sea fulfils exactly the conditions of the passage before us. To the northward it is hemmed in by a conspicuous mountain, terminating in a promontory, which projects far into the sea, and perfectly justifies the ancient appellation Baal-zephon, בעל־צפון "promontory of the north." The modern name is Gebel-Ataka, "the mountain of deliverance," in commemoration of the Exodus. The mountain to the southward is high, rocky, and precipitous. Its appearance, a jagged steep of white limestone, indented everywhere with caves and fissures, is also faithfully described by its ancient name, פידהחירת "the mouths of the caverns." Between these two mountains is a sandy plain seven miles broad. The Hebrew word Migdol, מגדל, means "a fortress." It has passed unchanged in sound or meaning from the Hebrew to the Egyptian language. Hieroglyphic, 𓂧𓈋𓏥𓏺𓇳 *migtol.* Copt. *meshtol.* It frequently appears in the battle-pieces on the walls of the temples, as the common appellative of the fortresses on the north-eastern frontier of the kingdom. In this sense it is evidently used in the present passage. It was afterwards made the proper name of a settlement on the Mediterranean coast of the Isthmus; Magdolum. The ancient versions have confounded the two, to the grievous increase of the previous difficulties of their geography of the Exodus. The Migdol of our text appears to have been a fortress built at the extreme point of the promontory of Baal-zephon, on the narrow plain between it and the sea, to defend this pass to the Wady-el-Tih (which was the high road to Heliopolis) from the desert tribes.*

The position of this first encampment of Israel is thus described in another place of Holy Writ.

"Then they removed from Etham, and turned again to Pi-hahiroth, which is before Baal-zephon, and they pitched before Migdol [the fortress]." Numbers xxxiii. 7.

This is by no means difficult to understand. Moses and Aaron, with the princes and elders of Israel, encamped at the foot of Baal-zephon, close under the walls of the fortress, with which they were at peace. The rest of the host thronged the whole of the valley up to Pi-hahiroth, and far inland. Here they remained in camp for three weeks and upwards. This would afford an opportunity for the stragglers, the weak, and the sickly to join the main body. During this time they would be

---

* The Red Sea was not at this time navigated by the Canaanites.

abundantly supplied from Egypt with water and provisions.

"Then was it told the king of Egypt that the people had departed. Then the heart of Pharaoh and his princes was made stout against the people; and they said, Why have we done this, that we have let Israel go from serving us?" Exod. xiv. 5.

Moses had already been forewarned of this occurrence. The change in the councils of Pharaoh had taken place when the Exodus was nearly completed. We may assume about three weeks as, probably enough, the time that had actually elapsed. In this interval the fearful consequences of the Exodus would be often and painfully discussed in the council-chamber of Sethos. All around them were fields desolated by the plagues, and never again to be restored to fertility by the hand of man, but to be left to the stagnant pools of the receding river, and to the sands of the desert. On every side of them were temples and other public works in progress, now never to be completed. The villages were without inhabitants, and in the cities was left desolation. Nor was the mischief that had befallen the kingdom of Egypt limited even by a judgment so fearful as the utter loss of two-thirds of her inhabitants. Her riches were also gone, and, still worse, the flower of every family that remained in the land, had been cut down by the scythe of the destroying angel. It would be in the midst of deeply mortifying and gloomy speculations upon these unparalleled circumstances of misfortune that the tidings would reach Ramses, of the encampment of Israel " over against Pi-hahiroth, between Migdol and the sea." A ray of hope, a vision of vengeance, would arise to the fierce, untutored, impulsive spirit of Sethos. Aha! they are in the toils, " they are entangled in the land, the wilderness doth hem them in." The deep blue sea is before them: on their right is the waste howling wilderness of the Red Sea, which they cannot traverse without perishing.

" And Pharaoh made ready his chariot and took his people [that is, his sons, his body-guard] with him. Also he took six hundred chosen chariots, together with all the chariots of Egypt, and three men of valour over every one of them; for Jehovah had hardened the heart of Pharaoh king of Egypt, so that he pursued after the children of Israel, when the children of Israel had gone forth with a high hand.

" So Egypt pursued after them, all the horses and chariots of Pharaoh, even his strong horses and his mighty men, and overtook them encamping by the sea, beside Pi-hahiroth, before Baal-zephon." Exod. xiv. 6—9.

This also Jehovah had done. He had spread the

net, he had hidden the toils wherein his adversary shall be snared and taken.

" Command the children of Israel to encamp before Pi-hahiroth, over against Baal-zephon; for Pharaoh will say of them, They are entangled in the land, the wilderness hath shut them in. And I will harden Pharaoh's heart, that he shall follow after them: and I will be honoured upon Pharaoh, and upon all his host; that the Egyptians may know that I am God. And they did so." ver. 2—4.

It is a fearful thing to fight against God. He turns the counsels of men into foolishness. No extent of earthly power, no subtilty of device, neither skill nor promptitude nor bravery of execution, avail ought against him. The councils of Sethos on this occasion lacked none of these qualities; yet did they conduct him and all his host to most inevitable destruction.

The design was a promising one. No time was spent in the assembling of an armed force. Pharaoh himself with his body-guard, commanded by his sons, and the princes and nobles of Egypt, each also with their attendant, went forth at once to the eastern border in chariots. The ancient Egyptians used the horse only for war, and in no other manner than yoked by pairs in the war-chariot, which held three men. The sons and attendants on the nobles of Egypt accompanied their chiefs in chariots, in the same manner as the body-guard of Pharaoh.

The pomp and state of Pharaoh was always warlike. He moved from place to place in his war-chariot, armed to the teeth. His court accompanied him similarly conveyed and accoutred. No time was therefore required for the assembling of the force with which he meditated the execution of his daring stratagem. Neither was there any necessity for disclosing it to his subjects, who would, probably enough, have resisted any further attempt to brave the God of Israel: Pharaoh himself, his princes and his councillors execute the device which they themselves had planned; no one below the rank of noble was permitted to ascend the war-chariot. The numbers which would be assembled on this occasion may be safely computed at 3000 chariots and 10,000 men,—Pharaoh, his sons and near relatives, the princes and nobles, the men of might and valour, chosen from among the entire population, all trained together to the use of arms and from their earliest infancy. This was no contemptible force. They would scour swiftly over the grassy plains of Goshen and over the sands of the desert; for the horses of Egypt were renowned in the ancient world for courage, strength, and swiftness. They would cross the desert by different paths, for the convenience of water and provender.

The gathering-place was Migdol, the tower at the foot of Baal-zephon. Every man of the host was a trained soldier, marching through a country with which he was familiar: so that the army would assemble at the rendezvous as in a moment; and the first notice of danger to the Israelites would be the appearance of Pharaoh in his war-chariot, at the head of the war-chariots of Egypt in battle-array, and in the act of giving the command to

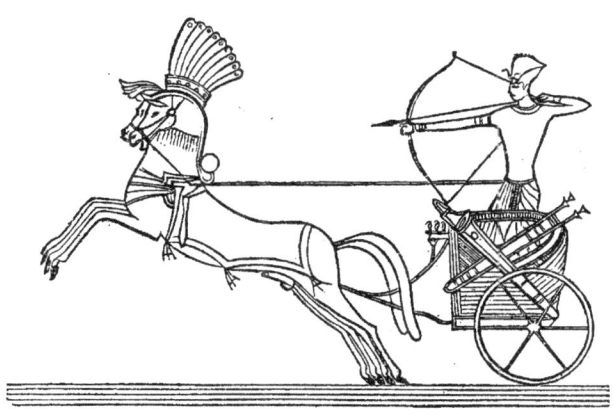

charge, when the whole host abreast would burst the feeble barriers of the camp, plunge into the midst of the multitude unarmed, unprepared, and in the act of retiring to rest for the night, and slay without pity or remorse, regardless of age or sex or condition, until the remnant surrendered unconditionally. The assault had been well planned, and hitherto skilfully and boldly executed.

THE EXODUS.

"Now when Pharaoh drew nigh, the children of Israel lifted up their eyes, and, behold, the Egyptians bent their bows against them, (נֹסֵעַ) and they were sore afraid: and the children of Israel cried unto Jehovah. Also they said unto Moses, Because there were no graves in Egypt, hast thou taken us away to die in the wilderness? Wherefore hast thou dealt thus with us to carry us forth out of Egypt. Is not this the thing that we did tell thee in Egypt, when we said, Let us alone that we may be slaves in Egypt? Yea, it had been better for us to serve in Egypt than to die in the wilderness.

"But Moses said unto the people, Fear ye not, stand still, and see the salvation of Jehovah, which he will shew you to-day: for the Egyptians whom ye have seen to-day, ye shall see them again no more for ever." ver. 11—13.

Never were fears better grounded. Israel knew full well the perfectly relentless character of the vengeance of Egypt. Many a fearful picture of the sufferings of the captives would arise before them. They would see, moreover their own utter impotence to resist the array that was coming against them. And now the word is given: the earth shakes beneath the hoofs of their bounding and impatient steeds, and already the fierce eyes of the warriors of Egypt gloat upon their prey, as they wave their glittering faulchions and draw the arrow to the head.

"Then the angel of God, which went before the camp of Israel, removed and went behind them: also the pillar of the cloud went from before their face, and stood behind them: yea, it came between the host of Egypt and the host of Israel. It was a cloud and darkness [to Egypt], but it gave light by night [unto Israel.]

"So the one came not near the other all that night." ver. 19, 20.

The children of Israel arose that night, and proceeded to strike their tents, to lade their beasts of burden, and to complete the preparations for their departure, by the light of God's own countenance: "for Jehovah did fight for them, and they were silent and at peace."

The Egyptian force passed the same eventful night in darkness. Their horses felt the present deity, and refused to approach the awful veil that waved mystically over their onward course. The charioteers were sore perplexed. To advance was impossible. They feared to remain; but they feared still more to return discomfited.

"Then said Jehovah unto Moses, Lift thou up thy staff, and stretch out thine hand over the sea, and divide it: and the children of Israel shall go on dry ground through the midst of the sea."

THE EXODUS. 413

"And Moses stretched out his hand over the sea, and Jehovah caused the sea to part by a strong east wind all that night, and made the sea dry, for the waters were divided." ver. 15, 21.

The gulf of Suez is about eight miles across, and of considerable depth at the point of Gebel Ataka, (Baalzephon). The act of God on this occasion was a stupendous miracle. It is worse than trifling with the sacred text, to attempt by any theory of tides to reduce it to anything less.

The host of Pharaoh felt the terrible storm that raged against them, they heard the surging and boiling of the fiercely-agitated sea, but they saw nothing. The wind did not dispel the blinding mist that hung over them.

"Then said Jehovah unto Moses, Wherefore criest thou unto me? Speak unto the children of Israel that they go forward. So the children of Israel went into the midst of the sea upon the dry ground, and the waters were a wall unto them on their right hand, and on their left." ver. 15, 22.

The entire space between the mountains Ataka and Abou Deradj was dry. At the former point the gulf is eight miles across, at the latter more than double that distance. The waters that had filled this broad and deep chasm stood in two huge mounds on the right hand and on the left. The light of God shone brightly on the astonished multitude. The word was given, and they advanced abreast; awe-stricken, but quiet and confident. God was before them to guide them on their steep and tangled path. God was behind them to hide them from their enemies. God was on their right hand and on their left; "he enlarged their steps under them, so that their feet did not slip." Thus, "by faith they passed through the Red Sea, as by dry land." Heb. xi. 29.

The host of Jehovah had more than half accomplished the passage of the Red Sea, before the muffling darkness that shrouded the Egyptian army was removed. The prey was escaped. They saw Israel by the light that blazed from the cloud of God's presence, journeying onward through the chasm, and leisurely forming their encampment on the opposite shore; and as the fitful gusts of the east wind swept past them, distant shouts of triumph, and songs of thanksgiving smote upon their ears. A frenzy from God seized upon Pharaoh and his princes. They saw not the mounds of water that stood quivering in heaps. Stung with disappointment, mad with rage, they lashed their fiery steeds, and rushed frantically down the yawning gulf.

"Then the Egyptians pursued and went in after them into the midst of the sea, all Pharaoh's horses, even his chariots and his fleet horses.

" And it came to pass, that in the morning watch Jehovah looked upon the host of Egypt from the pillar of fire and of a cloud, and threatened [hummed in the ears of] the host of Egypt. Also he turned aside the chariot-wheels [upon the axles] so that they drave heavily. Then said Egypt, I will flee from the face of Israel, for Jehovah fights for them against Egypt." ver. 24, 25.

Pharaoh and his princes had already reached the rear of the host of Israel, where Moses stood, when the morning dawned, and the Egyptians saw the wrathful tokens, and heard the appalling voice, of Jehovah.

The wheels of their chariots were at the same time fixed, so that it was difficult to proceed. They saw their mad folly. They turned to flee, but it was too late. This was the most fearful of all!

" Then Jehovah said unto Moses, Stretch out thine hand over the sea, that the waters may come again upon the Egyptians, upon their chariots, and upon their horses.

" And Moses stretched forth his hand over the sea, and the sea returned in his strength as the morning brake, and the Egyptians fled from it; for Jehovah shook Egypt [with fear] in the midst of the sea. Then the waters returned and covered the chariots, and the horses, and all the host of Pharaoh that came into the sea after him, there remained not so much as one of them ; but the children of Israel were walking [at the same time] upon dry land, and the waters were a wall unto them on the right hand and on the left.

" Thus Jehovah saved Israel that day out of the hand of Egypt. And Israel saw the Egyptians dead upon the sea-shore." ver. 26—30.

Thus fell Sethos II. It was his terrible destiny to leave to after-times the strongest exemplification of daring wickedness and mad impiety in his life, and of the vengeance of God in his death, that ever was enacted on the earth. Never had such a judgment befallen any nation, as his reign in Egypt. Accordingly the memory of this fearful event has never departed from among men. The gulf in which he perished is named Bahr-Kolzoum, "the sea of destruction," to this day.

The misfortunes of the Exodus, to Egypt, were perfectly irretrievable. The monuments discourse this truth silently yet eloquently. No temple remains in all Egypt which was begun by any Pharaoh who succeeded Sethos. There is but one to which his successors made any large addition. The kings of Egypt in these later times were poor both in revenue and subjects. Seven or eight of them managed with difficulty to excavate tombs for themselves in the valley of the kings. These are the only monuments of their reigns, and even this proved too much for their successors, whose mummies were in all probability interred in the vaults of their ancestors. So rare, in short, are the memorials of nearly all these later kings, that with the reign of Sethos II. the monumental history of the Pharaohs well nigh ceases.

The memory and name of Sethos II. were infamous in Egypt. His tomb was desecrated, and his sarcophagus publicly and judicially broken. The vault seems to have been used as a burying-place for slaves. The distinctive title of his name, *Sethos*, has been mutilated on all the monuments of Egypt. In Lower Egypt the mutilation has even been extended to the same title in the rings of his great-grandfather (Sethos I.), such was the deep abhorrence in which the name had fallen, after it had been borne by this wicked king.* His is the only one in the whole range of the monumental names of the kings of Egypt which has suffered this mark of public infamy. The fact of this mutilation of the name of Sethos has long been well known to all the students of our subject. The reason of it has not been before pointed out.

That the Greek tradition, as well as the monuments, should also have preserved some notice of the Exodus and its accompanying disasters to Egypt,

* e. g. the obelisco del Popolo at Rome, which is from Heliopolis, the Speos Artemidos at Beni Hassan &c.

would follow inevitably. An account of it, professedly copied by Manetho from the temple records, is related by Josephus.* Sethos is not mentioned in it. The onus of the transaction rests upon his father Amenephthis, whom it makes a very pious monarch, and who, wishing to see the gods, as his ancestor king Horus had seen them, applied to a prophet, his namesake, for information as to the mode of attaining this blessing. He received for answer, that it would be needful for him to expel all leprous and unclean persons from the boundaries of Egypt, and that this course would entail great misfortunes on the kingdom. In compliance with this injunction he banished more than 80,000 such persons, and employed them in the quarries on the eastern bank of the Nile. Many Egyptian malefactors were likewise in the same bondage. Sometime afterwards he set these bondsmen to work to repair a city in the eastern Delta, called Avaris. Here they conspired together, made a leprous Heliopolitan priest, named Osorsiph or Moses, their king, and swore allegiance to him. He gave them laws opposed in all things to the customs of Egypt, and commanded them to fortify Avaris against Amenephthis. He also formed an alliance with the Shepherds, who had been expelled from Egypt by Tethmosis, in their city called Jerusalem, and by

* Cont. Apion I. 25.

their aid invaded Egypt with a force of 200,000 men. Amenephthis perceiving that all this had been foretold by his namesake the prophet, resolved not to resist the gods, but fled into Ethiopia, taking his images and sacred animals with him, and also his son, who was named Sethos, or Ramses. The invaders then committed fearful havoc in all Egypt, sacking and demolishing both public and private buildings, so that their capital took its name from having been built with "the spoils of temples" (Ιερου-συλημ i. e. ιερου συλα.) Thirteen years afterwards Amenephthis and his son returned from Ethiopia with a great force, and expelled the invaders from Egypt.

There are parts of this fable which in all probability were invented at Alexandria about the times of Josephus, for the purpose of mortifying the Jews and amusing the Greeks, like the nick-names of the Shepherd-kings. It rests nevertheless upon a certain framework of truth.

The event upon which it fables is the Exodus. This is palpable and undeniable. The Exodus therefore took place after the times of king Horus, who was the last monarch of the 18th dynasty, as Lepsius very acutely observes, in reply to Bunsen, who assumes it to have taken place before: inasmuch as Horus was the king whose example Amenephthis wished to follow.

The city of Moses in Egypt was Heliopolis. This

is an important point, for Joseph also was of the same city.

The statement that the expelled strangers were leprous and unclean is repeated by so many other Greek authorities, that it seems to have been made for some better reason than that of mortifying the Jews. Such would be a very probable consequence of the hardships the Israelites underwent during the captivity. The minute directions regarding cutaneous diseases, in the Levitical law, seem also to point at the same fact. Lepsius has noticed this coincidence also.

Though, for the sake doubtless of misleading his foreign readers, Manetho makes Amenephthis the Pharaoh of the Exodus, it is nevertheless well worthy of note that he afterwards makes him the father of Sethos. They stand so connected on the monuments.

The disasters of the Exodus, if recorded on the temples of Egypt, would assuredly never be related by the priests to strangers. To obliterate, as far as possible, the remembrance of them, the narrative confounds Amenephthis with Ramerri, the obscure successor of Sethos II., and Sethos himself with Ramses III. the son or successor of Ramerri. These matters, however, bear not at all upon our present subject. They belong to the history of Egypt, and there we have discussed them.

This fable embodies, finally, another aggravation of the sufferings of Egypt after the Exodus. Vast numbers of Canaanites rushed across the Isthmus on hearing the tidings of Israel's departure, and Egypt suffered from them all the horrors of a foreign invasion. The story makes this to have lasted fifteen years. Our strong persuasion is that it continued much longer. This fearful anarchy was at length brought to an end by Ramses III., and he has recorded the exploit in a vast series of pictures on the external walls of the palace of Medinat Abou in Western Thebes. We are able, from a long and close examination, to state the fact, that Ramses never left the boundaries of Egypt in this his war, and that the pen and treaties with the invaders had really far more to do with the pacification in which it terminated, than the sword and victories: notwithstanding the vaunts of these designs. The second invasion of the Shepherds, as it is called, was in fact an immigration from Canaan to Egypt, whereby after many years of anarchy and bloodshed, the awful chasm which the Exodus had left in the population of the kingdom was at length in some measure filled up, and thereby Egypt was still enabled, though miserably diminished in power and glory, to maintain her independence. Without this supply, she would inevitably have fallen a prey to the savage tribes around her. The readiness of the

Canaanites to embrace the religion of Egypt we had before discovered.

It was doubtless on these same conditions that they were naturalized in Egypt on this occasion. We suspect the anarchy to have lasted more than forty years, and that the discomfiture which the Canaanites then underwent (as undoubtedly they did) from Ramses III, arose as much from the disasters which their brethren in Canaan were suffering from the sword of Israel, which cut off all succours from thence, as from any other cause. Numbers of fugitives would enter Egypt from Canaan during these wars also. These all were ultimately naturalized, though at first dealt with as foreigners. It was with their forced services, far more than with their prisoners of war, that Ramses built his one temple at Medinat Abou. It was moreover, by their labours that his tomb and the tombs of his seven successors were excavated and adorned. When they became naturalized, and no longer liable to forced service, all great constructions ceased in Egypt.

" And Israel saw that great work which Jehovah did upon Egypt: and the people feared Jehovah: yea, they believed Jehovah and his servant Moses.

"Then sang Moses and the children of Israel this song unto Jehovah:

"I will sing unto Jehovah, for he hath triumphed gloriously,
The horse with his chariot hath he thrown into the sea.
Jehovah is my strength and my song, he is unto me for salvation.
He is my God, and he shall dwell within me [in a temple*]; my father's God, and I will honor him [with worship.]
Jehovah is a man of war: Jehovah is his name. Pharaoh's chariots with his strong men he hath cast into the sea;
His chosen men by threes together, they have sunk in the Red Sea.
The roaring waves covered them, they sank to the lowest depths like a stone.
Thy right hand, O Jehovah, is glorious in power:
Thy right hand, O Jehovah, hath dashed in pieces the enemy.
In the greatness of thy majesty thou overthrowest them that rise up against thee.
Thou sendest forth thy wrath, it consumeth them as stubble.
Yea, with the blast of thy nostrils the waters were heaped up [as corn on the threshing-floor.]

* נוה "dwelt in a temple as a god," like the Greek ναος "a shrine."

The flowing waters stood upright in an heap.
Yea, the roaring waves congealed in the heart of the sea.
The enemy said:
 I will pursue,
 I will overtake.
 I will divide the spoil.
 My lust shall be satisfied upon them.
 I will draw the sword.
 My hand shall lead them captive again.
Thou didst blow with thy wind,
The sea covered them:
They sank as lead in the mighty waters.
Who is like unto thee among the gods, O Jehovah?
Who is like unto thee, glorious in holiness, fearful in praises, doing wonders?
Thou didst stretch forth thy right hand,
The [depths of the] earth swallowed them up.
[But] thou leadest [by the hand of] thy mercy,
This people which thou hast ransomed;
Yea, by thy strength [right hand] shalt thou bring them
Unto the habitation of thy holiness."

" The people shall hear and be afraid,
The inhabitants of Palestina shall assemble their forces.

Then the dukes of Edom shall be amazed;
The mighty men of Moab, trembling shall take hold on them;
All the dwellers in Canaan shall melt away.
Fear and dread fall upon them;
At the lifting up of thine arm they are still as a stone;
Until thy people pass through thee, O Jehovah,
Until thy people pass through, whom thou hast purchased! *
Thou shalt bring them in,
Yea, thou shalt plant them in the mountain of thine inheritance,
The place, O Jehovah, thou hast made for thee to dwell in,

* The nations specified in this sublime passage were all the inhabitants of the southern districts of the land of Canaan. The apprehensions so powerfully described in it, and the tidings of the depopulated state of Egypt, doubtless led to the vast emigrations from those countries across the Isthmus, which the Egyptian priests have called the second invasion of the shepherds. That Egypt was hereby saved from extinction, as a kingdom, is one purpose of God in it, which we have already explained. It also served another divine purpose. It saved vast multitudes of individually unoffending members of the human race from the sword of the avenger, which the accursed and cannibal idolatry of the land had at length provoked the long-suffering, even of Jehovah, to draw against its inhabitants. Bad as was the mythology of Egypt which they then embraced, miserably as it perverted the few religious truths it concealed, it was nevertheless by no means the confection of human blood, and scarcely human lust, which reeked to the nostrils of the foul idols of Canaan. This purpose also will be seen very clearly by those who rightly appreciate the character and attributes of the true God.

The sanctuary, O Jehovah, which thy hands have established.
Jehovah shall reign for ever and ever."

Exodus xiv. 31 ; xv. 1—18.

Here our work is at an end. The labour will not have been in vain should it produce or aid the conviction in the mind of any man, that the persons mentioned in the Bible were men and not metaphors ; that the events it has recorded were actual occurrences and not fables; and that even the numbers which are found there (when they have not been tampered with by weak and wicked alterations) are real dates, and not geological indefinites.

APPENDIX A.

PRINCIPAL CANAANITE NAMES ON THE TEMPLES OF EGYPT.

[hieroglyphs] *rt-n* Heb. ארודין *Arvadites*. Arab. *ruad*. Arvad was one of the sons of Canaan. The tribe was named after him. Gen. x. 10. They built the city of Zidon, which they named after the firstborn of Canaan, who probably died childless (v. 15). They afterwards built Tyre, (see Ezek. xxvii. 8.) and still later the city which they named after themselves *Aradus*. They were the great trading power of the ancient world. Herodotus the Greek historian says, (lib. i.) that their intercourse with Egypt was the earliest traffic of which any record remained. The monuments of Egypt fully confirm this statement. So great had been the immigration of Arvad into Lower Egypt, that Saites married an Arvadite princess : and on this account his kingdom is named upper Arvad, and Memphis an Arvadite city, in the hieroglyphic account of the capture of it. The same document leaves us to infer that Arvad was the first of the Canaanite nations to make peace with the Theban Pharaoh. In all other hieroglyphic records, Arvad is in alliance and trading with Egypt. Herodotus tells us, that in his day the commerce of Arvad with Egypt was very extensive, and that a Syrian settlement existed in the vicinity of Memphis. (lib. ii.)

𓊖𓏤𓈖 *thi* Hebrew חִתִּי *the Hittites.* The descendants of Heth, the second son of Canaan. (Gen. x. 15). The possessions of this powerful tribe were in the south of Canaan. They had also large possessions in Egypt at the time of the capture of Memphis by Amosis. But in the days of his successors (the 18th dynasty) they had been expelled from the Delta by the Xoite kings confederate with Arvad, and probably with Israel. In the pretensions of Heth, to those possessions in Egypt, originated the wars of Sethos and Ramses.

𓉐𓏤𓈖𓏤 *shasu.* Hebrew זוּז the Zuzim; probably a sept of the Hivites, inhabiting the mountains of Siddim or the Dead Sea. They had been among the first of the Canaanites to cross the desert of Suez and form settlements in the Delta. In the times of Abraham, they were on this account entitled "the Zuzim that dwelt in Ham." [i. e. Egypt.] Gen. xiv. 5. For this reason also their name in the provincial language of Egypt had become the common appellative of "shepherd," with all its degrading associations. This nation had been dispossessed of their territory in Siddim by the children of Lot, sometime before the Exodus. (See

Deut. ii. 20, 21.) The monuments seem to indicate that their possessions in Egypt also had been ceded to Moab and Ammon. This war seems to have taken place while Sethos reigned in Egypt In his first year the Zuzim were a very powerful nation: but in the wars of his son Ramses, they were much diminished, and confederate with him against Moab.

[hieroglyphs] *sht-n.* The geographical identification of the enemies of Egypt who bear this appellation, with Moab in the mountains of Sheth, we published long ago.* We are now in position to confirm this identification unanswerably. In the long inscription at Abu Simbel, the Shethites are declared to be [hieroglyphs] of "the race of the Mubith," that is, מֹאבִית "Moabites" in Hebrew. In the decree of the 21st Ramses expelling Sheth from Egypt, the princes of [hieroglyphs] Ar Moab (Num. xxi. 28 &c.) [hieroglyphs] Moab-Dannah (Jos. xv. 49.) and [hieroglyphs] Aroer, (Jer. xlviii. 19.) represent the Shethites. We need scarcely remind the reader, that all these are cities of Moab, mentioned in the Bible.

These are the four principal Canaanite nations mentioned on the monuments of ancient Egypt. Many others are likewise named casually. We have given them at length elsewhere.†

* Egypt: her testimony, pp. 130—136.
† Ubi supra. Also monumental history of Egypt, Vol. II. Trans. R. S. L. &c.

APPENDIX B.

COREGENCIES IN EGYPT DURING

N.B.—The letters over each name refer the figures, to their

LOWER EGYPT.

C 14
Othoes 6th dyn. lists.

D 8
Saites son of Othoes: conquered Memphis (16th dyn. lists.)

C 15
Aphophis, Phiops, or Apappus, son of Meris. Crowned king of Lower Egypt, and many years co-regent with his father. Afterwards king of all Egypt. Reigned for 61 years.

APPENDIX B.

THE SOJOURN OF ISRAEL.
to the planes of the chamber of Karnak, succession there.

UPPER EGYPT.

Amuntimæus C 12
(12th dy. lists)
lost Memphis
to Saites.

Amenemes IV. B 13
co-regent and
successor to
Amuntimæus.

Shepherds in Up. Eg.

 C 16
Meris, father of
Aphophis: expelled
Skeniophris from
Crocodilopolis.

Menecherian Pharaohs.
B 14
Skeniophris
expelled
from the
Faioum
by Meris.

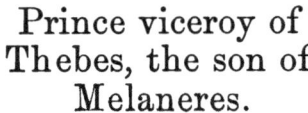
Melaneres son of
Aphophis conquered
all Upper Egypt.

B 15
Prince viceroy of
Thebes, the son of
Melaneres.

13th DYNASTY.
E 1
Menthesuphis II.
E 2
erased.
E 3
erased.
E 4
E 5
E 6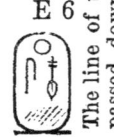

Five successive kings in this line during the reign of Aphophis. They were his sons and grandsons.

H 1

H 2

H 3

The line of the Menecherian Pharaohs passed down 10 descents during the reign of Aphophis

432 APPENDIX.

LOWER EGYPT.

The immigration of Israel late in the reign of Aphophis, either in the 51st or 54th year.

 Iannes succeeds Aphophis at Memphis, reigned 50 years (lists).

Six descents of Shepherds at Abydos in friendly co-regency with the 18th dynasty.

G 3

 Son of H 5.

 Asses : the son of Iannes, and for many years his co-regent. Whole reign 49 years lists.

Actual duration of the reigns of Iannes and Asses 60 years.—Asses probably perished in the attempt to maintain Memphis against Amosis ;—about the 70th year of the immigration.

APPENDIX. 433

UPPER EGYPT.

F 1

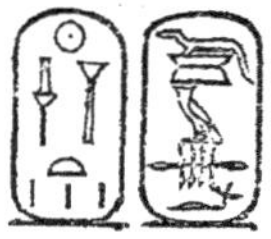

F 2
erased.
F 3
erased.

H 4   The bursting of the lake in the reign of this king.   F 4

F

F

H 5    The father and father-in-law of Amosis.   F 7

18th DYNASTY.
I.
 Amosis, who expelled the Lower Egyptians from Memphis.

2 F

434   APPENDIX.

LOWER EGYPT.

Shepherds in Middle Egypt. *Not in Lists.*

14th DYNASTY XOITES.

G

H 6

 Qu. the son of Asses, He devoted himself to the worship of Sephris  the builder of the 2nd pyramid, and took his name.

H 7

G 5

H 8

G 6

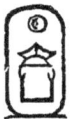 This king conquered Memphis again.

 The tomb of one of the officers of this king at Essiout.

G 1

G 7

G 2

G 8 erased.
The father-in-law of Thothmosis, in whom this line merged.

No more names of the Xoite Pharaohs known until Si Phtha. They are named on the monuments princes of Upper Arvad and Moab.

APPENDIX.

UPPER EGYPT.

18th DYNASTY THEBANS.

I
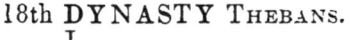Chebron Amenophis.

III
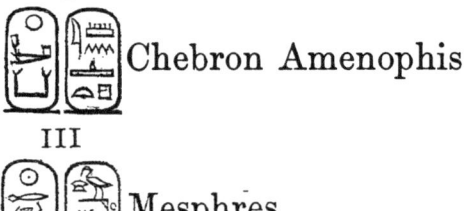Mesphres.

IV
Achencheres.

V
Amenses.

VI
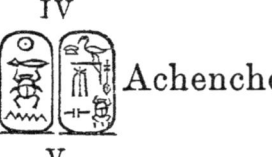Thothmosis, the final expeller of the Shepherds, *lists.*—Married the daughter of the Shepherd king of Abydos. Chamber of Karnak, and recovered Heliopolis from the Lower Egyptians.

VII
Acherres.

VIII
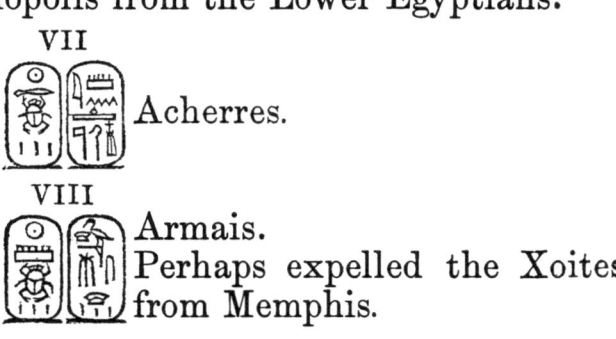Armais.
Perhaps expelled the Xoites from Memphis.

436   APPENDIX.

LOWER EGYPT.

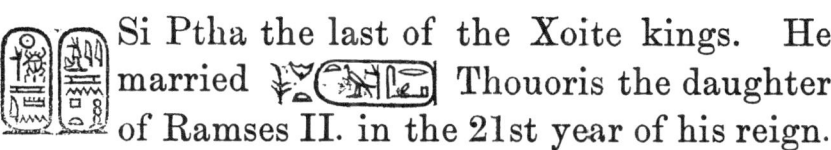 Si Ptha the last of the Xoite kings. He married Thouoris the daughter of Ramses II. in the 21st year of his reign.

The duration of the 18th and 19th dynasties was tion of Israel to the capture of Memphis by Amosis. vears.

APPENDIX.

UPPER EGYPT.

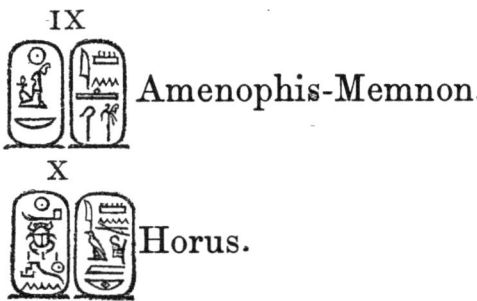 IX Amenophis-Memnon.

X Horus.

These ten kings reigned for 205 years.

19th DYNASTY I THEBANS.

 Ramses I.

II
 Sethos I.

III
 Ramses II. The King that knew not Joseph.

IV
 Amenenthis.

V
 Sethos II. Who perished in the Red Sea at the Exodus.

365 years, which gives 65 years from the immigra-
Our calculation of the same interval makes it 67

www.ingramcontent.com/pod-product-compliance
Lightning Source LLC
Chambersburg PA
CBHW040326300426
44113CB00020B/2670